THE SEARCH FOR
OMM SETY

Also by Jonathan Cott

STOCKHAUSEN

CITY OF EARTHLY LOVE

CHARMS

FOREVER YOUNG

PIPERS AT THE GATES OF DAWN

CONVERSATIONS WITH GLENN GOULD

DYLAN

THE
SEARCH FOR
OMM SETY

A Story of Eternal Love

Jonathan Cott

IN COLLABORATION WITH

Hanny El Zeini

DOUBLEDAY & COMPANY, INC.
GARDEN CITY, NEW YORK
1987

A Dream of the Past by Dorothy Eady (a.k.a. Omm Sety) first published in 1949. Reprinted by permission of the Egyptian General Authority for the Promotion of Tourism in Cairo.

Excerpts from *Abydos: Holy City of Ancient Egypt* by Omm Sety and Hanny El Zeini. Copyright © 1981 by L L Company. Reprinted by permission of L L Company of 2066 Westwood Blvd., Los Angeles, California 90025, with special thanks to Arthur Wallace. Two photos by Hanny El Zeini reproduced by permission of L L Company.

Portion of "The God Osiris" from *Omm Sety's Abydos* by Dorothy Louise Eady first appeared in the *Journal of the Society for the Study of Egyptian Antiquities* (Volume X, fascicles 1, 2, and 3). Copyright © 1982 by The Society for the Study of Egyptian Antiquities (SSEA). Reprinted here by permission of The Society for the Study of Egyptian Antiquities, with special thanks to Roberta Shaw.

Excerpt from "A Question of Names" by Bulbul Abdel Meguid ("Omm Sety") from *Newsletter of the American Research Center in Egypt* (Number 71, October 1969). Reprinted by permission of American Research Center in Egypt.

"And he was the demon of my dreams . . ." by Antonio Machado, translated by Robert Bly. Copyright © 1983 by Robert Bly. Reprinted by permission of Robert Bly.

"Let her come to the lotus pond" from *Her-Bak: The Living Face of Ancient Egypt* by Isha Schwaller de Lubicz, illustrated by Lucie Lamy, English translation by Charles Edgar Sprague. Copyright © 1954 by Isha Schwaller de Lubicz. Reprinted by permission of Inner Traditions International, Ltd., Rochester, Vermont.

"Our Story" from *Stories That Could Be True* by William Stafford. Copyright © 1976, 1977 by William Stafford. Reprinted by permission of Harper & Row Publishers, Inc.

Excerpts from *Helen in Egypt* by H.D. Copyright © 1961 by Norman Holmes Pearson. Reprinted by permission of New Directions Publishing Corporation.

Letters from Omm Sety to M. Tracey reprinted by permission of M. Tracey. Grateful acknowledgment to M. Tracey for use of photos from her private collection.

Entries from Omm Sety's diaries reprinted by permission of Hanny El Zeini. Grateful acknowledgment to Hanny El Zeini for use of photos by him.

Painting of ancient Egyptian garden by H. M. Herget from the October 1941 issue of the *National Geographic.* Copyright © National Geographic Society. Reprinted by permission of *National Geographic Magazine.*

Library of Congress Cataloging-in-Publication Data
Cott, Jonathan.
    The search for Omm Sety.
    Includes index.
    1. Omm Sety, 1904–1981. 2. Egypt—Antiquities.
3. Seti I, King of Egypt. 4. Parapsychology and
archaeology. 5. Reincarnation. 6. Egyptologists—Egypt—
Biography. I. El Zeini, Hanny, 1918– . II. Title.
PJ1064.O46C6 1987   133.9′01′30924 [B]   86–24095
ISBN 0-385-23746-4

Contents

Remind me again—together we
trace our strange journey, find
each other, come on laughing.
Some time we'll cross where life
ends. We'll both look back
as far as forever, that first day.
I'll touch you—a new world then.
Stars will move a different way.
We'll both end. We'll both begin.

Remind me again.

—"Our Story"
(from *Stories That Could Be True*
by William Stafford)

· I ·

Bentreshyt
("Harp-of-Joy")

Remind me again

In the holy city of ancient Abydos—where the celestial green valley of the Nile gives way to the bleached, coppery sands of the Western Desert—there has long stood a beautiful white limestone temple. Known for its mysterious L-shape, its seven vaulted chapels dedicated to the major gods of ancient Egypt, and its peerless and delicate bas-reliefs depicting these gods, the temple was once adjoined on its southern perimeter by a luxuriant garden.

At the center of this garden was a rectangular lotus pool, bordered by beds of jasmine and oleander, mimosa and dwarf chrysanthemums, mandrakes and bindweed, all of which were encircled by pomegranate, date palm, and sycamore fig trees. It was here one morning, about three thousand years ago, that a golden-haired, blue-eyed, fourteen-year-old girl named Bentreshyt ("Harp-of-Joy")[1] was out walking under the radiantly blue sky picking flowers and singing a song very softly to herself:

[1] The spellings used to render the Arabic and ancient Egyptian names and places mentioned in the text—with the exception of quotations from other authors—are consistent with those employed in the various writings of Dorothy Eady/Bulbul Abdel Meguid/Omm Sety.

"Let her come to the lotus pond,
My beautiful loved one,
In her transparent shift
Of fine linen.
Let her bathe herself near me
Among the flowers,
So that I may behold her
As her limbs emerge from the water."

It so happened that on that same day the man responsible for the building of this temple—the Pharaoh Sety the First ("Mighty of Bows in All Lands," "Bringer of Renaissance")—was paying a visit to Abydos to oversee the ongoing construction of the monumental shrine that was intended to house his spirit, as well as to inspect his immense temple estates with their staffs of priests and servants. Passing by the garden with his retainers, the Pharaoh, a man then in his fifties, was struck by the sound of a melodious voice, and caught sight of the young girl, Bentreshyt, who glanced up to see him through blossoms and leaves. Trying to bow respectfully to His Majesty, the nervous girl made a clumsy gesture. Charmed by her awkwardness, Sety laughed and called her over to him.

"Stand up, Little One. What is your name?" he asked her.

"Bentreshyt, Your Majesty," she replied nervously.

"Do you know who I am? Do you know my name?"

"Nisou-Beti Men-maat-Ra." (This was one of the King's five official names.)

"Who are your parents, Little One?"

"I am an orphan, *Nisou-Beti.* My mother was a vegetable seller. She died when I was three years old. My father is a soldier . . . he is now in Wasit [Thebes] in a garrison."

"And what are you doing now?"

"I am a priestess to our lady Isis. I am studying with Master Antef, our high priest, in order to participate in the sacred Mystery Play about the birth, death, and resurrection of our lord Osiris."

Then came a long moment of silence, during which Sety scrutinized this young blond girl with blue eyes who looked so different from the rest of the people standing reverently at his side. In Memphis, Thebes, or the other principal cities of Egypt, it was not at all unusual to encounter blond girls or blond priestesses . . . but in Abydos this was quite exceptional. Everybody in the temple, however, knew that Bentreshyt's father's grandfather was a foreigner

. . . an Achaean, one of those whom the Egyptians used to call the "Sea People," who originally came from the Greek islands.

For her part, Bentreshyt found it hard to meet His Majesty's eyes directly, though she soon became aware that he was quite handsome; and although his look was intense and penetrating, she thought it neither disturbing nor unkindly. After their first meeting, she caught a glimpse of him on several occasions as she made her way to or from the garden.

One night the Pharaoh was sitting alone by the lotus pool when Bentreshyt happened to walk by—perhaps on purpose, perhaps not. His Majesty smiled at her and said, "Come, Little One, and sit beside me." When she did, he took hold of her hand and kissed her. The girl was scared, and His Majesty told her to run . . . run very quickly and not come back. So she ran, but she did not run far enough. At the end of the park she turned around and saw him sitting with his head in his hands. Slowly, she went back to him.

Sety found one excuse after another to delay his departure from Abydos, and all the while Bentreshyt would meet him in the garden after dark. And here they "ate the uncooked goose"—the ancient Egyptian term for "eating of the forbidden tree." "Forbidden" because Bentreshyt was vowed as temple property, and nobody was allowed to touch her. If Bentreshyt had been divorced or a widow or a free woman, the situation would have been tolerated since it would have been considered an honor to become the King's concubine. But since the girl was a virgin priestess of Isis, the affair was regarded as a horrific breach of the religious laws of the time.

Bentreshyt was constantly under the close scrutiny of the high priest Antef, his junior priests, and the other priestesses. When one of them informed Antef that Bentreshyt was "in a family way," the priest made her go down to the tomb of Osiris under the island of the Osirion—behind the Temple of Sety—and tried to force her to confess her crime. The girl refused to answer his questions at first. When he compelled her to place her hand on the statue of Osiris, however, she was unable to lie; and she finally shouted out, "Yes, I have a lover!" . . . but she refused to name the King as her fellow culprit.

It was at this time that Sety was finally obliged to leave Abydos because of some trouble in Nubia and the gold mines in the Eastern Desert. He told Bentreshyt that he would come back soon and stay for a longer period. A few days later, events began to move very quickly. As the last ship of the King's cortege disappeared, Antef again sent for Bentreshyt for a final cross-examination, during which she was coerced into admitting that the King was her lover. The priest, with Spartan bluntness, told her that her crime against Isis was punishable by nothing less than death.

By law there could be no death sentence without a fair trial. This presented Antef with a dilemma; if the legal procedure were followed, the secret could not be kept. So Bentreshyt, suddenly realizing how serious the whole business was, decided to save the name of the only man she had ever loved and to take her own life. She committed suicide. And when Sety returned to Abydos and asked about her, he was shocked and heartbroken to hear of her death. "I will never forget her," he vowed to himself.

For three thousand years, he never did.

FROM THE *SECRET DIARIES* OF OMM SETY

April, 1972

His Majesty came last night at about 1 o'clock after midnight. I was still awake. I had put out the big light, but could not sleep, and was feeling rather fed up. Sety lay down beside me, and put his arms around me, and said, "Bentreshy, my Little Love, I had to come to you, I cannot bear to be far from you!" He began kissing me, and I returned them, but soon he became so passionate that I thought it wiser to change the subject. I said, "Beloved! do you want to lose me for another 3,000 years? Stay quiet for a while. Please tell me by what road you come to me." He sighed deeply, and after a little silence, said, "You are a wise Little One, and I am a bad man to let my desire endanger our eternal happiness. But I love you so much; forgive me, Bentreshy." I said, "There is nothing to forgive, your love is very precious to me, but we must be wise and patient for just a little time longer." He got up, and led me to the chairs, and we sat down side by side.

I said that I wanted to ask a question, but if it was something that I should not know, to please forgive me, and forget that I asked. He said, "Speak, Bentreshy." I said, "Do you remember your death, and what was it like?" He looked at me very seriously, and replied, "Do you not remember your own experience, Child?" I shook my head. "So," he said, "I will tell you. The feeling is wonderful, just as you feel when your akh [astral body] is released from your body. But one's thoughts and feelings remain the same. I was torn by longing, by doubt and fear. I longed, I even dared to hope, that I should find you waiting for me. But I also realized the full measure of my sin. For a brief while I was aware of my earthly surroundings. I saw my lifeless body, lying on the same bed and in the same room which you know. I saw my friend Hora, weeping, and I saw my son Ramesses lying on the floor weeping bitterly and calling on me not to leave him. This was a terrible experience. Please, Bentreshy, tell the people that they should not torture their dead in this way, if they love them truly. My daughter also wept a little, though she did not love me deeply, but her mother, whose beautiful eyes were dry, tearless and hard as agate stones, forbade her to kiss my dead forehead in farewell. Then the scene faded and I found myself out under the starry sky. . . .

"You must understand that after my arrival in Amenti [the West, the realm of the dead], I was a man maddened with sorrow. I thought that I would find you, but I did not. I searched, I questioned, but to no avail. My friends among the priests cast pitying eyes upon my grief, but they were forbidden to answer my questions or to give me any word of comfort. In despair I even braved the wrath of the Council, and they replied, 'She whom you seek is not here, nor is she upon earth.' When I tried to ask more, they said one word, 'Begone!' Then I began a search."

I asked when it was that he knew that I had returned again to earth. He said, "After long ages of suffering, Our Lord Osiris had mercy upon me, and the Council summoned me and said that you were 'sleeping in the blackness, and that one day, you would be re-born.' That comforted me a little. Then much later, I was told that you had been re-born on earth in almost the same form as you had before, and I was permitted to search for you as an akh wandering all over the world, and saw many strange places and things, until at last I found you, and the rest you know."

·II·

Dorothy Eady

Though thou goest thou comest again.

—*Book of the Dead*

In 1907, when she was three years old (she was born on January 16, 1904), Dorothy Louise Eady fell down a flight of stairs. While her mother, Mrs. Caroline Eady, looked on in shock from the upper landing of the family's flat in the London suburb of Blackheath, the little girl slipped and careened down the steps, ending up motionless on the floor below. Rushing down after her, Mrs. Eady lifted up her daughter—her only child—and saw she was unconscious. The frantic mother immediately sent for the doctor, who examined the girl with a stethoscope, held a mirror, then a feather up to her mouth, and pronounced her dead.

Mr. Reuben Eady, Dorothy's father (a master tailor by profession), had by now been summoned home; he promptly telephoned his mother- and sister-in-law, who hurried over to try to console his then prostrate wife. The doctor, meanwhile, had carried the dead little girl to her bedroom and informed the grieving family that he would shortly return with a nurse to lay out and wash the body, and that he would bring a death certificate declaring that the girl had died of a brain concussion in an accidental fall.

The doctor and a nurse came back in an hour and went to Dorothy's bedroom. Instead of finding a corpse, however, they saw a fair-haired, chocolate-smeared child, sitting up and playing on her bed. Dumbfounded, the doctor examined the girl, observed no obvious injuries, tore up the death certificate, swore to Mr. Eady—who was furious about the family having been needlessly upset—that the girl *had* been dead, then hastily took his leave.

Soon after her accident Dorothy began to have recurring dreams in which she saw a huge building with columns, a garden filled with fruits and flowers, and tall trees nearby. During the day her parents —to whom she had spoken about these visions—would often find their daughter sitting in her room or under the dining-room table and weeping for no apparent reason. "Why are you always crying?" Dorothy's mother would ask. The little girl would answer: "I want to go home." "Don't be silly, dear, you *are* home—*this* is your home," Mrs. Eady would reassure her. Dorothy continued to cry, pleading to be allowed to go home. After a few months of this her parents, exasperated, began to tease their daughter, asking at odd moments, "Where *is* your home, Dorothy?" She, seriously, would reply, "I don't know, but I want to go there."

One day, when Dorothy was four, her parents decided to take Mrs. Eady's younger sister to the British Museum. Knowing that every time they left their daughter alone, however briefly, or with a baby-sitter, some minor disaster would befall the child, they thought it best to take her with them.

The Eadys thus found themselves dragging their petulant and bored daughter around the museum from one exhibition to another. Upon entering the Egyptian galleries, though, Dorothy suddenly let go of her parents' hands and went running crazily through the rooms, kissing the feet of all the statues that she could reach. Catching up with her, the Eadys calmed her down and continued their tour of the Egyptian collection upstairs. Again, breaking away from her parents, the little girl walked right up to a mummy in a glass case, sat down on the floor beside it, and refused to budge. "Well, she's tired," the parents thought, relieved she had at last become tranquil. So they left her there and took Dorothy's more tractable aunt to view some other exhibitions.

When they returned a half hour later to the mummy room and called out to Dorothy that it was time to go, she just remained where she was, immobile and oblivious to their voices. "Dorothy, we *must* be leaving!" Mrs. Eady insisted. But Dorothy wasn't moving. Mrs. Eady bent down to pick her up. As she did so, the girl grabbed the side of the glass case and, in an unrecognizable voice that sounded to her mother eerily like that of a strange old woman rather than that of a little girl, announced: "Leave me . . . *these* are my people!" Mrs. Eady was so surprised and horrified that she immediately dropped the child, who had to be removed from the museum kicking and screaming.

A few months after this incident Reuben Eady happened one afternoon to be passing a bookshop. In the window was a display of sample pages from Arthur Mee's *The Children's Encyclopaedia.* Thinking that it would be an instructive present for his daughter as she got older, he went in, bought part of the *Encyclopaedia,* and took it home. (This popular, lavishly illustrated reference work—filled with practical information; lessons in grammar and arithmetic; versions of fables, legends, and stories—was issued in fifty fortnightly parts between 1908 and 1910 and had an enormous effect on children in every English-speaking country during, and even after, the Edwardian era. It was eventually translated into other languages, such as French, Italian, Arabic, and Chinese.)

As chance would have it, the part of the *Encyclopaedia* that Mr. Eady had purchased contained photographs and drawings of ancient Egypt. The moment Dorothy caught a glimpse of them she knew that they were pictures from home. For weeks afterward, whenever someone came to visit the Eady household, Dorothy would run up to the unsuspecting visitor with a copy of the relevant pages in her hand and implore the person to "please read to me about Egypt." Mrs. Eady got so fed up with her child's incessant importuning that one day she said to Dorothy, "If you want to read, I'll *teach* you to read." The young pupil learned extremely quickly.

Her mother could not understand why Dorothy persisted in placing a magnifying glass over one particular page in *The Children's Encyclopaedia* that reproduced a full-page photograph of the Rosetta Stone (the famous black basalt tablet, now in the British Museum, whose trilingual inscription led to the decipherment of the Egyptian hieroglyphs). "Even though you can read a *bit* now, Dorothy," Mrs. Eady commented to her daughter, who was lying on the floor poring over her favorite page, "what makes you think you could ever read *that?* It's a language you don't know." The then six-year-old girl, without looking up, replied almost wistfully, "I *do* know it, but I've just forgotten it. If I could only copy it down, perhaps I might remember it."

When Dorothy was seven, she first began to understand (or remember) what her recurring dream image of the huge building with its columns and garden and trees was all about. One evening her father had come home after work with some magazines. While lying on the floor idly going through their pages, Dorothy suddenly became transfixed by a photograph whose caption read: *The Temple of Sety the First at Abydos, Upper Egypt.* It was as if she couldn't breathe. Clutching the magazine, she ran up to her father and waved the photo in front of him, shouting, *"This* is my home! *This* is where I used to live!" Then, looking more fixedly at the picture, she added sorrowfully, "But why is it all broken? And where is the garden?"

Mr. Eady, irritated and more than a little disturbed, said firmly: "One should never tell lies, Dorothy. You *know* you've never been there. That is a photograph of an old building—thousands of years old—and it's broken because it *is* so old, and there's no garden because it's in the desert and they don't have gardens in the desert, there's only sand there. . . . So, no more lies, if you please!"

As if this weren't bad enough, Dorothy, soon after discovering the building of her dreams, came across another photograph—this one showing the extraordinarily lifelike and well-preserved mummy of Sety the First, Pharaoh of the Nineteenth Dynasty. Once again Dorothy, unable to restrain herself, rushed over excitedly to her father, and this time *swore* to him that she really *did* know the man in the picture, and that he was a nice and kind man. Reuben Eady had had enough; now he too wound up yelling that she certainly didn't know and couldn't possibly *ever* have known the man in the photograph, that he was "some old king" who had been dead for three thousand years, that he probably wasn't at all a nice man, and that she should and must stop all of this nonsense once and for all!

Dorothy, like a girl who has heard her father irrevocably denounce her one and only love, ran weeping into her bedroom and slammed the door.

* * *

Dorothy's parents undoubtedly realized that their daughter's accident had affected her in some unknown and peculiar way. In the Edwardian era, though, one did not send healthy and functioning young children off to psychiatrists or neurologists just because they seemed eccentric or entertained "childish" delusions. Of course Dorothy was an unconventional child. (She detested wearing shoes, for example, and would frantically pull them off on entering her house, even before removing her hat and coat.) Her obsession with Egypt was bizarre, to say the least. Otherwise, she was a precocious, bright, curious, clever, headstrong, good-humored—if often lonely—little girl. Certainly, the Eadys thought, she would eventually "outgrow" her exotic oriental fantasy. So the parents resisted, but after a while almost took for granted, their daughter's *idée fixe.*

Most people with whom Dorothy came into contact outside her home, however, were hardly as tolerant of the girl's single-minded obsession. When the Eadys sent their daughter to Sunday school—a place that bored her to tears, though she was fond of the parts of the Bible that concerned Egypt—Dorothy told her teacher that, since Egyptian religion was thousands of years older than Christianity, *it* must be the true religion and Christianity merely its copy. After all, she asserted, weren't Osiris and Jesus both resurrected? Hadn't the Virgin Mary adopted some of the same characteristics as the goddess Isis? And didn't Joseph, Mary, and the infant Jesus closely resemble Osiris, Isis, and their son, Horus the Child? The Sunday school teacher's response was immediately to make an appointment with Mrs. Eady to request that she keep her "heathenish" daughter away from class.

Dorothy was also expelled from a girls' school in Dulwich (on the southeast outskirts of London) when she refused to join in singing a hymn that beseeched God to "curse the swart Egyptians." Taking the offending hymnal, Dorothy threw it at the teacher and abruptly stalked out of the assembly hall.

The Eadys, therefore, occasionally found themselves having to search around for an "appropriate" school for their daughter. Once they had the inspired notion that a convent school in Belgium might be just the thing to make a little lady out of her. Dorothy, needless to say, was hardly delighted by such a prospect; so she confided to her aunt that she indeed couldn't *wait* to be sent to that school, since from there she would easily be able to run away, journey on foot across Europe until she reached the Hellespont, and then—like Leander and Lord Byron—swim across it, and again start walking until she came to the land of Egypt. The aunt promptly informed her sister of Dorothy's scenario and that was the end of the convent school idea. "Poor nuns!" Dorothy Eady later said, regarding this incident. "They didn't know what they were saved from!"

When she got a little older Dorothy used to enjoy going to Catholic mass on Sundays because the ritual, incense, and music reminded her of the "old religion." At one of the churches she frequented an eagle-eyed priest, who carefully observed all the parishioners going in and out of his services, stopped her one morning and asked: "I don't think you're a Catholic, are you?" Dorothy realized that she must have done something inappropriate during the prayers, and she replied, "No, I am not a Catholic." "What are you, then?" he questioned her. Dorothy informed him that her parents were Protestants. "And they don't mind your coming to this church?" he inquired. *"I* like your church," Dorothy told him; "I find the sermons and rites and ceremonies very satisfying to me." "But you're a Protestant," the priest said. "No, I'm not," Dorothy hesitantly admitted. "I told you my *parents* are Protestants." "Well, then," the priest pressed on, "are you a Jew?" "No," replied Dorothy. "Well," asked the perplexed and by now suspicious prelate, "if you're not a Catholic and you're not Jewish, what *are* you?" Again, the girl hesitated. "Well, if you *really* want to know, *I follow the ancient Egyptian religion!"* As Dorothy later recalled: "The poor man absolutely got the foam up to the eyebrows. He got my address out of me; and a few days later he turned up at our house and he gave my mother a good talking to, saying, 'My dear lady, do you want your daughter to go to hell?' My mother said to him, 'No, but I expect she will!'

"You see," Dorothy Eady once explained, "my mother [who was born Caroline Mary Frost in 1879] was always criticizing me for doing things she didn't consider the right thing to do. She'd say, 'Can't you behave like a lady?' And I'd ask her, 'Well, why did you marry an Irishman?' Because my father was half Irish, and much more liberal-minded than my mother. But neither of my parents, nor anybody in either of their families, had any interest whatever in the East . . . except for my mother's great-uncle, who was a missionary who went to China and tried to convince the Chinese that the Christian religion was better than the Buddhist one. But one Chinaman settled the argument with a big stick, and that was the end of my uncle! . . . As a matter of fact, my grandmother said it was a mercy that he died before seeing his grandniece grow up to be a pagan!"

Dorothy Eady finally found someone who accepted and encouraged her devotion to ancient Egypt. When she was ten, she would often play hooky from school and wander over to her beloved British Museum to moon about the Egyptian galleries. One day, while examining some hieroglyphs on a relief, a short, stout, white-haired older gentleman, who had noticed this little girl in the museum many times before, went up to her and asked her why she wasn't at school where she belonged. Dorothy replied that she *was* supposed to be at school but that school didn't teach her what she *really* wanted to know. "And what might that be?" the gentleman inquired. "Hieroglyphs!" she fervently exclaimed. He smiled at the intense-looking young girl and said, "Well, in that case *I'll* teach you what you want to know."

This white-haired guardian angel who befriended Dorothy Eady and offered to act as her unofficial tutor ("He aided and abetted me," as she would later put it) was none other than Sir E. A. Wallis Budge, the Keeper of Egyptian and Assyrian Antiquities at the British Museum—an extraordinarily prolific and controversial Egyptologist, many of whose works on Egyptian history, language, religion, and magic, though today considered somewhat outdated and flawed, are still in print and widely read. To his amazement, his young pupil revealed a natural gift for drawing, and she quickly learned how to write the hundreds of basic hieroglyphic characters that he taught her (though, in later years, Dorothy Eady realized the imperfections in Budge's system of transliteration and compensated for them by adopting other scholars' more accurate methods). Soon, at her mentor's suggestion, she began to try her hand at deciphering certain texts of the so-called Egyptian *Book of the Dead* (magical funerary prayers and spells intended to guide the dead of ancient Egypt on their journeys through the netherworld, originally inscribed on the walls of tombs and preserved on papyri—the finest collection of which is in the British Museum).

Whenever Dorothy now visited Dr. Budge, he would give her a short hieroglyphic passage from the *Book of the Dead,* which she would then take home. A few weeks later, when she appeared with her "translation" written out in her notebook, Dr. Budge would go over and check Dorothy's version against his own famous translation and transliteration of the text:

auk	*er*	*heh*	*en*	*heh*	*aha*	*en*	*heh*
Thou shalt exist	for	millions	of	millions of years,	a period	of	millions of years.

Dr. Budge was both pleased and amazed by his pupil's rapid mastery of this material. And while complimenting her one day on her remarkable "progress," he also happened to wonder aloud how she had been able to learn and understand so much so quickly. Dorothy explained to him simply that she had actually known the language a long time ago, that she had only forgotten it, and that, with his help and guidance, it was now all coming back to her.

"Dr. Budge was quite a character," Dorothy Eady reminisced many years later. "The young people working in the British Museum today occasionally look upon me as a prophetess because I used to know the old boy personally! And when *I* knew him, he must already have been quite old. In appearance he was short and very fat, and he had snow-white hair that came down to his shoulders. I suppose he looked like a forerunner of the hippies, and his face was round and rosy like the faces of cherubs, and quite unlined, almost like the face of a baby. Over his long white hair he used to wear a top hat made of black fur—I think it was what used to be known as a beaver hat— and then across his large, round stomach he wore a huge gold watch chain—big and strong enough to have tied a bull with—and in the middle of it was an enormous gold coin. He had very small, soft white hands, unveined—not at all like those of an old person—and he had an enormous scarab ring that reached from his knuckle to the joint of his finger.

"Whenever I could escape from school and go to the museum, he would call me to his office and give me a glass of milk and a bar of chocolate. He was very nice to me . . . even years later when I would occasionally pay him a visit. I remember one particular day— I must have been in my twenties then—I entered his office and found it full of boxes. In them were Sir Leonard Woolley's finds from the royal cemetery of Ur in Mesopotamia, with all the jewels of Queen Shub-ad . . . and they hadn't yet been on exhibition. 'Ah!' Dr. Budge said when he saw me. 'You're just in time. Come on here and I will make you a queen!' And he proceeded to place on my head this crown of Queen Shub-ad with all its golden flowers and what looked like a bunch of golden bananas on each side, and then the necklaces and the bracelets as well. And there I was, simply going down under the weight of all this gold![1] Now, I thought they were pretty and all that, but I didn't like them and I wouldn't have cared to keep them . . . I mean, I didn't feel at home in them at all. Years later, how- ever, when I was working on an archaeological dig in Egypt, they found a gold bandlet belonging to a lady of high rank; and when I

[1] About Queen Shub-ad's extraordinary headdress—dating from c. 2700 B.C.—Sir Leonard Woolley, who discovered it in the Queen's tomb, has written: "Its basis was a broad gold ribbon festooned in loops around the hair [covered by a thickly-padded wig]. . . . Over this came three wreaths, the lowest hanging down over the forehead, of plain gold ring pendants, the second of beech leaves, the third of long willow leaves in sets of three with gold flowers whose petals were of blue and white inlay; all three were strung on triple chains of lapis and carnelian beads. Fixed into the back of the hair was a golden 'Spanish comb' with five points ending in lapis-centered gold flow- ers. Heavy spiral rings of gold wire were twisted into the side curls of the wig, huge binate earrings of gold hung down to the shoulders, and apparently from the hair also hung on each side a string of large square stone beads with, at the end of each, a lapis amulet, one shaped as a seated bull and the other as a calf. Complicated as the headdress was, its different parts lay in such good order that it was possible to recon- struct the whole and exhibit the likeness of the queen with all her original finery in place" *(Ur of the Chaldees: A Record of Seven Years of Excavation).*

put *that* on—and *that* was so heavy that it almost gave me a headache!—I didn't want to ever take it off."

If she could have had her way, Dorothy Eady would have lived in the British Museum; and between the ages of ten and twelve she spent as much time there as she could. These were the years 1914 to 1916 with World War I now in progress. Dorothy was forced, as usual, to attend school—though she still skipped classes in order to visit her second home and generally carried on as if the disturbances of the outside world were more a nuisance than a cataclysm.

One night she and her parents hurried out onto a balcony in order to watch the first German Zeppelin flying overhead. "It looked so lovely in the cross searchlights," Dorothy Eady recalled years later, "—just like a great big silver cigar. I was admiring it up there, and then suddenly I saw this beautiful thing burst in the middle and take fire. I began to cry, and my parents promptly gave me a good hiding because I was supposed to have cheered. But I didn't like seeing beautiful things broken."

Two years into the war, however, German war planes started bombing London at night; and the usually nonchalant, fearless, unabashed twelve-year-old began to get scared. One time, during a particularly devastating raid, Dorothy closed her eyes and found herself praying—much like Lucius in Apuleius' *The Golden Ass*—to the goddess Isis:

"O Holy Blessed Lady, constant comfort to humankind whose beneficence and kindness nourish us all, and whose care for those in trouble is as a loving mother who cares for all her children—you are there when we call, stretching out your hand to put aside that which is harmful to us, untangling the web of fate in which we may be caught, even stopping the stars if they form a harmful pattern. All other deities, whether bountiful or merciless, do reverence to thee. It is Isis who rules the world, stamping out the powers of evil, arranging the stars to give us answers, causing the seasons to come and go, commanding the winds to move ships, giving the clouds to water the growing seeds so that we may have food. If I had one thousand mouths and one thousand tongues within each, still I could not do justice to Your Majesty. Yet I will forever remember your help in my time of need and keep your blessed image deep within my heart."

"And from that moment on," Dorothy Eady would later affirm, "I was never afraid of anything ever again."

One Saturday morning she was taking a bus from Blackheath into London to get to the dancing institute Mrs. Eady insisted she attend every weekend to lose weight ("I certainly was as big and fat as a cow!" Dorothy would later say about her early adolescent figure). Suddenly the bus pulled to a halt as sirens began sounding an alert— it was the first German daytime air raid over London—and everybody hurried off scattering for shelter. Dorothy took cover in a sweetshop, bought some chocolates, and, from the doorway, looked up at the aerial dogfight taking place in the sky. "It was most thrilling," she would later testify, "with airplanes attacking and swerving. Then one was hit, and I cheered—though no one knew whose plane it was." Presently the German bombers were driven off; and after a few minutes the "all clear" sirens sounded. Everybody rushed for the buses; but Dorothy, who hated the thought of having to go to dancing school, let the crowds push on ahead of her. Dawdling for a while, she finally boarded an empty bus, got off at Southampton Row, and began to walk the four blocks to the school. Suddenly, out of the blue, she saw and heard a bomb dropping not far ahead of her —the German war planes had returned to attack civilian targets. "The force of the explosion was like a great hand on my chest and pushed me down," she later recalled. "But I wasn't hurt—I wasn't even frightened, I even thought it was a great joke. When the noise subsided, I walked along, taking my time, to the school. And when I arrived there, all I saw was a huge cloud of dust, and in place of the school was an enormous crater."

With her insouciant black humor, Dorothy realized she wouldn't have to take dancing lessons anymore. What disturbed her was that the British Museum might have been destroyed. So she rushed off to Great Russell Street to make sure it was still there, saw that it was, then continued on to New Oxford Street to check up on a friend who owned an antique shop where she spent her pocket money on inexpensive Egyptian figurines and jewelry. Finding that he and the shop were safe, she decided to pay a visit to her aunt's London flat. Upon arriving there and entering the living room, she saw her father trying to console his hysterically weeping wife. Having heard about the bombings near Southampton Row, the Eadys had rushed to the dancing school, where they found emergency workers digging bodies out from under the rubble of the demolished building. Told that all the students had been in attendance, they assumed Dorothy had been killed. Now, seeing their daughter sauntering into the flat, Mr. Eady grabbed her and gave her a fierce hiding for not having called home to report she was alive. Dorothy only remarked: "I just had to see if the British Museum was all right."

* * *

The Eadys had now seen their daughter escape death a second time, but the grief and aggravation attendant upon her miraculous "resurrections" were too much for them. So they decided to send the twelve-year-old—for her own safety and for their own peace of mind —to her grandmother's farm in the Sussex countryside. Since her beloved British Museum had now been closed because of the German bombardments, Dorothy, for once, did not resist being exiled from London for a while. In fact her stay in the country was to make her extremely happy.

"I had a grand time there," she once said about her days in Sussex. "All that Granny had on the farm was a decrepit old man and a half-witted boy of sixteen who wasn't at all interested in farming; and I was a big, hefty child, and strong, and had a way with animals. So I looked after the horses, helped milk the cows, and churned the butter. I remember starting a lovely racing game with all the other neighboring farmers' boys when we took the milk in great big churns to the station. It was like Pharaoh chasing the Israelites—I being Pharaoh, of course! I was driving a cart, and I tied the reins of my horse around my waist, as I'd seen in those pictures; but the animal wasn't sufficiently trained in Egyptology, I suppose, and one time she pulled me out of the cart and I lost quite a large area of skin."

There was another horse in her grandmother's stable—a beautiful white one—and Dorothy baptized it Mut-hotep (which was the name of a chariot horse that had belonged to Sety the First's son, Ramesses the Second, and which means "The Goddess Mut is satisfied"). "We got along very well," she once said, adding: "Mut-hotep was the only creature I could talk to freely and without reserve."

Dorothy attended a country school, which she tolerated because, after classes, she knew she'd be able to hurry home, saddle up her horse, and ride eight miles across the Sussex Downs until she reached the coastal resort town of Eastbourne, with its three-mile-long esplanade and nearby chalk cliffs. Once in Eastbourne, she would make her way to the public library and borrow a number of books on subjects Egyptian, then ride back to the farm to take care of the animals.

She also loved to volunteer for certain chores that turned out to be excuses for mirth and mischief. Not far from the farm was a smock windmill called the Polegate Mill where people went to grind their flour. As Dorothy later recounted, "I was a perfect pest to the poor miller, a man named Mr. Katz. I'd insist on riding on the grand stern. Worse than that, while the sails of the mill were turning, I'd jump out from the little window, where the workmen would go to mend the sails, and then clutch one of the sails and ride round . . . which of course meant that I was upside down. Oh, my God, you should have seen the face of that poor Mr. Katz!"

Dorothy adored being in the country. When once she had to travel to London to spend three days with her parents (she also took a nostalgic walk past the still closed British Museum and witnessed another two air raids over the city), she couldn't wait to get back to the farm, the green fields, the rolling downs, and to her favorite friend, Mut-hotep.

To avoid hearing about the war, Dorothy buried herself in her Egyptological books and studiously avoided reading all newspapers. She couldn't help finding out about the brutal events taking place on the European fronts from the people in the village, and she occasionally suffered from nightmares in which she saw long stretches of farms filled with barbed wire and soldiers flying over them—"as in one of those crazy Salvador Dali paintings," she would later remark —and people, looking vaguely familiar to her, being "blown to pieces."

One day a soldier who was suffering from mustard-gas poisoning was brought, amidst much commotion, to the village. When Dorothy saw the ravaged face of this young man she almost fainted. "His was one of those faces I often saw in my nightmares," she later said. "And now, for the first time, I was finally made aware of the horrors of war . . . and I knew that this was something quite different from the fun I used to have watching those aerial dogfights in the skies above London. I understood how really silly I had been."

* * *

It was the fall of 1918, the war was slowly coming to a close, and the Eadys decided it was time for their daughter to return to London. Back at home, Dorothy was exceedingly unhappy. She missed the Sussex countryside and Mut-hotep. Now fourteen years old, she had no close friends and was a moody, misunderstood, ungainly, and often bored adolescent. Aside from her inextinguishable fascination with Egypt, life seemed weary, stale, flat, and unprofitable.

After one particularly dispiriting and routine-laden day, Dorothy came home from school feeling unusually tired. She ate a light din-

ner—saying only a few words to her parents—then excused herself
and went to her room. Getting undressed, she put on a nightgown
that her mother had recently bought her and that Dorothy herself
had decorated with beadwork—sewing around its border the name
of Isis in hieroglyphs. She got into bed with a book about ancient
Egypt and had hardly opened it when, already half asleep and too
tired to read, she decided it would be best just to turn off the light.

What happened next was so startling that, when she recalled it
some fifty years afterward to a trusted friend, it seemed to her as if it
had taken place only the night before. "I was asleep, and I half woke
up, feeling a weight on my chest. Then I fully woke up, and I saw
this face bending over me with both hands on the neck of my nightdress. I recognized the face from the photo I had seen years before of
the mummy of Sety. I was astonished and shocked and I cried out,
and yet I was overjoyed. I can remember it as if it were yesterday,
but still it's difficult to explain. It was the feeling of something you
have waited for that has come at last, and yet it gives you a shock.
. . . And then he tore open my nightdress from neck to rim.

"My mother was sleeping in the next room, and she heard me cry
out. After a minute she came in and asked me what was the matter.
And I replied matter-of-factly, 'Nothing, I had a nightmare.' Then
she said, 'Who tore your nightdress?' And I said, 'I don't know, I
must have done it myself.' But I *knew* that I hadn't.

"You see, the figure of Sety had appeared to me—though how
could I have explained that to my mother?—and his face was the
dead face of a mummy. The hands moved and the arms moved, but
he didn't talk . . . he didn't say a single word. And I will never
forget the terrible look in the eyes. I don't know how to describe it.
You can only say that the eyes had the look of somebody in hell who
had suddenly found a way out."

From that time on, Dorothy Eady hoped that she would somehow
be able to get in touch with this presence again. And shortly after the
night of Sety's visitation she began to have a recurring dream. She
would see herself as a young Egyptian girl in an enormous room on
rush mats that had been laid on the floor, and with her in this room
were many women and girls. While they were lying down, a very old
man, carrying a lamp, would come into the room and peer at them
with a nearsighted squint to make sure that they were all in their
proper places. Then the dream would switch to an underground
chamber that was surrounded by a channel of water. In this chamber, whose floor was covered with pebbles of agate, carnelian, and
turquoise, was a statue of somebody lying on a bierlike bed. In the

dream the young Egyptian girl encountered a tall, severe-looking man dressed as a high priest and a number of other men and women who stared at her disapprovingly. When she refused to answer his incessant questions, the man would begin beating her with a stick . . . at which point Dorothy would wake up screaming.

Now, at the time that Dorothy Eady was having these dreams she was not aware—at least consciously—that immediately behind Sety's temple in Abydos was located what many archaeologists and historians consider to be the most unusual and mysterious building in all of Egypt. This structure, known as the Osirion, originally consisted of a large subterranean hall, built of monumental red sandstone and white limestone blocks, with monolithic red granite pillars—weighing about a hundred tons each—that supported equally massive architraves and a roof. In the center of the hall was a moundlike raised island surrounded by an artificial water channel, with two flights of steps leading down from it to the water. A cenotaph (or "false tomb") of Sety, the Osirion has also, at various times, been thought to represent the mythical ancient Egyptian Island of Creation emerging from the primeval ocean, and also the tomb of Osiris himself ("he who sleeps surrounded by water").

At the age of fourteen, Dorothy did not know why this strange underground hall was always appearing in her dreams, or why she was always being beaten by a frightening inquisitor who looked like a high priest. This recurring dream was so oppressive, and the screams Dorothy let out during it so piercing, that Mrs. Eady would often have to rush into her daughter's bedroom to comfort her. What upset and unnerved the mother most of all was the way the girl's voice sounded when she called out in her sleep—an agonized crying for help that seemed to come from a possessed sleeping creature whom Mrs. Eady could hardly recognize.

It was also around this time that Dorothy's mother began to notice that her daughter had a tendency to sleepwalk. Once, when the Eady family was staying at the farm in Sussex, Dorothy went riding at night in a torrential rain. When she returned to the stable she cleaned her horse. Back in the house, she took a hot bath, then undressed for bed. But suddenly she remembered that she hadn't bothered to lock the stable door. She started to put her clothes back on again; but her mother, seeing her fussing about, asked her why she was getting dressed. When Dorothy told her, Mrs. Eady just said, "For goodness' sake, don't worry, they're *awful* horses, nobody's going to steal them." Dorothy thought, "Well, all right," and went to bed. The next morning, when Mrs. Eady entered her room to wake her, she noticed that her daughter's feet and nightgown were all muddy. Dorothy didn't know how that had happened since she had gone right to bed. When Mrs. Eady went to the stable and found the door locked, she realized that her daughter must have been out walking in her sleep. Because of Dorothy's somnambulism and her persistent nightmares, the Eadys committed their daughter several times to a mental hospital for observation—though her stays there were of short duration.

* * *

By 1920, Dorothy was sixteen years old and was no longer required to attend school . . . which left her free to spend her days as she wished—reading books, collecting Egyptian antiquities, and visiting the British Museum. Dorothy's father was then going through a "mid-life crisis." Having become interested in the newly emerging cinema industry, he started thinking about giving up his career as a master tailor. Like his daughter, Reuben Eady also had "another" life. Little is known about his youth. In addition to being a tailor, he was also a part-time magician and conjuror who worked under the name of Brandon Dalmar at small clubs and cabarets, and had occasionally performed at larger music halls. Sensing that movies were likely to become a lucrative form of entertainment, he made up his mind, in 1920, to take a leisurely tour of the British Isles with his wife and daughter to search for theaters suitable for transformation into movie halls.

Dorothy loved what was, for her, a very grand tour. In every city the Eadys visited, she would find the main library and local museum and spend her time doing Egyptological research. Then one day, when the Eadys were driving through the Wiltshire countryside, they found themselves on the Salisbury Plain. There, they came upon the most magical place Dorothy had ever seen—the extraordinary circular setting of megalithic standing stones known as Stonehenge. Approaching the ruins of this ancient religious center and astronomical observatory (built during the Late Neolithic and Early Bronze Ages—c. 1800–1400 B.C.), Dorothy observed, in the pale, mist-suspended early morning light, a beautiful white horse grazing in the enclosed earthwork, and noticed the eerie, calm shadows cast by the lintel-capped trilithons and sarsen columns. The horse immediately reminded Dorothy of Mut-hotep; and, as she would later remark, she could "smell Egyptian work in that place."² The 35-ton, 16-foot-high Heel Stone that stands on the Avenue outside the entrance and on which the sun rises on Midsummer Day seemed to Dorothy to resemble "a stumpy Heliopolitan obelisk." (Heliopolis was the original ancient Egyptian cult center of the sun god Ra, who, under another name, was probably also worshiped at Stonehenge.) Dorothy was thrilled when she found out that, in the graves and barrow burial plots clustered around the area, blue Egyptian faience beads (known as mummy beads) had been discovered. As have others before and after her, she speculated that perhaps Egyptians, or their more hardy seafaring and mercantile neighbors from Minoan Crete and Mycenaean Greece, may have gone as traders to pre-Roman Britain, taking Egyptian beads and stones with them. At Stonehenge, Dorothy had an intuition of what was later to become her firm belief that travel in ancient days was much more extensive and common than is generally imagined.

In the twelfth century the English historian Geoffrey of Monmouth thought that the monumental stones of Stonehenge had originally been transported magically to their present site from Ireland! After traveling through England, Dorothy and her parents eventually arrived in Dublin. To the Eadys' dismay, their daughter immediately got caught up in an anti-British riot when she entered the fray on the side of the Sinn Fein rebels against the British Black and Tans. Her parents dragged her out of a street battle in the nick of time. Although Dorothy reminded her father that, thanks to him, she was part Irish and that she was just standing up for Irish independence, Mr. Eady—an authoritarian in matters of discipline—gave her a beating. (Irish nationalists were fervent supporters of the nationalist Egyptian Wafd movement and its leader, Saad Zaghlul Pasha, during the Egyptian rebellion of 1919.)

"You know," Dorothy Eady would later explain, "I really never felt at home in England. As Moses said in the Bible, 'I was a stranger in a strange land.' After the First World War was over and the 1919 revolution broke out in Egypt, that country sprang into the English newspaper headlines. I remember quarreling with my family all the time about the right of Egypt to have its independence. Once, I got very angry at my uncle, who kept telling me that if ever I went to Egypt I would find the British flag flying over the Citadel in Cairo.

---

² Describing his first visit to Stonehenge, the travel writer H. O. Morton once stated: "Inexpressibly remote those great stones seemed, standing up there in the faint light that was not the light of moon or sun but the spectral half-light that comes before day. I was reminded of Egypt" (*In Search of England*).

In my fury I told him that I hoped the day would come when I'd see it lowered and the Egyptian flag hoisted in its place. And I'm happy I lived to see that day!"

* * *

After completing his scouting tour of the British Isles, Reuben Eady decided to move his family to Plymouth, where he had persuaded a London consortium to provide him with funds to convert a skating rink/dance hall into a cinema. This cinema was so remarkable that, almost fifty years after its opening, Eady's entrepreneurial creation was commemorated in an article by the journalist and film scholar Robert Ainsworth for the local Plymouth paper, the *Western Morning News.*

Located on Ebrington Street, the New Palladium, as the movie house was called, seated thirty-five hundred viewers and allowed standing room for another thousand. Reuben Eady built the projection room brick by brick; and so spacious was the cinema that the projection room was a hundred and fifty feet away from the screen, making it necessary for the projectionist to use binoculars in order to focus the film.

The movie Mr. Eady chose to inaugurate his theater was Erich von Stroheim's *Foolish Wives.* It ran for two weeks, with more than three thousand viewers attending each performance. The New Palladium was an immediate success, and Dorothy's father became renowned as a "manager extraordinaire." During the summer months he had huge blocks of ice placed at various locations inside the cinema in order to make it "the coolest theater in town." He also installed an electrical vapor machine that not only made the building smell like a cathedral but also served to disinfect the cinema so that "diphtheria [could] not live longer than seven seconds in its fumes, and influenza germs [were] killed in four seconds."

The New Palladium also housed the first cinema organ in Plymouth—"The Home of the Pipe Organ," as the advertisements put it —which was used both for accompanying the silent movies and for occasional solo organ recitals. Three times a week a Plymouth orchestra would broadcast performances "live from the New Palladium" over the local BBC radio station.

On Friday nights, and as prologues and interludes at the screenings, Reuben Eady would devise, produce, and direct his own concerts and dramatic spectacles. On one occasion impresario Eady presented three girls dancing on roller skates in front of a pirate ship in full sail. Another time, colorfully bedizened American Indians in war paint rushed onto the stage to attack a group of covered wagons, while a musician jumped up from the pit and charged after the assailants, wildly firing blank shots at them. And in a memorable *tableau vivant*, the head of a demon with horns and flashing eyes stared down ominously at three ghostly figures who were flitting around a huge fire.

At calmer moments, there would be a musical interlude, during which a buxom girl named Dorothy Lincoln, dressed in exotic garb, would appear on stage and sing a popular music hall number, embellishing her performance with a full range of melodramatic gesticulations—to the accompaniment of a fifteen-piece orchestra.

Dorothy Lincoln was the stage name for none other than Mr. Eady's daughter. As an older resident of Plymouth has recalled: "Dorothy was a large girl and quite good-looking in those days. I well remember the prologue to the film *The Thief of Bagdad*, starring Douglas Fairbanks. Just before the movie began, Dorothy Lincoln appeared on stage wearing an oriental costume, and proceeded to give a rendition of 'Somewhere in the Sahara'—which was a popular song at the time—though Mr. Eady changed it for the occasion to 'Somewhere in Old Bagdad.' " Another longtime Plymouth resident "vividly" remembers a Dorothy Lincoln of "generous build" and "having that quaver in her soprano voice so popular at the time—but not so much to little boys like me! Reuben Eady used to stand at the back of the theater and just *dare* anybody to respond unappreciatively when Dorothy was performing on stage. He applauded wildly after each song."

Little boys may have disliked her voice, but some "older" Plymouth residents thought that Dorothy had a bit of talent. She worked with an amateur theater group that presented a dramatization of the Isis and Osiris story. Dorothy played Isis, and another girl played Isis' sister, Nephthys. The highlight of the play was a duet in which the sister goddesses bewailed their brother Osiris' death and entreated him to come back to life. The text for this duet was derived from an ancient Egyptian lamentation recited three thousand years before during the annual sacred mystery play in Abydos. It had been translated into German at the turn of this century, and soon afterward it appeared in an English version done by the remarkable folklorist and man of letters Andrew Lang (1844–1912), best known for his *Blue, Red,* and *Green Fairy Books.*

As Dorothy Eady recollected: "The printed German version of the 'Lament of Isis and Nephthys' had its own music, but the melody I used for the English text, which we sang in the play, was one that I used to hum over and over again when I was a kid, and it would drive my parents crazy! I never varied that tune; and when I first read the Lang poem, many years later, I found that it fit very well with it. The original version of the text, by the way, must have been written either at the time the Sety Temple was built or just afterward, because it refers to the 'sevenfold sacred shrine.' The girl who played Nephthys and I sang it on stage together, but I also remember that I performed it on my own at a singing contest in Plymouth not long after we'd presented the play . . . and I won a gold medal! Even in modern translation, the 'Lament for Osiris,' which is what Andrew Lang called it, has the power to stir our deepest emotions":

> Sing we Osiris dead,
> Lament the fallen head:
> The light has left the world, the world is gray.
> Athwart the starry skies
> The web of darkness flies,
> And Isis weeps Osiris passed away.
> Your tears, ye stars, ye fires, ye rivers, shed,
> Weep, children of the Nile, weep for your lord is dead!
>
> Softly we tread, our measured footsteps falling
> Within the sanctuary sevenfold;
> Soft on the dead that liveth are we calling:
> "Return, Osiris, from thy Kingdom cold!
> Return to them that worship thee of old."
>
> Within the court divine
> The sevenfold sacred shrine
> We pass, while echoes of the temple walls
> Repeat the long lament
> The sound of sorrow sent
> Far up within the imperishable halls,
> Where, each in other's arms, the sisters weep,
> Isis and Nephthys, o'er his unawaking sleep.
>
> Softly we tread, our measured footsteps falling
> Within the sanctuary sevenfold;
> Soft on the dead that liveth are we calling:
> "Return, Osiris, from thy kingdom cold!
> Return to them that worship thee of old."
>
> O dweller in the west,
> Lover and lordliest,

Thy love, thy sister Isis, calls thee home!
  Come from thy chamber dun,
  Thou master of the sun,
Thy shadowy chamber far below the foam!
  With weary wings and spent
  Through all the firmament,
Through all the horror-haunted ways of hell,
  I seek thee near and far,
  From star to wandering star,
Free with the dead that in Amenti dwell.
  I search the height, the deep, the lands, the skies,
  Rise from the dead and live, our lord Osiris, rise!

"In the play, after Nephthys and I had finished singing our lament, Osiris rose from the dead; and the other actors suddenly threw off the dark cloaks they were wearing and stood revealed in beautiful white robes!"

* * *

Those few people still living who remember Dorothy Eady's father describe him as being a "short," "rather tubby," but "imposing" and "imperious" figure who was always well dressed and who always kept a pair of scissors in his pocket to extract butts from a cigarette holder that he used to place between his lips, while turning his head in profile when he spoke in public, "as if he had just stepped out of an Edgar Wallace detective novel." A master showman, he was instrumental in organizing a reception for the visiting American cowboy star, Tom Mix, at Plymouth's Savoy Hotel, where Tom's horse Tony pranced in between the tables of the astonished guests. In his business dealings, Eady was—according to his former projectionist—a "fair and straight-speaking man."

No longer a lower-class tailor, the now genteel middle-class Reuben Eady was one of the first residents of Plymouth to own an automobile. He eventually moved his family from their flat, just above the cinema, to a caravan (what someone has described as an "opulent trailer") in the nearby countryside. Here, waking in the morning, Dorothy could see ravens, crows, rooks, and kestrels flying above the dramatic granite hills and woods of Dartmoor, where otters, weasels, foxes, and badgers had their lairs.

The late 1920s saw the arrival of sound films. Reuben Eady's movie house was eventually bought by Denham Picture Houses (now a part of the Rank Organization), which kept him on as manager of both the New Palladium and Savoy cinemas—a position he left, in 1931, to become manager of the new Gaumont Cinema on Union Street—Plymouth's answer to London's Soho—where, every night, sailors from the naval base would congregate to carouse at the more than one hundred pubs lining the thoroughfare. In this new age of talkies, however, Reuben Eady's flamboyant directorial skills and theatrical flair were no longer appreciated. In 1934—having lost his enthusiasm for what was now mostly administrative work, and having begun to suffer from bouts of severe depression—he gave up the film business completely.

The New Palladium cinema—along with more than eighty thousand other buildings in the city—was blitzed by German bombs in March of 1941. A parking lot now marks the site of this once hugely popular movie house—conceived of, built, and run by Dorothy Eady's remarkable father, who died in his caravan, ten years before his wife, on May 28, 1935, at the age of fifty-six.

* * *

Dorothy Eady's late adolescent and early adult years in Plymouth were those of waiting. *She* knew what she was waiting for, yet almost everyone who came in contact with her at that time inevitably thought of her simply as a dotty loner who sang at her father's cinema. They were sure she would end up as an old maid living forever with her parents in this stolid, provincial port city. (Little did they realize that she was waiting not for her ship to come *in* but for her ship to go *out!*)

No one in Plymouth was either aware of or interested in finding out about Dorothy Eady's "secret" thoughts and plans. On the surface, she was an unpretentious, heavy-set girl with blue eyes and straw-colored hair who had an exuberant sense of humor. Laughingly, she used to recount the story of how once a Royal Navy vessel, the HMS *Ark Royal,* got stuck in the mud off the Plymouth coast. Dorothy and her parents were out on a beach from which they could see naval personnel attempting to unground the boat. At the very moment Dorothy entered the water to go swimming, the vessel was floated off. The Eadys never let their daughter live that down, telling everyone, "Dorothy walks into the water, and what happens? She fills up the sea so much she liberates the *Ark Royal!*"

Dorothy was, by then, quite used to her parents' teasing. She sometimes resented having to sing publicly at the New Palladium and at weekend soirees her father organized at home. On her own, she became a part-time student at the Plymouth Art School, where she took classes in drawing—a talent that would serve her well in the future. She also attended meetings of a local group that met from time to time to discuss the possibility of reincarnation. Dorothy, who had no one to talk to about this subject, and thinking herself among kindred spirits, tried to communicate her feelings about having had a former existence in ancient Egypt. "But the members of the club," she later commented, "weren't sure if I hadn't really had *several* reincarnations, one of which was Joan of Arc. But why the hell should I have been Joan of Arc? I don't know. I did feel like fighting, and I was always annoyed when Egypt was in trouble, and I would have liked to have gone to fight for Egypt—it was the streak of the Irish in me. Otherwise there was nothing saintly about me."

About this time she also consulted with spiritualists about her perplexing feelings. They, repudiating the doctrine of reincarnation, suggested instead that at the moment of her "death," when she fell down the stairs, an ancient spirit had possibly entered her body and possessed her. Uncertain of the "true" explanation of her condition, Dorothy gave up asking why and simply focused her energy on her Egyptological reading and collecting.

Several British newspapers at the time reported that the Egyptian government was becoming increasingly upset about the massive, illegal flow of antiquities out of the country. There were articles about an Egyptian archaeologist named Selim Hassan who had just discovered the sarcophagus-shaped limestone tomb of the Fourth Dynasty Queen Khent-kawes located just southeast of the Great Pyramid.

Dorothy, then in her mid-twenties, had put together "a nice little collection of Egyptian antiquities—I mean, nothing really very valuable, but I loved them very much. When I read those articles, however, I got a guilty conscience about my collection, so I piled all the pieces in a box and sent them by post to Professor Selim Hassan, Department of Egyptian Antiquities, Cairo, Egypt. I didn't say from whom they came, I just sent along the quotation from the New Testament: 'Render unto Caesar the things which are Caesar's,' and I thought no more about it.

"Then, one afternoon, I came home to find my mother in a terrible state. 'I don't know what you've been doing,' she said to me, 'but the police were here asking for you about something to do with Egypt.' Now, at that time, I was all out in favor of Saad Zaghlul—the Egyptian nationalist leader—and my mother had visions of my being shot in the Tower of London as a traitor! So I tried to calm her down by saying that I'd go right down to the police station to see what the matter was. When I got there I asked the officer in charge why he had been asking for me. 'Did you send a box of antiquities to Egypt?' he inquired. I replied that, yes, I'd sent them to Professor Selim Hassan. 'So,' he said, 'it *is* you. We thought it was.' I asked him what was wrong, and he informed me that Professor Hassan had been very curious about who it was who had sent the package, and he had had nothing to go on but the Plymouth postmark; so he wrote a letter to the police department in Plymouth, asking if anyone there knew of a local resident who was interested in Egyptian antiquities . . . and the only person they could find out about was *me.*"

A year later, at twenty-seven, Dorothy went to London where—in spite of her family's disapproval—she got a job with an Egyptian public relations magazine, for which she wrote articles and drew political cartoons promoting the cause of Egyptian independence. Living in London then was a young man from an upper-middle-class family in Cairo named Imam Abdel Meguid, who was studying British educational methods in preparation for becoming a teacher back in Egypt.

"I met Imam in the House of Commons, of all places," Dorothy would later say about their fated encounter. "You see, the Egyptian students who were residing in London in the early 1930s were extremely active politically. You could see them everywhere—distributing pamphlets or fliers, making speeches, and explaining their views patiently (but most of the time impatiently!) to a dumb crowd of loiterers in Hyde Park. Most of the students were continually writing letters to the editor of every English newspaper they could. Since they caused no disturbances, the British government had no grounds or excuse to repatriate them.

"Imam, in particular, was always following the debates in the House of Commons whenever the Egyptian problem was on the agenda. He listened very attentively and wrote down the points of view of every speaker—those who were for and those who were against the Egyptian cause.

"Well, one afternoon I was sent by my editor to interview a certain member of Parliament at the House of Commons to try to convince him that Egypt was quite capable of running her own affairs. While I was waiting outside his office, two young Egyptians came in, and the only free seat was beside me. So one of them—who turned out to be Imam—sat down, while the other went off to interview another M.P. . . . So far so good. Then this chap next to me started to nod . . . and nod . . . and eventually he fell asleep and ended up with his head on my shoulder. So I gave him a little nudge, and he woke up. 'Oh, pardon, pardon!' he said. But he kept on doing this several times. He must have been tired because he really *did* fall asleep! I thought, 'Well, hell, let him stay.' So, when his friend came back, there I was with his buddy sitting beside me, his head on my shoulder, *snoring.* We woke him up, and both of us burst out laughing. Then we started talking; and since they told me that they were both leaving London for Cairo the next day, Imam and I exchanged addresses. And we corresponded. He wrote to me how he was interested in education and wanted to raise the standards of modern Egypt to that of ancient Egypt and all that. After a year of exchanging letters, he sent me a photograph of himself with the family group —decent, honorable, honest people—and asked me if I'd marry him.

"Now, until then, I had turned down several offers of marriage. My hand had been asked for by a respectable and decent Englishman, who, as an inducement, said he'd been offered a job as an officer in the Cairo police. . . . Well, I couldn't face *that.* Then a couple of Egyptians asked to marry me. But I couldn't face *them.* Because, you see, I had been carrying the torch for King Sety since I was fourteen years old and was always hoping to meet someone like *him.* However, I soon realized that they didn't make men like that anymore. Also, I thought I loved Imam—you know how girls are with romance. My parents, of course, objected because they had never met him, and they said absolutely no to the proposal. They could have saved their breath! I was *certainly* over age and always did what I wanted to. When they saw how determined I was, they had no choice but to give their consent."

So, at the age of twenty-nine, Dorothy Louise Eady wrote a letter to Egypt to say that she had agreed to become Mrs. Imam Abdel Meguid.

·III·

Bulbul Abdel Meguid

my mind goes on,
spinning the infinite thread;

surely, I crossed the threshold,
I passed through the temple-gate,
I crossed a frontier and stepped

on the gold-burning sands of Egypt;
then why do I lie here and wonder,
and try to unravel the tangle

that no man can ever un-knot?

(from *Helen in Egypt* by H.D.)

In 1933, Dorothy Eady booked passage on a boat going to Egypt, packed a few of her belongings, and excitedly began her long-anticipated journey. Her vessel departed from Southampton, and after ten days at sea it finally approached the coast of Port Said just before dawn. Unable to sleep the night before her arrival, Dorothy had lain awake in her cabin. At one point, noticing that the boat had stopped, and hearing a commotion above her, she got dressed and went up to see what was happening. In preparation for their landing, the sailors were hurriedly swabbing down the decks. "I went and leaned on the rail," Dorothy Eady later commented, "and I could just see the faint, darkish shape of the land and, here and there, little twinkling lights. One of the sailors said to me, 'That's Port Said, miss.' I knew it was. Oh, I stood on the rail laughing and crying. When I got down off the ship, I knelt and kissed the ground and said, 'Mother, I've come home!' And I swore I'd never leave."

With her husband-to-be, who had come to meet her at Port Said, Dorothy boarded a train to Cairo. And throughout the journey she stood transfixed, staring out a window and taking in the colors of her land: the bright, lambent, celestial green fields of the Nile Valley with its squares of black soil; the opalescent violet shadows in the curves of the faraway desert sand drifts; and the unmitigated, brilliant amber light of the sky, worthy of the greatest of sun gods.

In every field were ox-drawn plows driven by the first farmers of the world—the Egyptian fellaheen in their blue galabias—and just behind every plow a flock of snow-white egrets "clearing" the upturned soil of parasites and vermin. Everywhere Dorothy looked she could see shiny black water buffaloes, cows, donkeys, horses, sheep, and goats. "Nothing like this in England!" she thought to herself, hardly realizing how little she was saying to the man whom she was shortly to marry.

On entering Cairo—at that time a green picturesque city of only one million inhabitants—she caught sight of young schoolboys in tarbooshes, women elegantly dressed in the latest Parisian styles or else traditionally veiled, merchants in peach-colored kaftans, and vegetable and fruit sellers in galabias-rayés.

In the heart of Cairo a few Englishmen—some in their knickerbockers and felt hats—were out strolling with their families, while young Egyptian university students stared at them with a mixture of contempt and disdain. "Although we spoke the same language," Dorothy Eady would later confess, "I felt, from my very first week in Cairo, totally distant and estranged from my British countrymen—as if they were creatures from an alien world. And I quite deservedly earned the wrath of the city's British community because of my attitude toward it."

Almost immediately upon arriving in Cairo, Dorothy and Imam Abdel Meguid got married; and the bride's father-in-law gave her the first name "Bulbul," which means "nightingale" in Arabic (perhaps on account of her mellifluous singing voice). But some of the first notes uttered by this "dryad of the trees" created a discordant melody, as the newlyweds quickly engaged in their first row.

Imam's family, it seems, owned a house that backed onto the Citadel in the old part of the city. And from this residence Dorothy would observe gray and black crows resting on top of sycamores and majestic kites soaring over eucalyptus trees; watch clouds of pigeons flying above cupolas, domes, and minarets; hear the cries of the muezzins calling the faithful to prayer; and, in the distance, make out the lateen sails of feluccas drifting down the Great River.

It was here that Bulbul wanted to live. "Oh, it was lovely, and so high up," she would later recall. "Wonderful air. You could see right over the city as far as the pyramids in the distance. But my husband wouldn't live there. He was a governmental official, and this was an Old Cairo quarter, and he insisted that we reside in Manya El Roda [in the early thirties, a beautiful residential section of Cairo whose houses overlooked gardens of palms, carob trees, and cassias]. But I wanted to be close to the ancient monuments, and this area was full of very snooty English people—you know, the bra and brown boots and no-breakfasttime set. Oh, my dear, awful, awful people! I mean, the husband of one of the families there was a chauffeur. In England he had been a chauffeur, too; but here, because he was chauffeur to some pasha, he thought he *was* a pasha. . . . My God, if there was ever a boring place, it was Manya El Roda!"

Imam Abdel Meguid quickly realized that his wife was a bit more headstrong than he had bargained for. But he did assume that she would, in the nature of things, be a good cook. On this score, too, he was unfortunately in for a surprise. Once, for instance, while attempting to prepare some *dholma*—one of his favorite dishes, which consisted of vine leaves rolled and stuffed with rice and minced meat —Mrs. Abdel Meguid found herself unable to handle the vine leaves properly; so she decided to tie them up with sewing thread, threw them in the water, where they immediately came apart, and then capped off her triumph by overboiling the ill-fated concoction.

Bulbul's cooking prowess became legendary. Neighbors of hers vividly remember one of her *"kushari"* parties. This was a dish— made with whole lentils, rice, onions, and hot tomato sauce—that *she* was particularly fond of; but it required an exact ordering of ingredients and precise timing in its preparation. Absent-mindedly, she mixed everything together in slapdash fashion and put the concoction in the oven. What emerged an hour later was described as "a thick magma of unidentifiable color" with a "unique" taste. One guest suggested that the cook use it to "paint the apartment an original color"; another said that he would try out a sample as a rat poison; and the hostess herself, unperturbed, suggested that each of her friends take a bit of it, for external use only, as an "ointment" for boils and abscesses.

"Poor chap, poor chap. The way I made that poor fellow suffer!" Dorothy Eady would later sigh, recalling her husband's desperate domestic situation. "What with nearly killing him with my cooking —you know, English cooking is pretty bad, but mine was the worst! —I also bored him to tears with my talk about ancient Egypt. He liked everything modern, and I liked everything old . . . so it was all too much for him."

Mrs. Abdel Meguid was now pregnant ("very quick work, that," she once commented). Mr. and Mrs. Eady took this occasion to come out to Egypt in order, in Dorothy's words, "to see the lay of the land and to meet my husband." They were, according to their daughter, "charmed with him, and my mother said that he was much too good for me!" The Eadys then stayed on to witness the birth of their grandchild—a baby boy who *they* thought should be named George, but whom their daughter insisted on calling Sety. (The father of the child, it seems, had no say in the matter.)

By now, Imam Abdel Meguid had ineluctably realized and accepted the fact that his wife was not only uninterested in and unsuited for any normal domestic "routine" but was also an extremely *peculiar* person, to and around whom the strangest things were likely to occur. Imam's father—whose sanity his son had no reason to doubt—happened to walk into his daughter-in-law's bedroom one day when she was recuperating from an illness; and suddenly people in the house observed him running from the room, yelling that "there was a pharaoh sitting on Bulbul's bed!"

A month or so before she was due to give birth, Bulbul and her husband were invited to a wedding party in another quarter of Cairo called Shoubra, but she felt tired and didn't want to go. So Imam told her that if it got too late he would spend the night at a flat belonging to his mother a short distance from the party. His wife did not object. "It was summer," Dorothy Eady later recollected, "and my mother and father were given our bedroom, and I was sleeping on a mattress on the terrace that adjoined the bedroom. (There was a glass door that opened onto the terrace, but it was a private terrace, and nobody could get onto it except through our flat.) So I went to sleep on my mattress, and my parents retired to the bedroom.

"Now, my mother, always an early riser, got up as usual the next morning. Since she could never do anything until she had her cup of tea, she went to boil some water, then came and brought two cups to my mattress on the terrace. 'Mother, sit down and drink your tea,' I told her. She said, 'I've already had mine.' I asked, 'Why the two cups then?' She replied, 'One for you and one for Imam.' Then I said, 'But Imam didn't come back last night, he stayed at Shoubra.' (I had told my mother he probably wouldn't be returning home.) She insisted, 'No, he came last night. I woke up and saw him standing near your mattress and looking at you.' 'What was he wearing?' I asked her. 'A white galabia and a blue cloak, or something over it . . . dark blue.' So I said to her, 'You *know* Imam's dressing gown is dark red.' Again she insisted, saying, 'It *must* have been him.' 'It wasn't him,' I told her. 'Then who *was* it?' she asked. 'Well, if you really want to know, it was King Sety the First.' . . . She was speechless for a while, but then she looked at me, terrified, and said, 'My God,

Dorothy, come away from this country, it's not a safe place to be in!' "

* * *

Years later Dorothy Eady would attempt to explain this phantasmal occurrence by stating that shortly after her arrival in Egypt "His Majesty" began to appear to her once again. And "His Majesty," Dorothy revealed, appeared to her in Egypt not in the guise of a mummy—as he had previously done when she had been a fourteen-year-old girl in Plymouth—but in what she claimed was his "normal" form and appearance. "Every time I tried to touch him or he tried to touch me, however," she added, "it was as if there were a thick pane of glass between us. It wasn't until several years after his reappearance that he first spoke to me. I had difficulty in understanding him, and I used to make funny mistakes when I talked. If I heard people moving about and wanted to say 'Keep quiet!' the words 'Shut up!' would come out instead. But one night he discovered that by placing his hand on me—and especially by *holding* my hand—I could understand and speak properly to him, as if some intimate power from His Majesty had entered into me."

* * *

Unlike Dorothy's mother and father-in-law, Imam Abdel Meguid had never caught a glimpse of this "apparition." Since the birth of his son, he had grown increasingly distant from his wife, whose interests, concerns, and visions were far removed from his own, and whose ever more bizarre behavior both amazed and frightened him.

During the second year of their marriage he would wake up in the middle of certain nights—usually when the moon was full—and would watch, totally astonished and almost without breathing, his "nightingale" spouse rise up out of the bed in a kind of half-conscious, half-trance state and seemingly *float* over to a desk next to the window, where, by the light of the moon, she would begin to write—as if being dictated to—some kind of fragmentary hieroglyphic messages.

"Most of the time when I was writing," Dorothy Eady would later say, "I was rather unconscious, as though I were under a strange spell—neither asleep nor awake. I *was* being dictated to. The 'gentleman' who was narrating my story—his name was Hor-Ra—really took his time. He would just tell me a few words, then be absent for a fortnight or so, then come again—always at night—and relate to me a couple of other lines or episodes . . . and after that his voice would just die away. It was as though this Hor-Ra were bored to death, as if he were fulfilling a mission that filled him with loathing. Every night when he came, I felt as though something were shaking me in order to wake me . . . just as in a dream. When I was writing the bits and pieces of the story I felt I was hearing a soft voice . . . without being able to see anybody. The nights were always moonlit, and somehow I was able to see my own handwriting. While I was being dictated to, I felt I understood every word; but later on, when I started to decipher the scribblings, I found they were quite difficult to understand. In fact, in the mornings when I woke up, everything seemed so vague, so uncertain, that if I hadn't been absolutely sure it was my own handwriting, I would have said it was somebody else's. The bits and pieces were there, and when finally Hor-Ra stopped coming I started to piece together what looked to me like a big jigsaw puzzle.

"It took this Hor-Ra almost a year to finish the story. During that time I was in great trouble with my husband because I was unconsciously hiding from him what was being dictated to me, and he was wondering what I was doing in the middle of the night, writing down something he never saw. I didn't want to further upset Imam, who already had every reason to complain about my cooking and the neglecting of all my housecleaning. He was extremely disturbed that I didn't tell him what these 'dictations' were all about right from the beginning. I wasn't sure he would believe it . . . and I wasn't sure anybody else would, either.

"After I'd finally translated and pieced together all of the writings —they came to about seventy pages—this is what I found out . . . and I think it's true because of things that I remember. My parents, it seemed, were of very humble origin. My mother was a vegetable seller who used to sell produce to the troops, and my father was a soldier stationed in Shunet El Zebib, an archaic fortress that had been turned into a military barracks about a mile to the north of Sety's temple. Beautiful ancestry! I don't know if they were married . . . possibly not. Maybe he gave her a potsherd with a few inscriptions to use as a marriage certificate. If they were married, it was short-lived. When I was born my mother called me Bentreshyt ('Harp-of-Joy'), but she died when I was a little over two years old. My father, who had previously been sent on missions for weeks or months at a time, was soon transferred to Thebes [Luxor]; and since he couldn't drag a then three-year-old baby along with him, he took her to the ancient temple at Kom El Sultan (just to the north of

Sety's temple, which was just then under construction) to be brought up as a priestess.

"The high priest at the temple was called Antef, which is rather peculiar because that name wasn't fashionable at that time. He was tall, with a stern face, and he used to scare the wits out of all the priestesses whenever they heard his low baritone voice. His shaven head, his immaculate clothes, and his imposing figure commanded respect. He was the prototype of the Egyptian aristocrat—a very distinguished, but frightening, person indeed.

"When Bentreshyt was twelve years old Antef asked her if she wanted to go out into the world or remain in the temple. If she wanted to go out into the world and find herself a nice husband, well . . . good-bye and God bless you! But she didn't know anything about the world outside, and she was happy in the temple, so she said she would rather stay. Antef then explained to her that she must make a vow to remain a virgin because she would now become temple property. Being only twelve, Bentreshyt did not quite realize the meaning of it all; but having nowhere else to go, she took her vows.

"For the next couple of years, Bentreshyt was taught by the high priest himself the role she would be enacting in the drama of the death and resurrection of Osiris[1]—a role that only virgins, vowed as

[1] As Dorothy Eady once wrote: "The standard version of the story of Osiris, as it was known during the New Kingdom, was that Osiris, his two brothers Set and Horus the Elder, and his sisters Isis and Nephthys, were all the children of Nut, goddess of the sky, and Geb, god of the earth. Osiris married Isis, and Set married Nephthys. Osiris became King of Egypt, but at that time the Egyptians were a totally uncivilized people. They lived in temporary settlements along the edge of the desert, dressed in the skins of wild beasts, and lived by hunting and herding wild cattle. They also indulged in human sacrifices and cannibalism.

"Osiris taught his subjects the arts of agriculture and irrigation. He showed them how to build houses of sun-dried mud brick, and he erected temples of the same material so that they came to live together in harmony in settled communities. Osiris gave them laws and education and even the skill of writing, using the hieroglyphic script invented by his friend, the wise god Thoth.

"The goddess Isis helped her husband in every possible way. She persuaded the people to cultivate flax and taught the women how to spin thread and weave cloth so that they could wear clean garments of linen instead of animal skins.

"Both Osiris and Isis were dearly loved by their subjects. But their evil brother Set hated Osiris and was bitterly jealous of his popularity with the people. Set finally managed to pick a quarrel with Osiris, murdered him, and cut his body into fourteen pieces, which he scattered all over Egypt.

"As soon as she heard of this tragedy, Isis set out to search for the fragments of her husband's body, embalmed them with the help of the god Anubis, and buried them in the spot in which they were found. (According to this version of the story, the head of Osiris was buried at Abydos. The heart was buried on the island of Philae, near Aswan. The phallus was thrown into the Nile and was swallowed by a fish. For this reason the eating of fish was forbidden to the priests.) Another tradition says that

priestesses of Isis from their childhood, were allowed to play. They received a very arduous training—this Antef fellow was quite severe, a real fundamentalist, so to speak—because the priestesses were not supposed to make any mistakes whatsoever when reciting the religious hymns during the performance of the Mysteries.

"In the play, the part of Osiris was taken by a life-sized wooden statue of the god, adorned with gold and semiprecious stones. The role of Horus was traditionally performed by the King himself, although he sometimes delegated this honor to some important official. The other gods were personified by the priests and priestesses, and it was stipulated that women who played the parts of Isis and Nephthys must be virgins. The 'crowd,' representing the followers of Osiris and the followers of Set, were played by certain members of the crowd themselves, who fought together with stripped palm branches . . . and one wonders how many heads were broken and how many old scores were paid off!

"Each episode of the play took place on a separate day and in a separate place. But the murder of Osiris was too sacred, too tragic and harrowing, for public presentation; and this took place inside the temple. The search for the body of Osiris, however, was enacted on the banks of the canal where the original incident was supposed to have occurred. The two women impersonating Isis and Nephthys, their hair unbound and their faces and robes smeared with mud, ran wailing along the banks of the waterway. Finally, they 'found' the god lying on the ground. Isis threw herself upon him, weeping and lamenting; and the two goddesses together then sang the heartrending 'Lament of Isis and Nephthys.'

Anubis and Isis assembled the embalmed fragments and buried them all at Abydos. In the oldest versions of the story, which are found in the *Pyramid Texts*, and date from the Fifth Dynasty, it is merely stated that Set murdered Osiris in Abydos and left his body lying on the bank of the canal. It was found by Isis and Nephthys, embalmed by Anubis, and buried at Abydos.

"At the time of his murder, Osiris and Isis had no children, but by mystical means, Osiris achieved a physical resurrection for one night and slept with Isis. By this means she conceived her son Horus, who was later to avenge his father's death.

"Set seized the throne of Egypt and ruled as a despotic tyrant. Isis fled away to the north, where she hid herself in the vast marshes of the Delta to await the birth of her son Horus. She was joined by her sister Nephthys who, horrified by the crimes of Set, left him forever.

"When Horus had grown to manhood, he challenged the right of his evil uncle, Set, to the throne, and, after many legal battles, actual wars, and trials of strength, eventually overcame him, avenged the murder of Osiris, and regained the throne of Egypt. Horus ruled Egypt in the same high traditions as his father, Osiris, and became the type of the perfect Pharaoh. In fact, until the end of the Pharaonic Period, all the rulers used the name Horus as one of their official titles."

"To the pilgrims, it was as if the ancient tragedy were taking place before their very eyes. After all, this was the same canal beside which Osiris was slain; over yonder were the same unchanged mountains to which the real Isis had raised her tearstained face. And sometimes, even today, when the wind blows across the ruins of Abydos, one can imagine that it echoes with the sobs and wails of the pilgrims mourning for their murdered god. . . .

"Anyway, as Hor-Ra continued my story, I was told about His Majesty's visit to Abydos in order to inspect the work on his temple, and about how he passed by the garden and saw Bentreshyt collecting some flowers. . . . And the rest you know."

* * *

For three years Imam Abdel Meguid remained married to his wife of many lives (who, for her part, described her husband as a "very patient and very decent man"). But when, in 1935, he was invited to work in Iraq as a secondary school teacher for a year, he readily— and with much relief—accepted the offer. His wife did not accompany him. And not long after his return to Egypt in 1936 he divorced her and married his cousin. As the ex-Mrs. Abdel Meguid, who legally kept her married name and Egyptian citizenship, would later describe their amicable parting: "His cousin was a good cook and didn't like monuments. I married the Egyptian Antiquities Department. So everybody was happy."

* * *

"We've all known people who have dreamed about the pyramids or had visions of a previous life in Egypt," an Egyptologist friend of Dorothy Eady's once stated. "But those kinds of obsessions last three months or a year, and then they're over and the people are on or off to something else. Dorothy Eady really *lived* the whole thing. She also was an endless source of fascinating information, suggestions, and theories about ancient Egypt because she really stayed put and learned her subject step by step the hard way."

Her husband having departed for Iraq, Dorothy immediately left her home in Flower City (as she disparagingly used to refer to Manya El Roda) and, with her little son Sety, pitched a couple of tents near the Giza pyramids and camped out in them briefly before taking up residence in a simple apartment in Nazlet El Simman—a tiny hamlet consisting of not more than twenty houses, located at the foot of the Giza plateau looking out onto the pyramids and the Great Sphinx. She soon got a job as a draftsman with the Egyptian Department of Antiquities—Dorothy Eady was the first woman ever to be hired by the department—and began working for Dr. Selim Hassan —the same Selim Hassan to whom, seven years earlier from Plymouth, she had anonymously sent her little Egyptian antiquities collection.

A world-famous Egyptologist, Selim Hassan (1886–1961), was responsible for the discovery of the Fourth Pyramid; and his excavations in the Giza area were among the most important archaeological undertakings of this century. (His magnum opus, the ten-volume *Excavations at Giza,* gives "special mention, with sincere gratitude," to Dorothy Eady for her drawings and for her editing, proofreading, and indexing contributions to three of the volumes.)

An imposing figure, Selim Hassan was once described by Dorothy Eady as looking "very much like an Old Kingdom vizier. I was exceedingly fortunate to have made my 'debut' with such a distinguished scientist as Professor Selim Hassan. He was hardworking and very systematic, though I'm afraid he didn't have much in the way of a sense of humor. I always felt terribly indebted to him for having so patiently taught me so much. At first he charged me with arranging his library. He was a very meticulous man—he just hated to see anything not in its proper place—and many times I was very severely rebuked. But I learned rather quickly, really, because I was scared stiff of him and wanted to avoid making any mistakes. I was also studying hieroglyphs and wanted to prove myself a good student.

"You know, it was really through watching him that I first understood what a systematic dig should be. He never jumped from here to there—he was, as I said, a very methodical man. When he started to work on a site, he proceeded to clear the surroundings and to dig every inch of the area until he reached the native bedrock, which he then ordered to be cleaned with brooms, leaving nothing else underneath. He made very remarkable finds, including two intact Fourth Dynasty tombs, both of them belonging to children of Khafra [known as Chephren, builder of the Second Pyramid and the Valley Temple].

"My first job for Dr. Hassan in Giza was to copy some details from another important tomb he had also excavated. Like everything else in my life, I had to start with something quite extraordinary—in this case, the Old Kingdom tomb of Ra-wer, an enormous burial complex, discovered in 1929, just to the south of the Sphinx. This Ra-wer was a very interesting personality. He started as a nobody and was promoted to become the barber of the King [the Fifth Dynasty King Nefer-ir-ka-Ra]. Then, I suppose, he kept talking—talking all the time he was shaving the King and cutting his hair, like all barbers—and he must have managed to 'talk' his way to become high priest of Heliopolis. . . . And, like its owner, it was a very interesting and unusual tomb; and it was really a pleasure to work in there because the scenes depicted were extremely beautiful.

"Now, during this time I also used to copy inscriptions in the Temple of Isis and tidy up some mummies. This wasn't official work, but it was all marvelous training. Because, although I had had lots of book learning and all that, it was Professor Hassan who really taught me to sort everything out scientifically. He used to insist that if you wrote anything you should never say: '*This* is so,' but rather, 'It *probably,* or *maybe,* is so,' because tomorrow you might turn up something that disproves it. Which, of course, is quite true."

In her early years in Giza, Dorothy Eady also had the chance to meet other great Egyptologists such as Hermann Junker (who was Selim Hassan's teacher and who did pioneering work at the cemeteries and mastaba field at Giza and at the Temple of Philae) and George Andrew Reisner (who, in 1925, discovered the unplundered Old Kingdom tomb of the Fourth Dynasty Queen Hetephares—the wife of Snefru, builder of the Red and Bent pyramids, and the mother of Khufu [Cheops], builder of the Great Pyramid).

"Reisner was, at that time, almost blind and almost paralyzed," Dorothy Eady once reminisced, "but his brain was anything but blind and paralyzed. He was a brilliant person, and a dear old person, too; and he had a very nice secretary, Miss Perkins—a big, fat woman with a deep voice like a man's—who, at one point, I believe, had been the headmistress of a girls' reform school. . . . And then there was Dr. Junker, who was working with the Austrian Expedition. He was a priest, but [!] he, too, was a very nice person, and very jolly. And we were all friends, and they all seemed pleased with me because I liked the antiquities so much.

"I also used to go to the Cairo Museum quite often during those days as well. I remember meeting an Australian named Alan Rowe, who was an expert in scarabs; and, also at that time, I met a Jewish scholar named Lipovitch.

"Now, Alan Rowe, like many Australians, was very rough in his speech and given to cursing and swearing, while Lipovitch was just the opposite. One day we were discussing a particularly perplexing hieroglyph—it was like an egg with two ears on each side. Alan Rowe wasn't sure about it, so I said that I thought it was a determinative for a smell, a perfume, or anything of that sort. Lipovitch intervened and commented, 'I beg your pardon, but I think it is what is vulgarly known as a *stink.*' 'Bloody hell!' was Alan Rowe's retort. Another time I entered the rotunda of the museum and saw Alan Rowe standing by an open case that contained a new collection of scarabs. He turned around, and as soon as he saw me he called out, 'Here, you, come here, can you tell me anything about this little bastard?'

"Alan Rowe then disappeared. In fact, he was quite a legend. He would work for a while and then vanish, and nobody would know where he'd gone. Then, out of the blue, he'd return. I knew an Englishwoman who knew Alan Rowe for thirty years [he died in 1968], and she said that his appearance never changed, he never got any older. And some of us thought that he was dead and that it was just his spirit that kept returning!

"Speaking of the Cairo Museum, I used to have a little problem, though, with a curator named Engelbach [Reginald Engelbach was Chief Keeper of the Cairo Museum from 1931 to 1946]. He was a clever man, and I admired his work very much. But he was one of the most uncouth people I have ever met, and we had no end of rows. One day I went to the museum with my son Sety, who was a tiny baby, about three weeks old. I got tired of carrying him and wanted to take some notes, so I just put him down on the floor. At that moment Engelbach came along and shouted at me, 'What are you doing there? What are you putting that child on the floor for? Take it up and get out!' So I told him to go to hell and mind his own business. Again, he yelled, 'Get out of here!' And I said, 'It's not *your* museum, it's *mine!* I'm an Egyptian citizen, and you're a foreigner, so *you* can get out!'

"Sety was a delightful baby. He rarely cried unless there was a good reason for it—he was not the grumbling type of child, and everybody in Nazlet El Simman loved him. I had no problem with the boy. I took him along with me when I worked in Giza. Have you ever seen a mare pulling a cart and the little colt running alongside? Well, that was me and my son. I got so absorbed in my work that occasionally I forgot his feeding times. When he was hungry, poor darling, he just yelled like hell, and the *ghaffir* [watchman] would come running to me at top speed and shouting with all his might, '*Ya sitt Bulbul, ya Madam Bulbul,* the boy is hungry.'

"When Sety was older—about three or four—he used to play in the sand with Selim Hassan's son, who was the same age. One morning Sety asked me where we were going that day. I was planning on visiting the Temple of Isis, so I said, 'We're just going up that hill to see the lady Isis.' When we got there the little boys were playing about, and every so often Sety would come over to ask, 'Where is the lady Isis? When is she going to come?' Just at that moment, one of the village wives—a very elderly Egyptian lady all dressed in black and carrying baskets of food on her head—appeared over the ridge; and Sety came rushing up to me to announce, 'Mommy, Mommy, here comes Lady Isis!' "

When she wasn't working in Giza, Dorothy Eady spent many of her days in the libraries at the Cairo Museum and at the home of Selim Hassan, where she read voraciously, continued her hieroglyphic studies, deciphered the magical spells of the Fifth Dynasty *Pyramid Texts,* and wrote out in longhand the hundreds of pages of hieroglyphic transliterations and meanings contained in the great German/Ancient Egyptian dictionary, *Wörterbuch der Aegyptischen Sprache.* She also found time to collaborate with Mrs. Selim Hassan on ten enormous tapestries that depicted ancient Egyptian maps, lists of kings, and battle scenes. (Selim Hassan was supposed to have made the original outlined drawings, while his wife and Dorothy Eady did the embroidery—though a number of people claim that it was Dorothy who took on most of the work.) After Dr. Hassan's death, these elaborately detailed four-by-seven-foot and eight-by-ten-foot tapestries were purchased by the late oil tycoon, engineer, and amateur archaeologist John Dimmick—a patron of and participant on several important digs at the site of the ancient city of Memphis. Dimmick eventually donated nine of these tapestries to the Brooklyn Museum, where they are now displayed in the Wilbour Library. He personally presented the tenth tapestry—scenes from the famous Battle of Kadesh in which Ramesses the Second (the son of Sety the First) defeated the Hittite army—to Mrs. Anwar Sadat, who, in her turn, gave it to the Foreign Office in Cairo, where it now hangs.

* * *

During the day Dorothy Eady developed her research, drawing, and archaeological skills with a practical-minded assiduousness, exactitude, and concentration. At night, however, the "other" side of her being would manifest itself. Villagers from Nazlet El Simman often noticed "the eccentric English lady" going out on certain evenings to pray in front of the Sphinx, where they would see her, for hours on end, "making queer gestures" and "mumbling strange words in an unknown language" and presenting offerings of beer, flowers, and incense to this numinous lion-bodied/human-headed rock figure that has haunted and puzzled tourists and scholars for thousands of years. Many modern Egyptologists suggest that the Sphinx may be a representation of the pharaoh Chephren (Khafra) in leonine form. In one of his "visitations," His Majesty had informed Dorothy that the Sphinx was a representation of the god Horus,[2] so she considered it and its surroundings to be a holy place . . . and would never pass the door on the eastern wall without taking off her shoes.

Occasionally, too, she would enter the Great Pyramid late in the evening—something that, as an employee of the Antiquities Department, she could do without much difficulty—and spend the night by herself in the King's or Queen's Chamber, only to emerge at dawn. No one knew what Dorothy Eady experienced in these chambers. But it is interesting to recall that when Napoleon visited the Great Pyramid on April 12, 1797, he asked permission to remain alone in the King's Chamber; and when *he* emerged, he was observed to be extremely pale and distraught. He refused to comment on his experience inside, insisting that the incident never be mentioned again. Years later, in exile on St. Helena, when he considered speaking about the matter to a friend, he finally decided against it, saying, "No. What's the use? You'd never believe me."

"I know this will sound unbelievable," Dorothy Eady herself once told a friend, ". . . and I don't know whether it was a dream or not, but one night when I was living in Giza I found myself in a nightdress walking on the plateau beside the Great Pyramid. Suddenly I saw King Sety, who was wearing a plain white pleated robe with a wide gold collar, and he came out to me and asked, 'What are you doing?' I replied, 'I'm just walking.' He said, 'It's all right . . . come and walk with me!' So I went with him, and all of a sudden he started to climb up the east face of the Great Pyramid. You know, of course, that the proper way to climb this pyramid is from the northeast corner; but he began climbing it from the middle of the east face, and he looked back and said, 'Follow me . . . and where I put my foot, you put your foot.' So I started to climb up behind him. . . . I was keeping my eyes fixed on his feet, and I could very well see his shapely feet and ankles at the edge of his pleated robe. When we got halfway up he began to walk along one of the steps, and I followed; and when we were exactly in the middle he pulled out a stone—not

---

[2] The Egyptologist Mark Lehner of the American Research Center in Egypt, who is completing the first detailed, photogrammetrically aided map of the entire Giza plateau, has recently suggested that the Sphinx represents the pharaoh Chephren as Horus, god of kingship, presenting offerings to the sun god in the adjacent Temple of the Sphinx.

completely, of course, since nobody could possibly do that—and he then said, 'All right,' and we went down again and walked to the edge of the plateau. 'Go home and go to bed,' he told me. I did.

"When I woke in the morning, the edge of my nightdress was all dirty and my feet were dusty, as if I had really been walking (I had probably been sleepwalking), and my arms were aching as if from the strain of pulling myself up the pyramid, which always happens when I climb it. But the curious thing was that early the next evening I was visiting some friends in Nazlet El Simman, and a gentleman named Abdel Salam—a courteous old soul—insisted on seeing me back home. When we were crossing this big maidan [square] in the village, I happened to look up. And there in the middle of the pyramid—just about the place where I had been the night before with Sety—there was a blue flame,[3] like the flame you get from kerosene stoves. Noticing it, I said to Abdel Salam, 'Can you see anything on the side of the pyramid?' And he looked up and exclaimed, *'A'ooz Bi Allah!* [May God be my refuge and my protector]' 'What's the matter?' I asked. He replied, *'Mish Kuwayess!* [This is not good at all!]' While we were looking at the flame, several people passing by also saw it and said, *'A'ooz Bi Allah!'* Then the old man excused himself and went home.

"Well, early that night, as I was getting ready for bed, I heard a lot of women crying and wailing. I went outside to see what was the matter, and somebody told me that a man had just fallen from the Great Pyramid. It appears that some workers had been sweeping away the sand that accumulated on the steps of the pyramid. One man who had reached the place where Sety and I had been the previous night—at least where I *imagined* Sety and I had been . . . though I'm sure we were—had slipped and fallen.

"What I couldn't understand was the connection . . . I mean, it didn't make sense . . . there wasn't anything in Sety's character that would make him kill or injure an innocent person. If it hadn't been for the fact that I saw Sety pull the stone out, I wouldn't have connected the two events. That light, everybody knew about it—a lot of people saw it and the whole village was talking about it. Perhaps when the man got to the center of the pyramid he thought of this

[3] It has been said that on the day Hitler invaded Poland in 1939 and on the night before the Americans dropped the first atomic bomb on Hiroshima in 1945, many people observed this same blue light on the Great Pyramid. About this "light," Dorothy Eady once commented: "I don't think it has anything to do with either Hemuewen, who built the Great Pyramid, or Khufu [Cheops], for whom it was built. I think it's some spiritual entity that has attached itself to the pyramid without having originally been connected to it."

light and became frightened and fell. The only curious thing is that
the spot from which the man fell was exactly the place where Sety
had pulled out the stone!

"At Giza I had quite a number of other spiritual encounters, if
you want to call them that. You know, when you walk to the Sphinx
from the Great Pyramid, there's a very deep hole called Campbell's
Tomb from the Saite period [664–525 B.C.], and there's a woman
who haunts that place. One night I was at Selim Hassan's house. It
was about half past ten—quite a good moon was up—I had my dog
with me, and we started back down to the village. All of a sudden,
the dog started barking and rushing at somebody, and I looked and
saw a woman standing near Campbell's Tomb. From the distance, I
couldn't see who she was; but I could make out that she had long,
lovely black hair. And when I got near to her, I saw that she was
dressed as an ancient Egyptian, all in white. I called my dog back,
but she wouldn't come—she was rather a savage dog—and she
jumped at this woman as though to catch her by the throat. She
jumped right *through* her, and yet that woman looked perfectly solid!

"Although it was a still night with no wind, the woman's hair and
dress were blowing as if there *were* a wind. The strands of her hair
blew across her face, and she pushed them back and looked at me
and laughed as she pointed her hand to Campbell's Tomb. My dog
was frantic, and Dr. Selim Hassan heard her and thought I was being
attacked by robbers. So he sent out one of the *ghaffirs* [night watch-
men], who shouted, '*Ay, fi ay* [What is the matter]?' 'Nothing,' I told
him, 'it's only an *afreet bas* [just a ghost].' Later I asked the villagers
about this apparition, and they said, yes, she hadn't been seen for
several years, but she was known to them; and they said that she
chased people until they fell into a tomb shaft and were killed. I
didn't believe this, because she looked perfectly good-tempered—a
nice sort of a woman—and I think she must have just followed people who, when they got frightened, ran away and fell by mistake into
the shafts. I saw this woman on three occasions, always at the same
place and always pointing to Campbell's Tomb; and when I tried to
speak to her she never answered, she only laughed. She was quite
friendly.

"One of the archaeologists working in Giza had an assistant who
used to go back home to Cairo every Friday morning and come back
that same evening. One night, when the assistant returned to Giza,
he happened to catch sight of this woman . . . and he was scared.
She even followed him to the house in which he was living near the
pyramids and sat down on a chair beside his bed. He was terrified

that somebody might see her and say something to his wife back in the city!"

Seeing a genial ghost or two was not something that tended to discombobulate Dorothy Eady. She had encountered a number of them on the pyramids plateau but, except for the woman near Campbell's Tomb, they never did anything to attract her attention; and most disappeared as soon as she came face to face with them.

Much more astonishing and exciting to her was the night she spent in a tomb in Cairo, in which the mummies of some of the pharaohs were temporarily being stored. Dorothy had pleaded with her ex-husband to help her; and with his generous connivance, he convinced the guard, an acquaintance of his who was responsible for watching over this underworld gathering, to allow her to gain admittance to the crypt. The guard let Dorothy in before eight o'clock in the evening and told her that she could only come out at sunrise. So Dorothy settled herself inside this tomb with a thermos of tea and a packet of biscuits and walked among the glass cases all covered with black velvet. Lifting up the veil of one of these cases, she found herself staring into the face of Sety the First . . . and she stood looking at him for hours. "But by two in the morning," she would later recollect, "I was getting a bit weary. So I had a cup of tea, recited the offering formula for Their Majesties, and then lay down on the floor beside the Sety case—with Ramesses on the other side—and had a little nap."

* * *

In 1939, Imam Abdel Meguid—who, though a patient and tolerant person, did, after all, come from a conservative Muslim Egyptian family—decided that his son was not being brought up in an "appropriate" manner. "Too much playing around with mummies and such things," he told his ex-wife; and he took custody of the five-year-old boy. By rights, the former Mrs. Bulbul Abdel Meguid could have made a fuss and legally kept her son until he was twelve years old, but she realized that the kind of life she had pledged for herself was not suitable for a child. "So I let him go," she later commented, adding—in her acerbic, bittersweet way: "I suppose I've always preferred cats to children anyway." She now began to devote most of her affectional life to an ever increasing menagerie of cats, dogs, geese, donkeys, birds, and snakes. For, ever since her days in the Sussex countryside, she had known that she could communicate more intimately, and feel less lonely, with animals than with most human beings.

A peregrine falcon had its nest on a sycamore tree just next to her house in Nazlet El Simman, and Dorothy used to place a piece of meat on the window sill every day for her to eat. When someone asked her why she did such a wasteful thing, she replied, "It's an offering for the god Horus" (often represented as a falcon or a falcon-headed man).

After Dr. Selim Hassan retired, Dorothy Eady moved into an abandoned tomb in Giza. When she did, the falcon discovered where she had gone, perched itself on a rock close to the tomb, and waited expectantly for its usual meal. In this strange, temporary habitation, Dorothy also befriended and started feeding at least five vipers, as well as a number of cats—her favorite animals.

Eventually she moved back to Nazlet El Simman and began work as a research assistant to another renowned archaeologist, Dr. Ahmed Fakhry (1905–73), who was in charge of the Pyramid Research Project at Dahshur (the site of the Red and Bent pyramids). According to Dorothy Eady, Dr. Fakhry had more of a sense of humor than her previous boss. "Professor Hassan," she once commented, "would fix me with one of his famous angry stares, and I would just feel my knees sagging under me. But Dr. Fakhry would shake off the dust of the desert and welcome a good anecdote or witty joke. When I made a mistake in drawing an object that we'd found in Dahshur, he would draw my attention to it with great kindness and elegance." While working on these excavations, Dorothy Eady began to display a remarkable ability to guess at and fill in the lacunae of different texts and inscriptions. She also had great success in, and was much praised for, her cataloguing and fitting together of the sculptured fragments from a number of tombs and temples in the area.

Dr. Klaus Baer, Professor of Egyptology at the Oriental Institute and Professor in the Department of Near Eastern Languages and Civilization at the University of Chicago, met and became friends with Dorothy Eady in the early fifties when, as a recipient of a Fulbright Fellowship, he was assigned to Ahmed Fakhry's Pyramid Research Project. According to Professor Baer, "Dr. Fakhry, along with the late Labib Habachi [Dr. Labib Habachi, 1906–84, was also a friend of Dorothy Eady and a great admirer of her work], were the two leading Egyptian archaeologists of their generation—Fakhry was a skillful excavator, and Labib Habachi knew Egyptian antiquities better than any other individual at the time. Dr. Fakhry was very Egyptian—that is to say, very outgoing—an excellent lecturer and very enthusiastic; he would take himself off into the desert oases at various times and work there. He came from the Fayyum [the largest of the Egyptian oases, fifty-six miles southwest of Cairo], was of Bedouin descent, and proud of it. Straightforward and enthusiastic about his field, he wasn't inclined to tell people what they wanted to hear . . . he had a university professorship and was extremely independent.

"He spoke highly of Dorothy Eady and respected her . . . and he also felt an obligation to her because of what she had done with Selim Hassan. Now, I met her in the early fifties when she was working at Dr. Fakhry's combination office/storehouse and antiquities deposit, where she was engaged in filing, record keeping, and cataloguing and trying to fit together all of the fragmentary stuff that was coming out of the Dahshur sites. (And she was also spending some time helping out Selim Hassan on his publications.) In fact, she was more of a research assistant than a secretary, though she was making ends meet on a secretarial salary.

"When I knew her, she was living alone with, at that time, two cats—one of them named Iriru, after some ancient Egyptian gentleman, and the other one was named Mr. Brown. I used to visit her in the house where she was residing at Nazlet El Simman. It was called Beit El Basha [the Pasha's House], and she rented the upper two rooms and a balcony. The place had vaguely functioning plumbing but was by no means fancy. It had a little shrine with one statuette and the usual elementary furniture—things to sit on, a bed, a rickety table. In fact, she was living at poverty level. Seventy-five years before, this had probably been a guesthouse attached to a pasha's residence that no longer existed; but once the original inhabitants left, maintenance had been neglected, and it looked run down.

"I used to see her frequently. Now, I knew that she had intuitive experience and tremendous knowledge, but the subjects we talked about were the kinds of things you find in sources. She told me nothing about her 'former life' in Egypt, but she did tell me a good deal about her religious beliefs—her worship of Osiris and about an occasion when Osiris had appeared to her and the way in which the ancient Egyptian gods, whom she worshiped, had protected her. I knew at the time that her plan was to get herself transferred to Abydos, where she wished to spend the rest of her life.

"Dorothy Eady had visions, and she worshiped the ancient Egyptian gods. But she fully accepted scholarship because she thought that ancient Egypt (as scholarship showed it to have been) was what she *herself* considered to be what was best in the old religion. And she understood the methods and standards of scholarship, which is usually not the case with nuts, and she knew that she wasn't going to

convince anybody else about her personal beliefs, nor did she desire
to convert anybody. I remember that when we once went to the
pyramid of Unas in Sakkara [built by Unas, the last of the Fifth
Dynasty kings, and in which are to be found the most pristine exam-
ples of the earliest Egyptian magical inscriptions known as the *Pyramid Texts]*, she brought along an offering, and she took off her shoes
before entering the pyramid. She herself was personally a believer,
but she wasn't about to make a nuisance of herself forcing her ideas
on me or anyone else. I spent a good deal of time with her, and she
never tried.

"The impression one had of her in those days was quite different
from the way she appeared in her last years when she was shrunken
and very old. When I first knew her, she was a large, vigorous
woman, bubbling over with enthusiasm—*very* English, despite everything; and she had a lot of friends in the foreign community of Cairo
whom she used to take around to the monuments and sites. Her
Arabic was fluent, colloquial, and bad—she didn't have a very good
ear for it—but she was quick with her tongue. She was an Egyptian
patriot, and she lived in Egypt when the political agitation against
England was at its height. Dorothy Eady didn't look Egyptian. She
was once walking down a street in Cairo, in a lower-class area, when
some women started shouting, 'Go home, English whore!' She
promptly answered back, 'And leave all the customers to you?' That
was the end of that!"

Other people who knew Dorothy Eady during her years in Giza
have confirmed Klaus Baer's depiction of Dorothy Eady's vivacious,
feisty, and eccentric personality. Not everyone was equally enchanted by her unconventional behavior. A noted Egyptologist who
met her in the early fifties, and who once described himself as "un-
ashamedly pedestrian and old-fashioned in my moral attitudes" (he
preferred not to be identified), commented: "Dorothy Eady was a
very colorful personality who fascinated me at first. But it was difficult for me to like such an eccentric. And I was deeply shocked
when, one night, I attended a party that was given by Dr. Ahmed
Fakhry behind the Great Pyramid . . . and there, under the full
moon, was Dorothy Eady *belly dancing!* I couldn't believe my eyes!"

A neighboring couple who lived in a house overlooking Dorothy's
Nazlet El Simman apartment happened to glance out from their
balcony one early evening and saw their English neighbor sitting on
her balcony, wearing only a dressing gown. Hot, tired, and dusty
after a day at the excavation sites, Dorothy would customarily come
home, take a shower, and, after putting on her dressing gown, go

outside to relax and have a cup of tea. Not approving of women doing that sort of thing, the concerned husband and wife sent over to Dorothy Eady's house a servant, who knocked on her door and asked her if she would kindly not sit on the balcony in her dressing gown. Dorothy graciously agreed. The next evening her neighbors observed her sitting outside in her petticoat. Back ran the servant to ask her *please* not to sit like that in her . . . *underwear.* Again, she smiled and promised to oblige. When the next evening came around, Dorothy Eady, having had her shower, showed up on her balcony in her bra and panties. *This* time, when the servant returned, he asked if she would *please* just put her dressing gown back on again.

But one of the many surprising things about Dorothy Eady was the easy way she had of temporarily adjusting and adapting herself to whatever social world she happened to be frequenting. One evening she would be having dinner at an aristocratic gathering, whose guests included members of the Egyptian royal family; the next day she would be at an excavation site, sitting on the ground with the workmen eating a simple, dusty meal with her hands.

To supplement her meager income (she received about thirty dollars a month from the Antiquities Department), Dorothy began in the late 1940s to design dresses—based on ancient Egyptian styles—for a successful fashion house called Miss Egypt. Though her dresses were sold in shops in Cairo and Alexandria, she took little credit for her work. Similarly, she was notoriously generous—and anonymous—with regard to the writing and editing "contributions" she made to many students, journalists, and certain scholars who needed to have their articles, research papers, theses, and books published in English. Many well-known Egyptologists—English, American, and Egyptian—have publicly expressed their opinion that quite a few publications that came out under other people's names were largely edited and/or written by Dorothy Eady.

Dr. William Kelly Simpson, Professor of Egyptology at Yale University and Curator of the Department of Egyptian and Ancient Near Eastern Art at the Museum of Fine Arts in Boston, met Dorothy in the early fifties when he was working under the supervision of Dr. Ahmed Fakhry. In his opinion, "Dorothy Eady knew a great deal of Egyptology. She wasn't a totally trained Egyptologist, but, then again, who is? Some people know the Egyptian language backwards and forwards but don't have a sense of Egyptian art; others know Egyptian art but not the language. Dorothy Eady knew them both. She was a delightful person, very peppery and opinionated in her own way—she'd bait you with questions like, 'What do you think of this, of that? . . . Oh, you *do,* do you? Well, I *don't!'* I found her a wonderful and nice person to work with. I also think that a great many people in Egypt took advantage of her because she more or less traded her knowledge of ancient Egypt by writing or helping people out doing drafting for them for a pittance. I think she may have done some writing for Dr. Selim Hassan, and a little for Dr. Fakhry—but that was probably more in the way of 'Englishing' the text, since I know the latter's style very well."

T.G.H. James, the current Keeper of Egyptian Antiquities at the British Museum and the chairman of the Egyptian Exploration Society—who, though a skeptic about the Dorothy Eady "myth"—concedes that she "personally performed some extremely useful editorial functions for Dr. Selim Hassan and Dr. Ahmed Fakhry. . . . Their books were written in English, and this required a great deal of tact and skill; and Dorothy Eady deserves recognition for what was, I think, a matter of 'Englishing,' tidying up, and putting things into order." Dr. Labib Habachi once claimed that Dorothy Eady, later in her life, was responsible for the writing of a book that came out under another person's name. (Just as this "author" may be blameless, so shall he here remain nameless.)

Regardless of the "full" or "partial" truth of these surmises and allegations, what seems most important is that this basically self-taught woman, whose formal schooling in England had been less than rigorous, had now, in Egypt, developed into not only a first-rate draftsman but also a prolific and talented writer who, even under her *own* name, produced articles, essays, monographs, and books of great range, wit, and substance—all displaying the plain, unadorned, conversational style characteristic of her manner and way of being.[4]

While working in Giza, Dorothy Eady published short articles on social, educational, and political issues for the local English newspaper the *Egyptian Gazette;* an essay about the trial and judgment of the conspirators who plotted to kill the pharaoh Ramesses the Third; and, perhaps her most charming work, a marvelous fantasy-meditation entitled *A Dream of the Past,* in which the beautiful bas-reliefs of the tomb of Ti (a nobleman of the Fifth Dynasty) at Sakkara come

---

[4] Among her major works are: *Abydos: Holy City of Ancient Egypt,* cowritten with Hanny El Zeini and published in 1981 by the L L Company; *Omm Sety's Abydos,* originally published in 1982 by the *Journal of the Society for the Study of Egyptian Antiquities* in Toronto, Canada, and republished by Benben Publications; *Pharaoh: Democrat or Despot?,* also cowritten with Hanny El Zeini and still unpublished; and *The Omm Sety Manuscript (Survivals from Ancient Egypt),* edited by Professor Walter A. Fairservis, Jr., and still unpublished.

magically to life as the author stands in wonder before them. (This text, published in 1949 by the Egyptian State Tourist Department—and out of print since then—is reprinted, along with Dorothy Eady's accompanying drawings, as Chapter VII of this book.)

When *A Dream of the Past* was published, it was prefaced by a poem by the governor of the city of Suez, Ahmed Rassam, also a writer and a painter. In this dreamy, Swinburnian verse reverie, the poet sees "the goddess of my dreams,/Rising before my eyes/Through a dark cloud./There she stood on papyrus/Of ancient Egypt,/On the deck of a royal barque/She sailed sublimely." This "Goddess of Night, Leila, of the moonlight" sinks with her barque into a temple wall, becomes a bas-relief, and then magically reemerges and manifests herself "with a blue papyrus in her hand" as Dorothy Eady.

Apparently Dorothy was a fascinating, inspiring, and enchanting presence to many of her Egyptian friends. They respected her honesty in not making a secret of her true faith and in not pretending to be a Muslim or a Christian. Sensitive to the religious feelings of others, she would fast during the holy month of Ramadan, out of respect for her Muslim colleagues; and she would celebrate Christmas and New Year's Day—though never forgetting to remind her Christian friends that Christmas was really a continuation of the Feast of the Aton (or Sol Invictus, as this sun god was called in early Christian times); to inform everybody that the "real" New Year's Day fell, according to the ancient Egyptian calendar, in September; and to point out that the seventh of January, considered by the Orthodox Church to be the "true" Christmas, was also the date on which the annual feast of the erection of the Djed pillar once took place in ancient times. (This pillar, with its widened base and four crossbars at its upper end, is said to represent the backbone of Osiris and the support of creation . . . and may even be the model for the king piece in the earliest chess games.)

Dorothy Eady lived, worshiped, and worked in Egypt during a period of strong anti-British sentiment. "Just before the revolution in 1952," she once recalled, "Egypt was in an awful state. We had a new government every week, and each one was worse than the other. People were nasty to foreigners, which they're not, usually—Egyptians are not spiteful people. But it was horrible at that time.

"You know, there's a papyrus that comes from the Ptolemaic period [304–30 B.C.], and in it, it is said that the gods were angry with Egypt and were going to leave the country; that the signs of their going would be that the ibis bird, the lotus flower, and the papyrus reed would disappear; and that Egypt would be ruled by foreigners until the gods decided to forgive her. Then the ibis, lotus, and papyrus reed would return and an Egyptian would again rule over Egypt. When Lord Cromer, once British ambassador to Cairo and the real power behind the throne during the first half of this century, learned about this papyrus, he got scared stiff about its prophecies and immediately ordered it to be burned!

"Now, when I was living at Giza, among my neighbors were an Englishman and his sister—elderly people, neither one had married. The man had a garden of mango trees a little bit to the north of the pyramids along the Alexandria Road. One day he came to see me and said, 'You know, I saw a blue lotus on the canal.' I said that that was impossible, and he replied that, no, it really was true. The next time he visited me he brought me back a lotus. Not long after this, I heard that people had seen the ibis bird just south of Luxor. Soon after that, somebody else said that they had seen papyrus reeds on the islands in the Nile. Then the 1952 revolution took place, and an Egyptian ruled Egypt. The same Ptolemaic prophecy also stated that Horus would eventually rule Egypt, and then Osiris; and it also said that the nations of the world would come on their knees, begging the favor of Egypt—and I believe that it will come. Not in my time, and maybe not for a while . . . but it will come."

As if to fulfill the promise that she herself had made as a young girl to her Egypt-scorning uncle, Dorothy Eady, in the late forties, went to Cairo's Tahrir Square to witness the lowering of the British flag from the Midan Ismailieh barracks. When she saw the Egyptian flag raised in its place, she uncontrollably wept tears of joy, and—to the chagrin of the English bystanders—shouted out for all to hear: "Long live Egypt . . . long live Egypt!"

* * *

"I've always found it puzzling," T.G.H. James of the British Museum recently commented, "that Dorothy Eady never got to Abydos until the 1950s. If Abydos was her place of pilgrimage, why hadn't she hopped on a train at some point? I find that there's an anomaly there. But then again, she might have been frightened of going. You know, very often you don't want to achieve your ultimate goal because it may turn out to be an anticlimax. So one doesn't want to be too hard on her. But the fact is that she came to Egypt with this aim in mind."

Indeed, Dorothy Eady *had* come to Egypt with this aim in mind. A number of people have raised the same question. No one asking it could have possibly understood or accepted the bizarre and astonishing nature of the answer.

With the revolution of July 23, 1952, Egypt had begun to renew its independent destiny. It was then that Dorothy Eady decided that it was time to begin to fulfill hers. "I had only one aim in life," she had often said, "and that was to go to Abydos, to live in Abydos, and to be buried in Abydos." She had spent nineteen years in Egypt, but "something outside my power had stopped me from even *visiting* Abydos. When I was first married, I had the little boy on my hands; and when, early on, I was finally ready to make the journey, my son got the measles and I had to stay at home with him. Then my husband very kindly offered to let me take a trip from Cairo to Luxor one summer—I think, perhaps, it was to get rid of me for a bit. I remember dumping the baby on his granny; going along, with the necessary two Egyptian pounds clutched in my hands, to the ticket office . . . but the last train that was part of that 'package' tour had left the day before. My financial position later on didn't allow me to go gadding about the country."

It should also be remembered that for the first nineteen years that Dorothy Eady had spent in Egypt she had patiently set out to study, train, and work in Cairo, Giza, and Sakkara with the leading archaeologists and scholars of the day in order to master the complicated and multifaceted discipline of Egyptology. For she desired not only to "immerse" herself in her favorite subject but also to contribute something to it.

Her chief reason for delaying her ultimate and inevitable "return" to Abydos, however, had to do with her "passionate" involvement with her secret paramour, Sety the First. It is a story of astral travel ("The experience of leaving one's physical body and traveling freely abroad"), materialization ("The production in darkness by an unknown agency of temporary spirits or entities, in varying degrees of solidification, in the form, likeness, and appearance of human beings, in whole or in part, and said to be composed of ectoplasm"), and an uncanny relationship with the "ghostly lover" ("The woman's soul mate, her 'other half,' the invisible companion who accompanies her throughout life"). It is a story strange beyond telling.

For reasons unknown even to her best friends, Dorothy Eady took great pains to avoid spending the night at anyone's home. A woman friend recalls that once, after an unusually late dinner, she was finally able to convince an extremely reluctant Dorothy to sleep over at her house. In the middle of the night the friend woke up to hear a strange, persistent tapping on the window in her guest's room. Feeling that something was wrong, she got up and quietly entered the room, where, frightened and concerned, she observed Dorothy lying completely pale and lifeless on the bed. Thinking that she desperately needed air, the woman opened the window and watched amazed as her comatose guest came magically back to life. In the morning she tried to speak to her about this incident, and Dorothy finally confided that when she slept, her akh—and here she used the ancient Egyptian term for "astral body"—would often leave her physical body and would not be able to return unless the window in her room were wide open.

"When I first came to Egypt," Dorothy Eady once told her friend Hanny El Zeini—the only person to whom she confided the full story of her pharaoh lover—"His Majesty started to reappear. You know, ever since his first visit when I was fourteen years old I so much wanted him to come again, but he never did until I was married. I knew deep inside my heart that I would have to travel to Egypt to be able to contact him again, although I also knew damned well that distances meant nothing to him—whether I was in England, Egypt, or anywhere. He was bound by our ancient moral rules. While I was still married, His Majesty was allowed only to *see* me . . . and most of the time he didn't present himself in solidified form. I could just barely *feel* his presence, except on some occasions when, unfortunately, he was also observed by my mother, my father-in-law, and even once by my son . . . but apparently this displeased the Council very much.

"Now, about the Council: His Majesty told me that he had never seen its members; and, as far as I could tell, *nobody* had ever seen them. They were just voices in a great hall of black stone, and even from their voices you couldn't tell whether they were male or female. Apparently he didn't know exactly who they were. They seemed to be responsible to Osiris. Osiris he had seen, and he said that I had, too, but that I'd forgotten: I saw him at my Judgment [the weighing of the deceased's heart on the scale of justice]. It seems that this Council was sort of keeping order in Amenti [literally, "The West"— the realm of Osiris, the setting sun, the dead] under the jurisdiction of Osiris. I wanted very much to go there, but His Majesty wasn't willing, saying that it was very dangerous because I might be attacked by evil spirits on the way, since the astral body, in its progress from the earth to Amenti, is very vulnerable to evil.

"One night His Majesty sent this young priest named Ptah-mes to fetch me—that is, to fetch my astral body. I was asleep and awoke suddenly and saw this priest standing in my room. He beckoned to

me, I sat up, and he said something in ancient Egyptian that I didn't
quite follow, except for the words 'Our lord wants you.' I had three
cats then, and the moment this fellow appeared, all of them put up
their backs and spat and ran out of the room. I felt a queer kind of
sensation, as if I were sort of expanding. I got up and felt most
beautifully light. I looked down on the bed, and there was my body,
lying there with my flannel nightgown on, and appearing most un-
wholesome and unappetizing! And here was I, stark naked, but feeling gloriously light; and this chap said to me, 'Come!' and we walked
out, as if on air, and I looked down to see the pyramids far below us.
We passed through a patch of blackness, like thick fog.

"On coming out of this fog, we found ourselves in front of a palace
door, and the guards challenged us. We went in, and Ptah-mes—the
young priest—led me through a passage into a big L-shaped room.
The front part of the room was low—with a door that opened into a
garden—and a series of shallow steps led to a room that was apparently a bedroom. Sitting in this L-shaped part was His Majesty . . .
but as a man . . . and he spoke to me. I could understand him
perfectly. He told me to come and sit down. He got up, took a
cushion, placed it on the floor, and I sat on it and we talked. I asked
His Majesty about the Osirion, and he said, 'No, I didn't build it, it is
very much older and existed long before my time.' I also said to him
that, according to the researchers, the Great Sphinx was built by
Khafra [Chephren], and he said, 'Oh no, it's older, it's older . . . I
was told it was a monument for Horus himself.' I repeated, 'It's a
monument for Horus, but they say it was *built* by Khafra.' Again, he
said, 'Oh no.' . . . And then, after a while, before dawn, Ptah-mes
came back into the room to take me home. Every time that Ptah-mes
appeared again to take me to Amenti, the cats always spat and fled.
But I can't describe to you the marvelous feeling of freedom and
lightness when one's rid of one's body! The spiritualists say that
when people go out in their astral bodies there's a silver cord joining
them to their earthly bodies. In my case there was no silver cord. If
there had been, I most probably would have tripped over it!

"I traveled many times in my astral body to visit His Majesty, and
I had lovely evenings with him. I remember meeting the high priest
Mery and his silly wife, and also the high priest Wennefer, and even
some of Sety's officers. On one occasion Ramesses was there [Sety's
son and successor to the throne]—but Ramesses as a young man—
and he was playing with a headstall from a horse's harness and was
humming as he was doing it. Cheerful and nice. And *very* handsome,
too! . . . On that night His Majesty asked me if I would, from then

on, agree to his materializing himself as a man and visiting *me!* He wanted me to know what to expect—Ramesses was watching like a hawk, of course—and I said that I was willing.

"I asked His Majesty why he had been allowed to visit me as a *sahu* [mummy] when I was fourteen years old. He said that he had been given permission to do so only in the form in which he had last seen his own body on earth. Since he had known me first as Bentreshyt, he hoped to see me in exactly the same way as when we had first met—he as a man in his early fifties and I as a teenage girl. But he had completely forgotten that he had last seen himself as a *mummy.* His Majesty said he had been severely reprimanded by the Council for having scared me so much on his very first appearance. I suppose that was the reason why he had been forbidden to see me afterward for so many years.

"When His Majesty visits me now in his 'natural' form, he always appears to be a man in his early fifties . . . but very fit and well preserved. Yet he had turned sixty-three at the time of his death. Ramesses, who was about ninety when he died, appears as a young man of twenty-two or twenty-three years. I once asked Sety about this, and he told me that we are allowed to choose the age at which we prefer to appear, but we cannot be older than we were at the time of our death . . . so that a child, for example, cannot choose to appear as an adult. He said that most people choose to appear at the age at which, on earth, they were happiest—so Ramesses is eternally the young hero of the Battle of Kadesh. I asked His Majesty why he had not chosen the age at which he became king. I remember that he replied, 'It is not happiness to be a king—it is a bitter weariness.' He said that he chose to appear at the age when he first knew and loved Bentreshy—actually he said fifty-four years—because those few brief weeks were the happiest in all his life. He stressed that, within the limits of our age at death, we are entirely free to choose our appearance in the other world. Also, although our other-world body resembles our earthly body, it is in a perfect state. Persons who had lost a limb or who were blind or scarred or disfigured by an accident or illness during life would not be so afflicted in Amenti.

"During the first two years that I lived in Cairo, I was still married and was not a 'free woman.' His Majesty had been forgiven by the Council, but he was still not allowed to 'materialize' . . . that is to say, to come to me in solidified form without my personal consent. On that visit to Amenti, I gave my consent, because without having done so I would never have been able to see or touch him. My personal consent was indispensable because, for Sety to be capable of materializing, he had naturally to take some of my *sekhem* [spiritual power]. A certain portion of my physical force was also involved in the matter. You see, after each meeting in which His Majesty presents himself in the solidified form—however long or short our encounter—I always feel some sort of physical fatigue after he leaves me. Sometimes, when I'm tired or slightly indisposed or ill, I feel exhausted or extremely run down after His Majesty goes away. I suppose that's why he had to secure my personal consent before getting permission to come visit me on earth. I think it's a rule in Amenti not to let the dead interfere in the life of those still living on earth unless they accept the presence of the dead in the materialized form.

"I once asked him how he knew how to materialize himself, and he told me that he had learned to do that when he lived on earth. When he first came to me in solidified form, there was no need to ask him whether it was possible to have a relationship with him like a normal man and woman . . . because he *demonstrated* his sexual powers. There was no chance of having children, however, since nothing of him was allowed to remain behind when he left me early in the morning, always before dawn. He said he intended to marry me in Amenti; and though I told him that it wasn't necessary, he said it was. No question was ever raised about taking my astral body and going through some form of marriage there. So apparently His Majesty realized that he would have to wait until I was dead to make an honest woman out of me!"

* * *

Whenever Dorothy began to think seriously of moving permanently to Abydos, she herself realized that at that point she would once again become "temple property" and be subject to the religious laws that would make it impossible for her to continue her passionate affair with the man she loved. Because of this, she found any number of reasons to miss her train. But she also knew that it would only be a matter of time before she would have to make that predestined journey.

In 1952, in her spare time, she agreed to do some publicity work for the Egyptian State Tourist Department, "writing nice advertisements about coming to Egypt and all that," as she once put it. Counting up the extra Egyptian pounds she had earned, she finally decided to ask Dr. Fakhry for a few days off so that she could make a "pilgrimage" to Abydos. Dr. Fakhry agreed and even made all the arrangements for her. On *this* occasion, Dorothy arrived at Cairo's

Central Station in plenty of time to catch the eight o'clock morning train.

As she was traveling up the Nile, Dorothy stared out the window and observed a landscape and a way of life that had hardly changed in thousands of years: palm groves, sandbanks, fields green with maize and tawny with dura, slowly revolving water wheels, men in tunics working their *shadufs,* women with water jars on their heads, young boys leading and riding their donkeys and oxen and buffaloes —and above them all, wild geese, hawks, bee eaters, and paddybirds gliding and circling through the illimitable blue sky.

At five o'clock that afternoon the train arrived—two hours late— in Balyana, the stop nearest Abydos. Dorothy hadn't been able to make out the station name, which was written in Arabic; but as the train approached her destination she looked out the windows and, as she later commented, "At first sight, everything looked familiar to me as far as the distant limestone hills. My heart was beating very fast. I was as excited as a schoolgirl about to have her first dance at a big party."

Without asking if this were the right stop, Dorothy "hopped off the train," as she put it, crossed the tracks, and, with suitcase in hand, was about to head down the dirt road on her own when a man came running after her, calling her name. It turned out that he was one of the watchmen from the Antiquities Department who had been sent to look after her. He informed her that, unfortunately, there was no taxi available at the moment to drive them to Abydos, which was eight miles away, and suggested they wait for one to arrive. But Dorothy was too impatient and told him, "I can walk, it's nothing." The *ghaffir* looked at her incredulously, lifted up her suitcase, and said—in the Upper Egyptian *Saidy* dialect—*"Ya, moodame* [Oh, my lady], in less than an hour it will be sunset. With such a heavy suitcase we will never be able to cover the distance in less than two and a half hours. It is better to wait half an hour for the taxi." Dorothy was unwavering. The watchman pointed to his emaciated- looking donkey and desperately pleaded with her, saying, "All I can do now is to put you on the back of this donkey with your suitcase, and I will walk beside you. But really, *moodame,* the only practical solution is to wait for a taxi. I can leave the donkey with my brother here because the orders given to me were very strict: I must accom- pany you until you arrive safely at the rest house in Abydos. You have to be more patient. We are not in Cairo, and women do not walk here at night."

"Do you want me to mount with my suitcase on this . . . this *thing?"* she asked sarcastically, pointing to the underfed beast of burden.

The argument continued for a while; but Dorothy, as usual, had her way. The watchman attached the suitcase to the donkey's back, and he and *"Moodame"* began walking down the road to Abydos. He later recalled, "I had great difficulty keeping up with her. I have never seen a woman so stubborn and so strong. You know our village women are quite healthy and robust, but none like her!"

It was, as befitted Dorothy's arrival, a night of the full moon, with silvery light illuminating the irrigated fields and the acacia and palm trees, and yellow pompoms perfuming the air. Dorothy, the watchman, and his donkey walked in silence past hamlets of mud-brick houses and reed-built *zarebas*. When they were almost halfway to Abydos a taxi pulled up and the driver insisted on taking the two human passengers the remaining way.

They arrived at the inspectors' rest house—the residence of the Antiquities Department's personnel and guests—and Dorothy deposited her suitcase and then let it be known that she intended to visit the Temple of Sety right away. The watchman informed her that there were strict orders forbidding anyone to go inside the temple at night. Furious, Dorothy started swearing in her heavily English-accented Arabic. The watchman exclaimed, "You are really an obstinate woman. Aren't you afraid of the *afareet* [ghosts] that roam inside the temple at night? Nobody has ever dared to enter that place after sunset."

"Don't worry, *ya abeet* [you idiot]!" Dorothy retorted. "I'm used to *afareet*. They understand me better than people like you!"

The watchman had to laugh, replying, "If you meet the *afareet* and cry for help, don't count on me!" He opened the main gate of the temple.

Immediately Dorothy took off her shoes and made obeisance to the god Ptah (the creator god of Memphis, the architect of heaven and earth, and the patron of artists and craftsmen) by bowing her head and extending her two hands forward—as was the ancient Egyptian custom—toward the doorjamb of the gate. Then she went straight to the northern wall of the Second Hypostyle Hall. Here was to be found a beautiful limestone relief depicting Sety burning incense and pouring a libation of water into three vases shaped like hearts—a play on the ancient Egyptian expression "washing the heart," which means to fulfill a long-desired wish or ambition. "In his subtle way," Dorothy Eady once said, "Sety here proclaimed that he was fulfilling his great desire to adore Osiris in his own beautiful temple." Also nearby was one of the masterpieces of Egyptian relief sculpture—The *Adoration of Osiris by Five Goddesses* (Isis, Nephthys, Maat, Amentet, Renpet)—a scene of extraordinary grace and dignity. Here, like a visiting sixth goddess, Dorothy Eady spent the rest of the night burning incense for and praying to Osiris and Isis, her tutelary god and goddess who had brought her out of the land of England. The next morning when she emerged from the temple the watchman "swore" that "she looked twenty years younger . . . and she even had a few nice and kind words of gratitude for me!"

In the short time she spent in Abydos, Dorothy visited the nearby Temple of Ramesses the Second, the almost five-thousand-year-old archaic tombs, and the Osirion—which she immediately realized was the place she had repeatedly envisioned in her dreams as a teenage girl.

During this first visit Dorothy discovered that the Osirion was even more extraordinary than she had dreamed it was. "In the northeastern side chamber opening out of the Central Hall of the Osirion," she would recall, "was a rectangular well formed by the removal of one of the paving blocks in the chamber floor; and the water in it was amazingly clear and transparent. Now, when I visited Abydos in 1952, I was unable to read or write without glasses. For some reason, I suddenly decided to wash my eyes in the water of that well . . . and from that day on I never needed to use my glasses again. I remember there was a woman accompanying me around Abydos at that time—she was the wife of one of the inspectors of the Antiquities Department—and she was suffering from an incurable eye disease that prevented her from opening her eyes in any strong light. I told her what the water had done for me, and she didn't believe me; but her husband persuaded her to try it. Less than a half hour after she did so—we were then walking through the desert on our way to the Ramesses Temple—she suddenly cried out, 'I can open my eyes!' Sure enough, she could. What's more, the cure was permanent."

Dorothy took a bottle of this water—water that any sensible health official might well have considered slightly suspect—back with her to Nazlet El Simman, because one of her neighbors had a fifteen-month-old baby boy who suffered from epilepsy. The mother —the wife of the local butcher—had gone to see many doctors in Cairo, none of whom could help her son, and who had in fact told her that the child would probably die in a fit or would grow up to be an idiot. The distraught woman had asked Dorothy if she knew of some "ancient magic" that might be able to help her child. So, upon her return from Abydos, Dorothy advised the mother when the child had his next seizure to throw some of the Osirion water onto his face and make him drink a bit of it as well. The woman did as Dorothy suggested, and the child came out of his fit and never had another one.

* * *

Because of her work commitments back in Cairo, Dorothy Eady was able to spend only two days in Abydos. She did return for a second "pilgrimage" two years later in 1954—this time for two weeks. During that period—exploring Abydos more deeply and in a more leisurely fashion—she realized that "nothing was going to keep me in Cairo. It was only because wonderful people like Selim Hassan and Ahmed Fakhry, from whom I learned so much, were there that *I* was there. But Cairo never really meant anything to me. Abydos is where I belonged, and it was 'written'—*maktub!*—that I live there. I was a free woman, divorced, my son had gone to live in Kuwait. For me, it was either Abydos or nothing!" At the conclusion of her two-week sojourn—one of the happiest times of her life—she cried on the train trip all the way back to Giza.

Upon her return, she applied numerous times to the Antiquities Department for a transfer to Abydos . . . but to no avail. None of the officials would dream of sending her to that "godforsaken" Upper Egyptian village. In the mid-fifties Abydos had no electricity, no plumbing, no running water. (Water was obtained from two wells and was distributed daily, in goatskins, by men called *sakkas.*) Not one person in this hamlet of mud-brick houses and mud-dust lanes spoke a word of English. (In fact, the name of Abydos on the map was El Araba El Madfouna—meaning the Buried Hamlet!) It was not, in the opinion of the Antiquities Department, a place to send a person from London *or* Cairo—much less a single *woman*—to live.

Dorothy Eady, of course, was not to be dissuaded, saying, "Why worry about me? I know every inch of the place, and the people are quite poor but extremely hospitable and friendly." No one, however, paid her any mind. In early 1956, Ahmed Fakhry's Pyramid Research Project at Dahshur was terminated, and Dorothy was without a job. Dr. Fakhry himself gave her some sage counsel. "Listen to me," he told her one day, assuming a mock official manner. "What I suggest you do is climb the Great Pyramid; and when you reach the top, just turn west, address yourself to your lord Osiris and ask him, *'Quo vadis?'* And he will answer: 'Come to Amenti!' Then all you will have to do is jump westward, and your problem will be solved!"

Dr. Fakhry did, in fact, have two other suggestions: "He offered me the choice of a well-paid, comfortable job in the Records Office in Cairo, or a *not* well-paid and somewhat physically hard job (two dollars a day as a draftsman) in Abydos. Needless to say, I chose the latter!"

Although overjoyed at the prospect of leaving, Dorothy had, of course, a deep and secret regret; but of that only her lord and king were aware. Years later in an extraordinary diary entry, she would write the following:

> *From the first time that I had been able to speak with Sety, I had told him of my life-long desire to live in Abydos and work in his Temple there. He had always seemed very sympathetic to this, and sometimes when I was despairing of ever being able to fulfil this wish, he encouraged me, and said that it was inevitable that I should return to Abydos in order to work out our destinies. He appeared to me at the Pyramids a few days after I had received news that the Antiquities Department had at last consented to transfer me to Abydos, to work in the Temple. I told him the news, and he was very much moved, and said, "My heart is glad about this, my Beloved." He stayed with me all night, and made love to me in a surpassing way. Just before he left he said, "I will send a priest to bring you to me tomorrow night, for I have something to tell you, my White Lotus." That was the last night that we ever made love together, and it was the sweetest. He has slept beside me many times since then, and we have embraced and kissed, but nothing more, because now the Temple lies between us like a drawn sword.*
>
> *The next night the new priest came to fetch my astral body. When I reached his apartment, I found him alone, and in a very gentle but serious mood. He embraced me fondly and made me sit beside him. For many years I had always kept the Feast Days of Osiris and Isis, burning incense before their statues in my home. Now Sety told me that when I returned to Abydos, I must keep the Feast Days in the Temple (which I had intended to do). He said that I must burn incense and offer wine or beer, and recite the "Lamentations of Isis and Nephthys," these being the speeches of the Goddesses in the Mystery Play. I replied: "But I do not remember them, Lord." He said, "They are written in books, have none survived?" I said, "I have such a*

*book, but it is written in the language of the Barbarians." He
said that it did not matter, "The Gods know everything, they
listen to what is in the heart." He made me swear to do this.
I promised, and I have kept my word ever since.*

*For a while we sat in silence, then he took both my hands
in his, and in a serious but very thrilling tone of voice told
me that I must understand what had happened. He said,
"The chariot-wheel of Fate has turned to its full circle. From
now until the end of your earthly life you belong again to the
Temple, and you are forbidden to me or to any man." I
started to cry, and asked him if I should refuse to go to
Abydos after all. He shook me gently and said, "Little One,
are you going to make the same mistake all over again?"
Then he explained to me that this was the period in which we
were both to be tested. If we resisted temptation for the rest
of my life in Abydos, our original crime would be forgiven,
and I would belong to him for Eternity. I asked if I would
ever see him again, and he replied that he would certainly
come to me at Abydos. I said, "Will you come as an intangi-
ble spirit as you used to do?" He said, "No, Beloved, I shall
come to you as a living man, I cannot forgo your kisses and
the clasp of your arms." I said, "This will be a temptation."
He replied, "If there is no temptation there is no test, but O
Beloved, help me to be strong, and do not weep, I will never
leave you or cease to love you." He dried my eyes on the edge
of his robe. I said, "Why should I be forbidden to you? I am
going to Abydos to help restore the Temple, not as a priestess,
and you know well enough that I am not a virgin." He
replied that this was something ordained, and that I had just
vowed to him to be sure to recite the "Lamentations." He
kissed me and said that I was a good girl. He thanked me
for the years of happiness we had snatched while I was living
at the Pyramids. He said a lovely thing: "Your love is an
ointment poured on the wound in my heart." And I nearly
started crying again.*

But at that moment the usual clatter and dowsha *[noise]
told us that Ramesses had arrived. After we had all greeted
each other, Sety told Ramesses what had happened. He con-
gratulated us, but I thought he looked a bit worried. Sety
asked what he was thinking and smiled and said, "Do not
fear, my son, this time we shall both be strong." To which
Ramesses replied, "May the Gods grant it!" They both de-*

*cided that the occasion called for a drink. Ramesses brought
the drink-stand over to where we were sitting, and I poured
out the wine for them, as usual. There is no doubt at all that
Ramesses cheered us up and broke the emotional strain that
had been there before his arrival. And when my time was up,
and the priest came to fetch me, Sety was in a normal mood.
A few days after this, I left for Abydos.*

* * *

Having made her decision, Dorothy Eady packed her few belongings: a mattress; two large trunks filled with some clothes, sheets,
and books; and two of her favorite cats—Iriru (the eldest and "quite
a character") and a beautiful white creature that had been given to
her, Dorothy later recalled, "by a nice French lady. The cat didn't
speak Arabic or English, so the lady tried to teach me French to talk
to the cat with. The animal, being more intelligent than I, learned
English before I learned French!"

The night before her departure she was wide awake with excite-
ment. Being unable to sleep, she went out an hour before midnight to
climb the Great Pyramid. The night was pitch-black, but Dorothy
was used to seeing in the dark; and every step up the pyramid was
familiar to her. She remained at the summit until dawn, watching the
Nile Valley all bathed in mist; then began her descent as the first rays
of the sun turned the sky orange and gold and vermilion.

An astonished *ghaffir,* who knew her well, watched her coming
down. "What were you doing up there, madam?" he asked. "I was
praying," she answered quietly. Knowing that this was her last day
in Giza, he held out his hand, saying, *"M'a El Salama* [Peace be
with you]!"

Dorothy went to say good-bye to her neighbors and friends at
Nazlet El Simman. Most difficult of all was saying farewell to the
little boy who had been cured of epilepsy and who was now a
healthy, mischievous five-year-old. He came up to Dorothy and insisted on kissing her . . . as did his mother, who mumbled a few
words of affection and gratitude in the midst of her weeping. Then
Dorothy Eady, who had kept her composure until then, just broke
down. "I never felt at home in Nazlet El Simman," she would later
say. "It was not, however, easy to leave. I felt I was abandoning so
much love."

It was the evening of March 3, 1956; and the fifty-two-year-old

Dorothy Eady insisted on leaving the doors of her apartment ajar. She was then driven to Cairo's Central Station where she boarded the train, having purchased a one-way ticket for the 325-mile journey south to Abydos.

·IV·

Omm Sety

The truly silent man holds himself
apart. He is like a tree growing in a
garden. It flourishes; it doubles its
fruit; it stands before its lord. Its fruit
is sweet; its shade is pleasant; and its
end is reached in the garden.

(The Instruction of Amenemope)

"If thou journey on a road made by thy hands each day," an ancient Egyptian maxim states, "thou wilt arrive at the place where thou wouldst be." Having never wavered from the certitude of her heart, and having spent many years preparing herself intellectually for her journey, Dorothy Eady finally, and irrevocably, returned "home."

"Home" for Dorothy was the small village of Arabet Abydos (until recently known as El Araba El Madfouna), which is situated at the point where the alluvial Nile plain in the east meets the desert and a limestone mountain to the west. In this crescent-shaped mountain, which seems to cradle the village in its protective embrace, there is a strange cleft, known as Pega-the-Gap, through which the sun can often be seen setting in a blaze of gold-vermilion. To the ancient Egyptians, Pega-the-Gap led directly to Amenti—the realm of Osiris, the Lord of Abydos. (It was also thought that the Stairway of Osiris lay directly under the sand slope of this very gap.) Along with the neighboring villages of Ghabat to the north and Beni Mansour to the south, the present-day Arabet Abydos, with its mud-brick houses, arched gateways, and pigeon towers made of pots and bricks, is part of the holy city of ancient Abydos—a necropolis of temples, tombs, stelae, statues, and cenotaphs whose origins have been traced back more than five thousand years to predynastic times.

Abydos had begun to be the cult center for the worship of Osiris during the Old Kingdom (c. 2575–2134 B.C.). By the time of the Twelfth Dynasty (c. 1991–1783 B.C.), thousands of Egyptians were making an annual pilgrimage there to visit the tomb of Osiris (which was then thought to be in the archaic cemetery called Omm El Gaab, just west of Arabet Abydos) and to witness the sacred Mystery Play enacted there every year.

In ancient times Egyptians began to identify dead persons with Osiris himself—referring to "Osiris-Sety" or "Osiris-Bentreshyt"—thereby imagining that person, by this act of identification, to partake of the god's resurrected life. Pious Egyptians desired nothing more than to be buried in Abydos. Failing that, they erected small cenotaphs (false tombs) or commemorative stelae for themselves, so that they might more easily enter the realm of Amenti through Pega-the-Gap in the mountain west of the holy city.

It goes without saying that, as a follower of the ancient Egyptian religion, Dorothy Eady would have ardently wished to be buried in Abydos. The primary reason for her fervent desire to reside there had to do with her unfailing sense of being a revenant who was returning to the place where she had previously been born and raised. And the *particular* spot where she felt she had spent the most important part of her brief earlier life was the Temple of Sety, which stands on the eastern edge of the desert, dominating the village of Arabet Abydos.

Generally considered the most beautiful and best-preserved structure of its kind in Egypt, the Temple of Sety was the greatest artistic achievement of the former army officer who, on becoming pharaoh in his early thirties, proclaimed himself "Bringer of Renaissance" and attempted to reform the corrupt and inefficient government and to regain the empire Egypt had lost since the reign of the Eighteenth Dynasty heretic king, Akhen-Aton.

The Temple of Sety was built during the second half of this pharaoh's twenty-one-year rule; and its white limestone structure and delicate bas-reliefs—many of which still retain their brilliant color—were close to completion at the time of his death. (The decorative reliefs on the building's exterior and in the First Hypostyle Hall were carried out by his son and successor, Ramesses the Second, who also built his own temple slightly to the north of his father's.)

The Sety Temple differs from all other Egyptian religious shrines in two important aspects: first, instead of being designed according to the customary rectangular plan, the temple is L-shaped, thereby allowing the Osirion, which served as a cenotaph for both Osiris and Sety himself, to remain uncovered and intact; and second, instead of being dedicated to just one principal god (and that god's consort and son), the temple contains seven vaulted chapels—three for the holy family of Abydos (Osiris, Isis, and Horus); one each for the gods Amon-Ra of Thebes, Ra-Hor-akhty of Heliopolis, and Ptah of Memphis; and a seventh for the dead, deified Sety. In its attempt to represent and reconcile the demands and hopes of this world, the netherworld, and the empire, the Temple of Sety the First truly became a "national" as well as a "cosmological" shrine.

To Dorothy Eady, the temple was also a "personal" shrine. On one of her first visits to the building—sometime during her two brief pilgrimages to Abydos in the early 1950s—she remembered feeling "as if I'd walked into a place where I'd lived before." The chief inspector from the Antiquities Department was in Abydos at the time of one of Dorothy's first visits there, and he was aware of her peculiar notions of "familiarity" with the temple. So, along with an architect and another inspector, he decided to test her out.

As she later recalled, "I went to the chief inspector and said: 'I know this place, I know where everything is and where everything belongs.' 'That's impossible,' he told me, 'the temple hasn't been catalogued properly.' (At that time there weren't even any detailed guides to the building.) So we all went along to the temple; and when we got there he said, 'We'll tell you where to go; just stand in front of the scene we ask you to, and when you think you're there, call out and we'll come to see if you're correct.' They sent me inside.

"Now, it was nighttime, and pitch-dark, and I had no light at all—though they had electric torches. I went straight to the place they had instructed me to—the Chapel of Amon. I didn't fall over or bang into anything; and I stood in front of the scene and called out. When they arrived with their torches they were amazed that they'd found me in the right place. So they said, 'That's just chance, let's try again.' This time they told me to go to the Hall of the Sacred Boats, which I did, and called out; and again, they found me where I was supposed to be. They did this four or five times, and every time I was in the right place. At the end, they gave me a few dirty looks and wondered what they'd got on their hands!"

What they had "got," it turned out, was an extraordinarily knowledgeable and rapturous devotee of the Temple of Sety. Being both postulant and scholar, Dorothy Eady—like few others—had the ability to experience *and* explain the marvels and mysteries of this holy place—her shrine, her fane, her sanctuary, which she would enter always in a state of breathless adoration:

To pass through the great Central Doorway and enter into the Temple of Sety I is like entering a "Time Machine" of science fiction. One leaves the modern world outside in the glare of the sunshine, and, in the soft, subdued light of the interior, enters the world of the past which, for a time, becomes the present. It is also a world of magic such as the modern mind, and particularly the western mind, has difficulty in understanding.

Most people think of the temples of Egypt as being something like churches or cathedrals where people came to public worship and to make their personal prayers and petitions. But temples are not and never were like this. In ancient Egypt, that kind of worship belonged to the temple courts and porticos, to the small temples of local gods, and to the wayside shrines, for the Egyptian was always pious by nature.

The interiors of the great temples were, in truth, the holy houses of the gods, where emanations of the divine spirits worked ceaselessly day and night to ward off from the universe the ever-threatening return of chaos and to maintain the divine order of the world and the welfare of Egypt, the "Beloved Land." Prayers, hymns, and sacrifices were certainly made here. Ceremonies and ordinances were performed and offerings laid upon the altars. These were done not by ordinary people but by priests trained in voice and gesture to perform the magically-important ceremonies in exactly the correct manner that would render them acceptable and serviceable to the gods.

The ordinary folk were never permitted to enter the interior of the temple, and it is doubtful whether any of them ever dared to do so! Every element in the scenes on the walls had a magical significance. Nothing is there merely for the sake of a good presentation or for beauty alone. If they are beautiful as well as magically potent, it is because they were conceived by men of vision and taste, and brought into being by men who, even though working for wages, were above all proudly participating in two momentous projects. They were helping to create a suitable dwelling-place for the gods in the midst of their own city. They were honored to have a share, however insignificant, in the great work being carried out by their God-King, their "Horus Upon Earth."

The scenes on the walls were magically active in two ways. They were supposed to make permanent the action shown being performed. If the pharaoh offered a loaf of bread to Osiris, that loaf would continue to be presented so long as the representation remained both in this world and in the world of the gods. Likewise, if one stood before a figure of a god and uttered his name, a portion of the divine spirit would animate the stone, and the deity's attention would be upon the speaker, upon his actions, and upon the hidden thoughts of his heart.

One could imagine that these beliefs, held and practiced in this temple for more than a thousand years, have charged the very stones of the building with their potency. To be alone in the Temple of Sety is to feel watched over by benevolent, all-seeing eyes, and to know an overwhelming sense of peace and security.[1]

In Egyptian villages the local people have always considered it impolite to call a married woman by her real name, choosing instead to designate her as the mother of her eldest child. So in Abydos, Dorothy Eady/Bulbul Abdel Meguid now became known as Omm Sety (Arabic for "Mother of Sety")—a name that she would use, and by which she would be known, for the rest of her life.

Regarding the curious custom among modern Egyptians of calling a person by an "unofficial" or "false" name,[2] Omm Sety once observed that "the usual explanation for this custom is that it is considered shameful for anyone except close relatives to know any personal details concerning a woman. Actually there may be a deeper, subconscious reason for this. There are still in the villages so-called 'magicians,' who, for a small consideration, are willing to write a magic spell to harm an enemy. In order for the spell to be effective, the true name of the intended victim, and that of his mother, must be known to the magician. This belief dates back to pharaonic times, when a man's name was followed by that of his mother: for example, 'Nakht-Amon, Son of the Mistress of the House, Meryt.' . . . And

[1] From *Abydos: Holy City of Ancient Egypt* by Omm Sety and Hanny El Zeini.
[2] Omm Sety once stated that she had known three women who "rejoiced in the names of Gibna (cheese), Fakha (fruit), and Salamon (tinned fish); and no one except for their parents and brother knew what their real names were."

the ancient belief in the great importance of a person's name is the reason they erased the names of enemies from tombs and other monuments. To destroy the name was to destroy the identity of its owner and even imperil his welfare in the afterlife."

* * *

When she first arrived in Arabet Abydos in 1956, Omm Sety briefly resided in a small room attached to the rest house of the Antiquities Department in the northern part of the village. For the first week or so she hardly slept there, preferring to spend her nights wandering around the desert, where she was both astonished and excited to encounter several wolves. "A lot of people say that there are no wolves in Egypt," she once remarked. "When I first arrived here, in fact, I met a naturalist who swore black and blue and blind that there were no wolves here, and that what I thought I saw were actually jackals. Now, I've seen plenty of jackals, and they are *nothing* whatsoever like wolves, except for their coloring. What I had seen were definitely nice, upstanding, noble-looking wolves. So I told the naturalist that, if he wished, I would show him the tracks . . . and probably even a real wolf, too! 'Fine,' he said disbelievingly. So we went out to the desert by the mountain; and there, standing on a hillock, was a very excellent specimen of a wolf. I started to turn to the man, saying out loud, 'Well, if that's not a wolf, what is it?' But when I looked around, there, in the far distance, was a cloud of dust in which the naturalist was disappearing. The funniest part of it, though, was the wolf, who looked at the vanishing man, then at me, then back at the man, then back at me . . . as if he wanted to say, 'What the hell's the matter with him?' "

Several weeks after arriving, Omm Sety had the good luck to find a house in the middle of the village for sale. The price was seventy-five dollars. "You can imagine what it was like!" the purchaser would later declare. "It had one room—if you could call it that—which I did up a bit and tried to make livable . . . though, owing to my lack of funds, there wasn't much I could do. Eventually I had a little mud room built on top of it—just mud, not even mud-brick. When I got my first donkey, who was named Alice, she lived downstairs and I lived upstairs.

"Once, when I got an attack of phlebitis, of course I couldn't climb up and down the rather steep steps to my room. So I took up residence with the donkey. When the local doctor came to see me— he happened to be a Copt—he said to me, 'Haven't you anywhere better to sleep than in the stable?' I replied, 'What's wrong with a stable? Jesus was born in a stable. If it was good enough for him, it's good enough for me.' . . . I think he was rather shocked."

Alice, the donkey, was not the only one of Omm Sety's boarders. Throughout her entire life in Abydos she was always surrounded by a remarkably colorful and noisy menagerie that, at various times, included a gander named Snefru that served as Omm Sety's "watchman" and liked to drink Earl Grey tea with six lumps of sugar and a dash of milk, a goose named Nebet, a rabbit named Banouna that bit everyone and everything in sight, an unidentified "lazy" dog with a menacing baritone bark, several snakes, and, at all times, generation after generation of cats that bore royal ancient Egyptian names such as Teti Sheri, Ahmes, Hor-em-heb, and Ramesses. This last-named creature was an elegant, apricot-yellow tomcat that would deign to eat only cans of Japanese tuna—literally spitting at the macaroni and boiled eggs Omm Sety prepared for his other feline companions—and that, as befitted his namesake, would imperiously stand on the ledge of a wall and make disdainful gestures at everyone who walked by. Meanwhile, from around the neighborhood, dozens of cats would frequently happen by to check up both on Omm Sety and on her "mafia," as she used to refer to her feline family.

* * *

In 1956 the Temple of Sety was in the process of undergoing restoration under the supervision of Edouard B. Ghazouli, the late chief inspector of Middle Egypt. The houses in front of the temple facade had been pulled down; and when the southern part of the first pylon and its terrace were cleared away, Ghazouli and his workers discovered a small temple palace with its reception hall and magazines. The original stone doorways, columns, and window grills were all in fragments. Omm Sety, upon her arrival in Abydos, was given about three thousand of the inscribed pieces to catalogue and fit together and was then asked to translate the inscriptions. This was exactly the kind of task she had undertaken for Ahmed Fakhry in Dahshur; and her earlier training was now to serve her well. "You see," she would say on hindsight, "I really couldn't have come to Abydos until I'd learned properly the job I was intended to accomplish there. In other words, I was meant to do something good for the temple, not just merely flap about it."

Her work on this project took about two years; and in his monograph describing it ("The Palace and Magazines Attached to the Temple of Sety I at Abydos and the Facade of This Temple"), Edouard Ghazouli gives "particular" thanks to Omm Sety for the plans and drawings she contributed, as well as for her help in "preparing the manuscript." (She apparently "Englished" the entire text.) Ghazouli and other members of the Antiquities Department were also enormously impressed by her almost uncanny ability to estimate correctly the original height of the broken columns and to interpret many of the more enigmatic hieroglyphic inscriptions.

It was during this period that Omm Sety finally got her chance to prove her contention that the gardens she had always sworn once flourished near the temple—and about which Dorothy Eady had told her disbelieving and scornful father when she was a little girl—*had*, in fact, existed. "I had kept on and on about that garden until I came to work here," she would later say, "and then the foremen found it exactly where I said it was—to the southwest of the temple—tree roots, vine roots, little channels for watering . . . even the well; and the well *still* had water in it."

When not "rediscovering" things about the temple, and when not occupied with her restoration work, Omm Sety found time, in 1957, to write out for her personal use a calendar that listed the ancient Egyptian religious feast days and designated the requisite prayers and ceremonial duties to be performed. Having access to the temple now whenever she wished, Omm Sety would go to the shrine every morning and evening, remove her shoes before entering, walk to the Great Hall, and then burn incense and pray to the lord of the dead. On the birthdays of Osiris and Isis, and on the great feast of Osiris—marked on her calendar as being celebrated between the twenty-third and the thirtieth days of the month of Khoiak (January 3–8)—she would observe the ancient custom of not eating fish, beans, onions, or garlic before crossing the threshold of the "God's Mansion" and would bring offerings of beer, wine, bread, and tea biscuits to the Cult Chapel of Osiris. Here she would recite the "Lament of Isis and Nephthys" that she had learned, in its English version, more than thirty years before in Plymouth, England.

Early in 1959, without warning, Omm Sety was informed that she no longer had a job. The budget for the restoration project had been exhausted, and she was advised to return to Cairo where the Antiquities Department would offer her another assignment. Of course she refused. Two months later she realized that she had completely run out of money. With her last few coins she bought some eggs for her cats; and, not knowing what else to do, she went into the temple, where she prayed and explained her predicament to Osiris, saying, "If you want me here, find a way for me to live and feed my cats. If not, please give us a swift and easy death." Several hours later

Edouard Ghazouli came over to her house to tell her that he had just received a telephone call from Cairo informing him that her contract to work in Abydos was going to be renewed.

An overjoyed Omm Sety now continued to participate on more limited excavations of badly damaged but still impressive predynastic burial sites at the edge of the desert north of Abydos. She then spent many months in the Temple of Ramesses the Second (located almost a mile north of the Sety Temple), copying down every inscription and eventually getting to know the building almost as well as she did the shrine built by Ramesses' father.

In the Temple of Sety she turned one of the rooms near the Corridor of the Bulls into a personal office. Here she worked on a drafting table lit by a gas lamp; befriended an inquisitive cobra that began to visit her on a regular basis, dutifully feeding it—to the astonishment and horror of the temple guards, who despised these ominous, hooded, venom-spitting reptiles—a daily ration of boiled eggs and milk; and did her best to keep graffiti-scrawling tourists from defacing her "home."

Spending as much time as she did in the Sety Temple, Omm Sety was bound to experience some extraordinary things there. Perhaps the most unusual of these took place in 1958 when she was working in the Hall of the Sacred Boats, and she described this uncanny occurrence at length:

"At that time," she once elaborated, "work on roofing the temple was in progress; and although I had the keys to all the doors, it was easier to get in and out of the building by going up the stairs to the roof, walking along the top of the southern wall of the unroofed Western Corridor and down the scaffolding at the west of the temple.

"We then had an epidemic of Asiatic flu in the neighborhood, and I caught it. One morning I was feeling rather bad, and as a couple of aspirins and a short rest had no effect, I decided to call it a day and go home. I went up the stairs and started walking along the top of the wall, when I suddenly became very dizzy and fell, twisting my right ankle and hurting my left shoulder. I remember hearing a loud grating sound, like that of a grindstone at work, and I rolled down a fairly steep slope; the grating sound was renewed, and I found myself in darkness.

"After a while the dizziness passed off enough to allow me to stand up and grope for a wall. I touched some smooth limestone blocks and stood there wondering what to do next. Presently I sensed very faint threads of light filtering down from above, as though through cracks in the roof; and as my eyes became accustomed to the gloom I found that I was standing in a narrow passage less than ten feet wide. A narrow path, perhaps about twenty inches wide, ran along the base of the wall; but the remainder of the width of the passage appeared to be completely filled with boxes, offering tables, cases, bales of linen; and everything had the gleam of gold. Feeling my way along the wall, I limped along. The passage seemed to be endless, and, to my left, crowded with objects.

"I stumbled and fell, and, on trying to rise, saw what I took to be the god Horus himself bending over me, his hands raised as though in astonishment. From his waist down, he was standing upright, but from the waist upward he was bending over, his fierce falcon's face peering down at me, and his Double Crown [representing Upper and Lower Egypt] sticking out at right angles without any visible means of support. There I squatted meekly, thoroughly embarrassed and trying to think how one should address a god under such circumstances. Then I suddenly realized that 'Horus' was only a painted wooden statue, life size, and originally standing upright with the arms bent at the elbows and the hands raised. Insects had eaten away part of the front of the body, causing the upper part to lean over. Scrambling to my feet, I noticed similar life-sized statues of Osiris and Isis leaning against the far wall, apparently uninjured.

"Near where I stood was a golden vase about ten inches high. It had an oval body, a long neck, and a trumpet-shaped mouth, and stood in a wooden ring stand. By the faint light I could see a cartouche engraved on its body, but it was too dark to read it. But by the length of the frame, I knew that it was not the cartouche of Sety, but of one of the later kings, perhaps from the Twenty-sixth Dynasty. I picked it up. It was very heavy, and at first I thought I would take it as evidence of what I had discovered by accident; but I finally decided against it and put it down in its place.

"I began to feel very ill again but continued to limp along, half unconscious. Suddenly I found myself out in the open air, almost blinded by sunlight. I was standing beside the well in the Second Court of the temple, and approaching me was a young man, a stranger. He stared at me in frank astonishment and asked if I knew where the architect in charge of the restorations was. I told him and, still staring in surprise, he thanked me and left. I went to enter the temple by the main door, only to find that I didn't have the keys with me. I went around to the back of the temple in order to reenter the Hall of the Sacred Boats by the way I had left it, when I met two of the watchmen. They all cried out, 'Where have you been? You are all dirt and cobwebs!' And so I was; no wonder the young man had stared at me so hard! I replied that I had fallen down and hurt my ankle and had forgotten my keys. But I did not tell them anything more. I managed to crawl back to the Hall of the Sacred Boats; and there were the keys, just as I had left them, on the table.

"Two days later the Chief Inspector of the Antiquities Department for this area came here, and I told him about this experience. He was very astonished and interested, but neither of us could decide if it had really happened, or if it was just a hallucination caused by the fever; and to this day I do not know for certain. All that I am sure of is that I really fell, my ankle was swollen and painful for a week, and I had a big bruise on my shoulder. Also, I was really covered with dust and cobwebs; and having left the keys behind, there is no way in which I could have reached the front part of the temple except by going around from the outside, where the watchmen would have seen me, and where, moreover, I would not have collected any dust or cobwebs all over my clothes. If this really did happen, then there is only one possible explanation: I must have hit a stone with my shoulder as I fell, which turned on a pivot and opened into a sloping passage. This would account for the grating sound. But how did I get out again? All that I can suggest is that a deserted hyena's lair in the side of the wall may have communicated with the 'Treasure Passage.' Later, the lair caved in, but its place remains, still clearly visible. The chief inspector got interested and told me to try to find the supposed pivot stone. I looked for it in every possible place in the temple, including the 'Blind Rooms' [two rooms—one on top of the other—without windows or doorways, that are located immediately behind the Inner Chapels of the Osiris Complex], pushing and butting against the walls of these rooms . . . but with no results, except some more bruises!

"There is one significant point, however. The paving stones of some of the aisles in the hypostyle halls are large, single slabs that resemble those in the upper 'Blind Room.' These could well be roofing subterranean passages. But in all other places, the paving stones are smaller and irregularly shaped. One thing I am certain of: the Temple of Sety still holds some secrets . . . as a matter of fact, lots of them. One day a patient archaeologist may come to Abydos to investigate all its unknown and fascinating possibilities. And maybe he will stir the enthusiasm and admiration of the entire world with something bigger and more important than the discovery of Tutankh-Amon's mortuary treasures in 1922."

Less momentous events also occurred to Omm Sety in the temple. "One day," she once remarked, "I was so hot while working inside that I took off all of my clothes, since nobody was around. In fact, ever since I was a child, I've hated wearing clothes (and especially shoes). I never could see the object of wearing clothes unless you happened to be cold. I still don't. Children in ancient Egypt, by the way, didn't wear clothes until they were around twelve years old— you'd put clothes on when you came of age. (Sometimes you'd find the very young aristocratic children wearing clothes, but the lower- and middle-class children didn't.) . . . Anyway, back in the temple, suddenly I heard the watchman coming along with a visitor; and there I was with my clothes in some other room. So I dashed across the corridor to get my things . . . and *just* in time. You should have seen me, streaking through the temple. I think I may have been the original streaker!"

Most of the time, however, Omm Sety did give in to social conventions, dressing in an incongruous combination of woolens or, later in life, a twin set with a head scarf and a shawl, and imitation pearls, intermingled with a various assortment of Egyptian beads and charms and an ankh amulet—the hieroglyphic sign for "life"—hanging from her neck. Certainly, to both villagers and foreign visitors alike, this unusually bedizened woman, when noticed for the first time, cut a very strange figure.

Dr. Veronica Seton-Williams—research fellow at University College, London, and the author of the books *The Treasure of Tutenkamen* and *Egypt* (in the *Blue Guide* series)—remembers meeting Omm Sety in 1957. "I had driven with a friend from Luxor to Abydos," Dr. Seton-Williams recently recalled, "and I remember that we were having lunch under the water tower of the village, when suddenly there was a rattling of bracelets and a voice, in English, said, 'Prithee' (nobody had ever, or has *ever* again, said 'Prithee' to me!), 'Prithee, would you like some water?' So we looked up to see a woman with a water jar on her head. That was my introduction to Omm Sety."

Maureen Tracey—an exuberant English tour guide, tour manager, and the author of *English for Americans with a Sense of Humor*— first encountered Omm Sety when she was leading a Swan Hellenic tour to Luxor and Abydos a few years later. "I'll always remember that meeting," Tracey (as she is known to all her acquaintances) once remarked. "I was sitting at the rest house, and a woman next to me, who was wearing a charcoal-gray chalk-line suit—it looked as if it had been made out of some man's demobbed garment!—turned around to me and, in a very English voice, said, 'Would you like me to take you about the temple?' I exclaimed, 'Oh, my God, an English

Dorothy Eady in England in 1920. "Sweet 16 & still a virgin" she wrote on the back of this photograph—one of the few surviving pictures of her from her childhood. *(Collection of M. Tracey)*

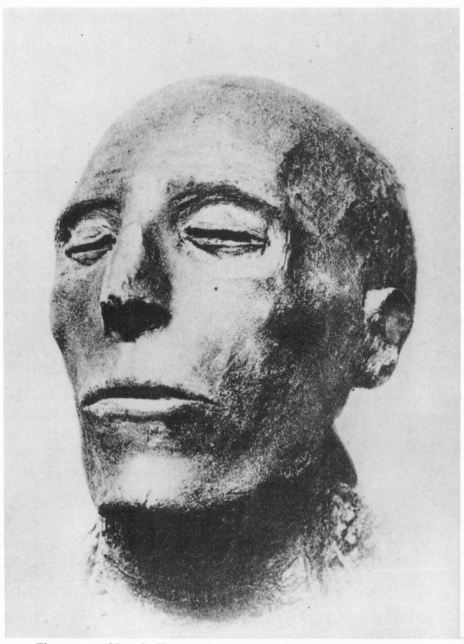

The mummy of Sety the First, now in the Egyptian Museum in Cairo. "When I was fourteen," Dorothy once confided to a friend, "I was asleep one night, and I half woke up and saw this face bending over me with both hands on the neck of my nightdress. I recognized the face from the photo I had seen years before of the mummy of Sety. I was astonished and shocked and I cried out, and yet I was overjoyed."

Dorothy Eady believed that in a "previous" life she had been a girl named Bentreshyt, who had been left to be raised at the Temple of Sety at Abydos when she was three years old by her soldier father (her mother—a vegetable seller—having died). At fourteen she became a vowed priestess of Isis and first encountered Sety the First in the garden of his newly built temple at Abydos. The painting by H. M. Herget reconstructs a formal garden at the time of Egypt's Middle Kingdom (c. 2040–1640 B.C.). With its ornamental lotus pool, encircling flower beds and rows of trees, it is a model of the kind of garden one would have found during the later reign of Sety the First (c. 1306–1290 B.C.). *(Painting by H. M. Herget, © National Geographic Society)*

During World War II, Dorothy Eady gave lectures about ancient Egypt to American troops who were then stationed on the Suez Road. This photograph was taken in Sakkara. "Don't you love the Deadheads?" was Dorothy's caption on the back of this photo. *(Collection of M. Tracey)*

When she lived in Giza during the 1940s and early 1950s, Dorothy Eady would often sleep on summer nights in this "doorway" in the causeway of the Valley Temple of Chephren, located just south of the Great Sphinx. Throughout her life, she would sleep outdoors or on the rooftops of her residences whenever she could. *(Hanny El Zeini)*

"I know this will sound unbelievable," Dorothy Eady once said, "but one night when I was living in Giza I found myself in a nightdress walking on the plateau beside the Great Pyramid. Suddenly I saw King Sety . . . and all of a sudden he started to climb up the east face of the Great Pyramid . . . and he looked back and said, 'Follow me.' . . . When we got halfway up he began to walk along one of the steps, and I followed; and when we were exactly in the middle he pulled out a stone—not completely, of course, since nobody could possibly do that—and he then said, 'All right,' and we went down again and walked to the edge of the plateau. 'Go home and go to bed,' he told me. I did." *(Hanny El Zeini)*

Omm Sety's first residence in Abydos, which she bought for seventy-five dollars in 1956. She abandoned the house in 1971, concerned that prying neighbors were intruding on her "privacy" with "His Majesty" (Sety the First) during his nighttime "visitations." *(Hanny El Zeini)*

View of the Osirion (or Tomb of Osiris) looking northwest—the mysterious subterranean structure whose construction resembles the Valley Temple of Chephren, located behind the Temple of Sety in Abydos. In the distance is the rest house of the Egyptian Antiquities Authority. Behind that is the desert path, along which Omm Sety often used to walk, known as "Pilgrims' Way," where, thousands of years ago, participants of the annual Mystery Play (reenacting the life, death, and resurrection of the god Osiris) would march in a funeral procession honoring that god—the Lord of Abydos. *(Hanny El Zeini)*

The village of Arabet Abydos (looking north) with the Temple of Sety on the left. *(by Hanny El Zeini, © 1981 by the L L Company)*

The village of Arabet Abydos (looking south). In the distance (left), the hill called "Lord of Offerings." *(by Hanny El Zeini, © 1981 by the L L Company)*

Omm Sety in front of the Temple of Sety, c. 1958. *(Collection of M. Tracey)*

For Omm Sety, the Temple of Sety was a holy shrine, and she would always remove her shoes before entering it. Here, a barefoot Omm Sety is shown giving a tour of the temple, 1974. *(Hanny El Zeini)*

lady! I'd *heard* there was an English lady living here.' She remarked, 'Well, hardly a *lady,* dear!' We immediately got on like a house on fire. We had the same sense of humor and laughed at the same things . . . though she believed in reincarnation, and I don't know whether I do or not—I'm waiting to be convinced. Omm Sety would often say to me, 'You know, Tracey, people come here thinking that they were once Cleopatra because they can see pictures of Antony in their mind. They've all been Cleopatra and Hatshepsut and Ramesses and Thotmes! But they've never been a *nobody.* I was just one of the old scrubbers, I was nothing—the daughter of a soldier and a vegetable seller, you know, who was left on the steps of the temple.' When I asked her if she minded living all alone in the village, she'd reply, 'Oh no, I'm never alone. Isis or Osiris is always hovering over me one way or another.'

"I don't know why we got on so well. Perhaps because she was an extrovert and I'm an extrovert. I would stay over at her house in the village for two or three days at a time; and at night we'd sit up in our dressing gowns, drink some beer, and chat about this and that for hours and hours. She was full of stories and gossip about the ancient times and about what was then happening in Abydos. When I had returned to London, she would send me these wonderfully racy letters that kept me abreast of the latest news about her cats. 'Baby Khufu—*definitely* a girl,' she once wrote to me, 'got the spring feeling, so brother Ahmes offered his services. He isn't very expert, and while he was messing around, along came Hasuna, their dad, hauls Ahmes off, and promptly gave an expert demonstration on how these things should be done! Ahmes stood by, obviously filled with admiration.'

"She would always give me the up-to-date news about a Coptic bishop from the nearby monastery whom she would call 'the Kissy Priest' because he always insisted on giving her a big kiss whenever he saw her. In one letter she wrote: 'I think I told you about the time I got mixed up with a mixed party of Coptic bishops. Well, the other day I was sitting in Foukay's place [an outdoor cafeteria], when in marched the Bishop of the Bishops! He gave me a great bear hug and a resounding smacking kiss on each cheek. He certainly was showing a truly loving Christian spirit! Foukay nearly choked. Foukay told the dishy Bishop that I was one of the lost sheep that strayed away after the old gods. I don't know if he was setting a seal of approval on my defection or trying to win me back into the fold.' "

Foukay, who was born in Arabet Abydos and who owned the outdoor cafeteria where Omm Sety used to go to have tea, coffee, or a beer with visitors and friends, once said, "This place was Omm Sety's second home, and she would often stay here all day long. Occasionally, she would bring along a white cat inside a cage and feed it with milk and eggs. Sometimes she spoke to it. She used to speak to me about the ancient monuments. She was a lovely woman. All the people here loved her just like they love their mom. She was one of us, and she was straightforward in her dealings with everybody. She would always tell the truth without being afraid of anybody!"

"You know," Omm Sety once remarked, "when I first moved to Abydos, I wasn't exactly welcomed here. The villagers were wondering why a foreign woman would come to live all by herself without her family and pass all of her time in the temple unless she were up to some kind of mischief. I really never blamed them for thinking that way, although *I* knew I didn't need anybody. I had already lived for more than twenty years in Giza and knew enough Arabic to be able to deal with the local grocer, butcher, vegetable seller, and so on. I was also proficient in insults as well as proverbs!"

The reason why Omm Sety was not "afraid of anybody" in Arabet Abydos was because most of the villagers had come to be afraid of *her* on account of her reputation for being an adept of Egyptian magic. "The local people regarded her as a kind of witch," Dr. Seton-Williams once commented, "and Omm Sety only managed to live in Abydos by herself all those years because the villagers, who are very superstitious, were terrified of her. They didn't attack her because they didn't know what powers she could call down on them.

"When I first began studying Egyptology," Dr. Seton-Williams added, "one of my university professors was Margaret Murray, who was interested in Egyptian magic and was known as 'the Witch'!" (Margaret Murray, it should be mentioned, actually discovered the entrance to the Osirion while working with Flinders Petrie's famous excavation team in Abydos between 1901 and 1902; and in addition to her Egyptological accomplishments, she was the author of *Witch-Cult in Western Europe,* published in 1921, which popularized the notion that witchcraft was the surviving pre-Christian religion of Europe.)

"I myself once saw Margaret Murray perform an act of magic," Dr. Seton-Williams continued. "In 1947, just after the war, we had a very cold winter in London, and there was little fuel around. Now, Margaret Murray didn't at all like Emanuel Shinwell, the Minister of Fuel and Power at that time. I remember that I was working with her in Regent's Park one day, and she made a wax figure of Emanuel

Shinwell, stuck it full of pins, put an appropriate spell over it, and placed it in a small fire she had built. The wax figure took all day to burn and finally melted away by evening. When we came out of the park to the Baker Street underground station the newsboys were crying out, 'Emanuel Shinwell Will Resign!' He never held a government post again. Maybe it was a coincidence, but it's a curious coincidence. . . . Omm Sety, too, had access to all the ancient texts on magic; and she had healing powers and also powers over snakes and animals.

"You know, most Egyptians are terrified of cobras, but certain Egyptian women can deal with them. When I was once working at Tell El Fara'in [the ancient city of Buto, home of the cobra goddess Wadjet], I came across women who had names like Miriam the Egyptian or Fatima the Egyptian. If you had a cobra in your house, you'd send for one of these women, called *rifaiea,* who would catch snakes by making them bite on milk-soaked cloths; then they'd pick them up and wrap them around their necks. To do this, these women would have to practice sexual abstinence and undergo purification rites for a month—and would repeat them every year—during which time they drank a thimbleful of snake venom every morning and were rubbed all over with the venom as well. . . . Omm Sety had a similar kind of control over snakes as well—but a control that, in her case, stemmed from her knowledge of ancient Egyptian magic."

In the *Instruction for Mery-ka-Ra* (c. 2060 B.C.), it is stated that the ancient Egyptian creator god gave "magic" to human beings as a "weapon" to be used only in cases of self-defense. ("He made for them magic as weapons/To ward off the blow of events,/Guarding them by day and by night.") According to Maureen Tracey, "Omm Sety wouldn't do any harm to anybody unless he or she did harm to her."

One day her gander Snefru disappeared. "I'll turn this village upside down until I find him!" an anguished and angered Omm Sety exclaimed to a friend, who advised her, "Don't try. . . . Snefru was very big and very appetizing, and he's probably in someone's stomach right now!" As Maureen Tracey commented, "She knew who had taken the gander, and she said to me, 'Oh, he'll get his comeuppance!' A while later she informed me that the person who had killed Snefru had been bitten by a water buffalo and had died of rabies. I think she put a spell on him. If someone did something cruel to her animals or to herself, she'd say, 'I'm going over to the temple and spill the beans to Osiris, and that will put *that* right!' Revenge or recompense usually followed. One man—an outsider to the village—

apparently once tried to forbid her permanently to enter the temple. So she just went to have a talk with Osiris; and soon after her conversation, that particular man was found dead—some say of a heart attack, others say of some other cause."

Omm Sety knew that the ancient Egyptians believed that the "unfettered" use of magic was antithetical to the "law" and contrary to the will of the gods. In fact, almost all of the "magic" that Omm Sety employed served the purpose of healing people and reversing or warding off the effects of evil spells.

"I can tell you of two occasions," she once declared, "when I tested out the *Pyramid Texts* [spells, incantations, and utterances dating from the Fifth Dynasty] . . . and they worked!

"One day some tourists were taking photographs outside the Sety Temple; and all of a sudden a cobra came out from a hole in the wall and caught a sparrow and started to eat it. A gentleman wanted to photograph this scene, but the policeman who was on guard at the time wanted to kill the snake. I told him to leave it alone and not to annoy it since it wasn't doing any harm. Now, the cobra was in the shade, and the tourist wanted to get it in the light, so I picked it up and put it in the sun—knowing full well that the cobra couldn't bite because its mouth was full with the sparrow. This damn fool of a policeman threw a stone at it. Well, the stone didn't hit the cobra, but it annoyed it. It dropped the sparrow and reared up and started puffing and spitting and wanted to attack everybody in sight. So I decided to try out a spell, meant to drive snakes away, which ended up with the word *seben*. I kept saying: *'Seben . . . seben . . . seben,'* and nothing happened—the snake just sat there laughing at me. But then I said it again, this time emphasizing the *en* sound: *'SebEN . . . sebEN . . . sebEN!'* At once the cobra put down its hood and returned into the hole from which it came. I think a lot of ancient Egyptian magic must have been based on vibrations that we don't understand, because it's important that you use the correct tone of voice when uttering the spell.

"Another time, one of my neighbors, who was newly married, had a problem with impotency. He and his whole family were in a real panic about this. First he went to a doctor—nothing doing. Next he went to the local sheikhs' tombs—nothing doing. Then one of his people asked me whether, by chance, I might know of some remedy for this problem from ancient Egypt. Well, I *had* noticed a spell in the *Pyramid Texts* that looked as if it might be appropriate. So I traced the spell out, which went something like: *'I am bound, thou shall unbind me . . . and the god Min* [the god of fertility] *shall protect me.'* I wrote all of this down on a goose egg, drew a picture of the god Min, and told the man to bury the egg under the threshold of his door. He did so, and that night all went well. . . . And after that, as you can imagine, anybody who was impotent came rushing to me for this spell; and every time it worked."

Omm Sety, who could, among other things, cast and ward off spells, tame cobras, and cure impotency, was, it seems, a true descendant of the ancient Egyptian magicians.

* * *

In every society where magic is practiced, its adepts are both feared *and* respected. Omm Sety, who was now admired in Arabet Abydos for her healing power—and trusted because she was also a woman—was soon spending a good deal of her time sitting and talking with the village wives about their customs, superstitions, and folk magic. Years before, when she was first married and living in Manya El Roda, Bulbul Abdel Meguid had, to the despair of her husband, preferred chatting and becoming friends with the servants rather than giving them orders in the manner of a "proper" lady of the house. Now in this Upper Egyptian village her sense of curiosity, her unassuming spontaneity, her knowledge of basic Saidy Arabic, and her recently won social acceptance by the local women allowed her to find out what she needed to know to become a first-rate folklorist —and one, moreover, who practiced what she knew.

One day, when Omm Sety and a friend were on their way to the Ramesses Temple, she saw two little girls playing a kind of hide-and-seek game in the narrow lane leading to the temple. The younger one, who was about five years old, stumbled over something, and, twisting her ankle, fell down. Omm Sety and her friend heard a dull thud, but the child didn't make a sound. Having hit her head against a stone fragment, she remained motionless, sprawled face downward. Suddenly the child's mother came running up, screaming. Omm Sety had been standing motionless, pale and tense, as if hypnotized. Her friend immediately ran to pick up the little girl and tried to make her swallow some water from his thermos. Fortunately, the girl regained consciousness very quickly, none the worse for her accident except for a red mark on her forehead. Starting to cry, she rushed quickly to her mother.

At this point Omm Sety did something very curious. She took the thermos from her friend, filled the plastic cover with cold water, and sprinkled it over the exact spot where the girl had fallen a few minutes before. "May Allah keep you, *Ya, Omm Sety* . . . and you too, sir," the mother said gratefully to both of them. When they reached the Ramesses Temple, Omm Sety had regained her composure, and her friend asked her why she had sprinkled the water on the spot where the child had fallen. "The girl could have hurt an *akh* [a spirit] when she fell," Omm Sety replied. "What I did has always been done in Arabet Abydos—and perhaps in every other village in Egypt since time immemorial."

Omm Sety was not, however, the first Englishwoman to find herself in the position of a practicing amateur folklorist. In 1862, Lucie Duff Gordon (1821–69), in an attempt to cure herself of tuberculosis, had moved from London to Luxor where she resided in a ruined house on the site of the great Luxor Temple for a period of seven years—the longest time a European woman had, until then, continuously spent in Upper Egypt. During these years she used both her rudimentary medical skills and common drugs like quinine, Epsom salts, rhubarb pills, and zinc sulphate to minister to local people suffering from gastric fever, dysentery, and eye infections. While gaining a reputation as "the *hakeemah* [woman doctor] of Luxor," she listened to and learned much about the customs of the villagers and peasants, whom she grew to love. (As she wrote, "One's pity becomes a perfect passion when one *sits among the people*—as I do, and sees it all.")

A skeptic, rationalist, and radical liberal by nature, Lucie was frequently, but gently, bemused by her patients' superstitions and magical beliefs. But she was completely astounded and taken aback by an incident that occurred one afternoon at her house. As she described it in *Letters from Egypt:*

"I was sitting here quietly drinking tea, and four or five men were present, when a cat came to the door. I called, 'biss, biss,' and offered milk, but pussy, after looking at us, ran away. 'Well dost thou, oh Lady,' said a quiet, sensible man, a merchant here, 'to be kind to the cat, for I dare say he gets little enough at home; *his* father, poor man, cannot cook for his children every day.' Then in an explanatory tone to the company, 'That is Alee Naseeree's boy Yussuf—it must be Yussuf, because his fellow twin Ismaeen is with his mule at Negadeh.' *Mir gruselte* [it gave me the creeps!], I confess, not but what I have heard things almost as absurd from gentlemen and ladies in Europe; but an 'extravagance' in a *kuftan* has quite a different effect from one in a tail coat. 'What, my butcher's boy who brings the meat—a cat?' I gasped. 'To be sure, and he knows well where to look for a bit of good cookery, you see. All twins go out as cats at night if they go to sleep hungry; and their own bodies lie at home like dead meanwhile, but no one must touch them, or they would die. When they grow up to ten or twelve they leave it off. Why, your boy Achmet does it.' 'Oh, Achmet! Do you go out as a cat at night?' 'No,' said Achmet tranquilly, 'I am not a twin—my sister's sons do.' I inquired if people were not afraid of such cats. 'No, there is no fear, they only eat a little of the cookery, but if you beat them they will tell their parents next day, "So-and-so beat me in his house last night," and show their bruises. No, they are not *Afreets,* they are *beni Adam* (sons of Adam), only twins do it, and if you give them a sort of onion broth and camel's milk the first thing when they are born, they don't do it at all.' Omar professed never to have heard of it, but I am sure he had, only he dreads being laughed at. One of the American missionaries told me something like it as belonging to the Copts, but it is entirely Egyptian, and belonging to both religions. I asked several Copts who assured me it was true, and told it just the same. Is it a remnant of the doctrine of transmigration?"

It is not surprising to learn that Omm Sety herself, many years later, reported similar incidents and stories to several of her friends. And throughout her years in Luxor, Lucie Duff Gordon often expressed her desire to collect "all the pretty stories I hear" and to publish a paper "on the popular beliefs of Egypt." Dying as she was of consumption, she was unable to realize this task. What remains instead are her fascinating and controversial *Letters from Egypt* (published in 1865 and 1875).

Lucie Duff Gordon's unaccomplished task was brilliantly taken up by another Englishwoman, Winifred S. Blackman—Fellow of the Royal Anthropological Institute—who, in 1927, published *The Fellahin of Upper Egypt.* Having lived with the peasants in Upper Egypt for six months annually between 1920 and 1926, W. S. Blackman was fortunate to witness harvest and fertility rites, weddings, funerary ceremonies, exorcisms, and the detailed operations of "medicine men" and "medicine women." In the concluding chapter of her revelatory book, she connects many of the customs and practices of the Upper Egyptian peasants—a great number of which can still be observed today—to those of the ancient Egyptians. As Lucie Duff Gordon had earlier commented: "You see the ancient religion cropping up even through the severe faith of Islam. If I could describe all the details of an Arab, and still more of a Coptic, wedding, you would think I was relating the mysteries of Isis."

Neither Lucie Duff Gordon nor W. S. Blackman, however—percipient as they were—was able to combine, as was Omm Sety, the practical *and* theoretical knowledge of both modern-day and ancient

Egyptian customs and rituals. And in the late 1960s, Omm Sety began to write a series of articles and reports for the American Research Center in Egypt that revealed the endurance of the ancient folk and religious traditions as they manifested themselves in the daily lives of her village neighbors. As Professor Kent R. Weeks—who is director of the Theban Mapping Project that has been producing unique three-dimensional maps of the Valley of the Kings—once described her work: "She would frequently take a quotation from the *Pyramid Texts* or from the *Book of the Dead* and write down an analysis of it—an explanation of it in her terms—and then go on to show how similar things seemed to crop up in modern folklore in Upper Egypt. And they were very interesting comments.

"It's amazing that Omm Sety did so much . . . and even more amazing when you realize that she was living in a village as a villager. She hadn't gone to a university, she didn't have access to a great research library, nor did she own things like typewriters and decent pens that we take for granted. So it really is astounding that she got so much material down on paper. She was a very keen observer—I don't think anything escaped her eye." Susan Weeks—an expert on and writer about Bedouin jewelry who visited Omm Sety many times in Abydos—added: "It's also amazing what television and plastic sandals have done to the Egyptian village. Someone recently commented to me that there really *is* no such thing as a village anymore. That's why Omm Sety's observations were so important. Where she lived, tourists would arrive for half a day and then leave. She remained there for almost twenty-five years and was a part of everything."

Both part of the village and yet still, in some sense, an "outsider" —just as she lived both in the present and in the past—Omm Sety found herself in the unique position of being able to participate in and to observe the life around her.

"The village women," Omm Sety would report, "although they can have free birth control, don't want it. If they miss one year without having a child, they go running around all over the place— even to the doctor! And if that doesn't work, they'll try all sorts of other things. In the Sety Temple, I've seen women approach a figure of Isis, touch her feet, and then rub their own tummys. I once asked a woman why she had come to the temple, and she said, 'Oh, I've been married for six years and haven't got a child, and my husband's going to divorce me if I don't have one.' 'Well, why did you touch *her?*' I inquired, pointing to Isis. And the woman replied, 'I don't know her name, but she's a good lady.'

"At Dendera, moreover [the site, sixty miles south of Abydos, of the Temple of Hathor], there's a large, full-faced relief of Hathor [the goddess of love and beauty] on the outer wall of the temple. There, the women who want to have children often bring an offering of some green vegetable, place it on the ground in front of the goddess, and call out to her, 'Mother of children, be kind to me!' It works. . . . Then, too, there's a sandstone statue of Senwosret the Third [a pharaoh from the Twelfth Dynasty] that's seated in the desert just south of Abydos. Actually, the upper half of the King's statue is missing. So the infertile women walk around him seven times, and then go and sit on his lap. But he's not reliable. I tell them they should go to Ramesses the Second instead—he had a hundred and eleven sons and sixty-nine daughters!"[3]

In ancient as well as modern times, in Egypt and elsewhere, the line differentiating "magic" and "medicine" or "priest" and "physician" was often hard to distinguish. (Isis, for example, was a goddess both of healing and of magic, and the highest-ranking ancient Egyptian physicians were also priests.) There is, moreover, evidence to suggest that the Temple of Hathor and the Temple of Sety were once known to be "curative" sanctuaries. The latter temple, like many others, contained what was called a "House of Life"—a kind of combination library, scriptorium, and teaching center where medical and magical books were compiled and written. It was here that people who were ill would spend the night to receive "therapeutic dreams." Omm Sety herself firmly believed that the Sety Temple still had extraordinary powers. "When I was a young girl," she once said, "I fractured my arm very severely; and from then on, whenever it got cold, the arm would always start to ache. Whenever I set my foot inside the First Court, the pain just disappears as if by magic . . . and I'm not sure it's entirely a psychological effect.

"You see, I could never get hurt badly inside the temple. I've fallen many times while walking absent-mindedly, or while reading or drawing some texts from the pillars or the walls. Several times I fell almost headlong from a portable ladder that I used during my work . . . and I wound up with not even a scratch. And I've never seen anyone *else* injured inside the temple, either. Quite a few tourists

---

[3] There is also a still persisting belief that just a few grains removed from the phallus of the god Min, as depicted on the walls of the Sety Temple, can, when mixed and swallowed with some water, cure impotency. And Omm Sety, when surveying the damage done to the by now almost completely hollowed-out image of the god's "member," would exclaim: "That idiot of a sculptor! If he had had any foresight he would have made the phallus of Min a hundred yards long!"

who get absorbed while taking photographs sometimes forget where they're going and fall down; and some of them have had their cameras completely broken. But no physical harm ever occurred to anybody. I even remember that, when the masons and workmen were preparing for the operation of roofing the temple, some of them fell from great heights, but none of them was injured. Another time, a watchman who was trying to chase some bats from the Chapel of Horus—where the droppings have done considerable damage to the painted reliefs—forgot that the floor of that chapel was uneven and so neglected to set the ladder properly on the ground; and he fell from a height of almost ten feet, and nothing happened to him. If this had occurred outside the temple, he would have immediately journeyed to Amenti!"

Omm Sety, as we have seen, also believed in the healing properties of the water in the Osirion. A friend of hers recalls visiting her one time in November when she was suffering from a very bad case of the flu and high fever; and watched, astonished, as she jumped into the chilly pool of the Osirion, only to emerge smiling, energized, and completely restored to health.

"There was an architect here in Abydos," Omm Sety once related, "who was charged with the repairs and maintenance of the temples —a very capable man. He had a small baby, and one night the baby was very ill. This was at a time when we didn't have a local hospital in Abydos, and the nearest doctor was fifteen miles away in Balyana. So the architect sent for me and asked if I could do anything for the baby, who had a high fever and was gasping for breath. I began to suspect that it might be a case of diphtheria, though the child had been immunized with a triple vaccine. But since I didn't know what to do, I thought of using the water of the Osirion.

"It was a dark night, and I took a water jar and went down into the Osirion well. The only light was starlight, and I felt my way along the wall. When I went into the room where the well was located, I saw a sort of white light shining through it as if it were moonlight. I felt quite awe-stricken because it was the first time I had seen this light coming just from inside the well itself—the room was in total darkness. I dipped the jug and filled it with the gurgling water; and, again, I was surprised to see that the water dripping from the jar was shining like diamonds.

"I took the water back to the architect, and we gave the child some of it to drink, then washed him with the rest of it. The mother was afraid that it might kill him, but I told her that it was well known that the water would reduce fever . . . and then I left them.

When I returned in the morning to ask how the baby was doing, the mother said there was absolutely nothing wrong with him anymore. Of course I know babies are like that—one minute you think they're going to die, the next moment you hope they will! But this was a very strange case. That strange light emanating from the well itself, plus the gurgling sound—those two things together might, in ancient times, have set the people to imagining that Geb and Nut [the god of the earth and the goddess of the sky] were perhaps conversing with each other and working together to cure ailing persons. This is a possibility one can hardly discard!"

Omm Sety herself had once suffered from a severe varicose ulcer. Walking in a field, she was bitten by a scorpion ("my lady Serket"— the scorpion goddess—was how Omm Sety referred to it). The next day, to her amazement, she noticed that the ulcer, which had been tormenting her for several months and which she had been treating unsuccessfully with drugs, had now disappeared. When it was suggested that she should have gone to the hospital, Omm Sety commented, "It's a miracle that the *scorpion* didn't die!"

She had become extremely knowledgeable about folk medicine, not only by reading the ancient texts but also by courageously trying out the remedies on herself. "One of the main interests I shared with Omm Sety," Dr. Kent Weeks once remarked, "was ancient Egyptian medicine. That required my going out to ask people today what plants and animal parts are still being used in treatments in order to discover parallels with the past, since a lot of modern Egyptians live in pretty much the same environment as the ancient Egyptians. Unlike Omm Sety, I'm not trying the 'cures' out on myself!

"There are sycamore fig trees growing outside our house here in Maadi [a suburb of Cairo where Dr. Weeks and his family reside]. Now, the fruits, of course, have always provided a food; but the sap and leaves of the tree are also used today for a variety of medical treatments—for rashes, burns, skin ailments. You can go back into ancient Egyptian texts and discover that the sap and leaves were used *then* for the same purposes. You can also discover that the sycamore fig was one of three trees in ancient Egypt considered especially sacred to gods like Hathor and Isis. You have to think that one of the reasons such medical importance was ascribed to this tree was not only because it cured skin ailments but also because it was closely allied to certain religious beliefs and was thought to be the dwelling place of several Egyptian goddesses. So you've got double strength—something that is chemically sound and religiously sound."

To Omm Sety, healing trees and restorative waters were truly manifestations of the gods whom she saw, lived with, and prayed to every day of her life, and who unfailingly rejuvenated her body and her soul.

* * *

In 1964, Omm Sety celebrated her sixtieth birthday. The eight years she had spent in Abydos had been the happiest of her life. Now, faced with mandatory retirement, she was again advised to return to Cairo to find part-time work. Once more she refused. (During her years in Abydos, Omm Sety visited Cairo only once, in 1960. She stayed for one day and one night and was "jolly glad to get back.") The Egyptian Antiquities Department decided to make an exception of her and allowed her to continue working in Abydos for another five years. There were no more extensions to be won, and in 1969, as she said, "they put the old mare out to pasture."

Her son Sety—who, now in his thirties, was the owner of a successful printing business and a counselor to the Kuwaiti Ministry of Education—paid a visit to this Upper Egyptian village to try to convince Omm Sety to come live with him in Kuwait. "He arrived in 1971," she would later recall, "and said: 'Mother, I could let you live in an air-conditioned villa, not a mud hut.' I told him, 'Well, I happen to prefer a mud hut in Abydos to an air-conditioned villa anywhere else.' But he couldn't see it, silly fool. To live in Abydos and to be buried in Abydos: the first half of my life's goal had been achieved—the gods had been kind to me. All that remained was the second half."[4]

Superannuated and having to make do on a pension of not more than thirty dollars a month, Omm Sety now realized that she was going to have to expand her activities. So she started making needlepoint embroideries of the Egyptian gods, scenes from the temple, and hieroglyphic cartouches; and these she would sell to visiting friends and tourists, who would also bring her much-appreciated presents of clothes, books, out-of-date magazines, tea, biscuits, chocolates, and vitamins.

In addition to working as a part-time consultant for the Antiquities Department, she now began guiding tourists through the Sety Temple. "People who came on cruises met me," she once commented, "and when they returned home they mentioned me as being

---

[4] Omm Sety never saw her son again. He died in Kuwait in 1982 at the age of forty-eight.

sort of among the monuments here; so when *their* friends showed up, they, too, wanted to see the horrible specimen in life." Omm Sety could immediately sense whether or not tourists were truly interested in the temple. If they were, she would devotedly spend several hours taking the "chosen few" around the holy shrine on a supererogatory tour, after which she would sometimes invite them to her home or to the rest house for a cup of tea.

In her bare feet, Omm Sety guided her visitors through the halls and chapels of the temple, describing and explaining the reliefs, while interspersing her remarks with jokes, anecdotes, feisty opinions, and folkloristic asides. Osiris and Isis, she would comment, were, of course, brother and sister, as well as husband and wife—"a good system," she would add, "since it did away with the mother-in-law!" Mer-en-Ptah, the pharaoh-grandson of Sety the First who often inscribed his name on monuments he was not responsible for building, found himself chastized by Omm Sety for his "overbearing boasting." The little Mert goddess of Upper Egypt, who is depicted on one wall with her arms raised to King Sety and crying out, "Come bring! Come bring!" was described as "a charming little lady crowned with a clump of lilies of Upper Egypt and wearing her hair in a long plait down her back. Sety gazes upon her with a kindly, indulgent smile."

Speaking of a scene in which Sety is shown receiving from the jackal-headed god Wepwawat the royal crook and flail, Omm Sety would state that the function of this god (whose name means "The Opener of the Ways") was "to show the newly dead the way from this world to the kingdom of Osiris." It was not surprising—she would inform her listeners—that Wepwawat should be represented as a jackal-headed man, or sometimes simply as a jackal, since "it is well known to the modern Arabs that if a traveler is lost in the desert, he has only to follow the footprints of a jackal and they will lead him to the cultivated land . . . and I myself have tried this out and have found it to be true!"

In a similar vein, when Omm Sety pointed to a scene on the southern wall that showed King Sety breaking some earthenware jars at the conclusion of a burial service, she would explain that this rite had been explained by many archaeologists as that of "killing" the vessels in order that they might be used by the dead in the Other World. If that was the reason, Omm Sety would wonder aloud, "Why was not the entire funerary equipment smashed up?" She would then speculate: "In reality it was done to prevent a possible hostile spirit from returning to earth and causing trouble for the living. This is proved by a modern Egyptian custom. If an unwelcome person visits a house, hospitality demands that he should be received, and offered tea or coffee. As soon as he leaves, his host will smash a pot, usually a drinking jar, behind him in the belief that it will prevent him from returning!"

Omm Sety would inevitably call attention to a portrait of a priest clad in a leopard-skin tunic and wearing "the side-lock of youth over an elaborately curled wig," and who was shown offering to King Sety "one spouted jar of water, and *two* tall jars of beer"—Omm Sety would emphasize the number "two," after which she would suggest that perhaps this indicated the "royal preference." Then pointing to another scene that depicts Sety addressing the god Soker—the falcon-headed Memphite god of the dead—she would regret the "deliberate distortion" in this particular portrait "of the handsome features of Sety." Why the "coarse and vulgar" bearing? she would ask. "That such a thing was allowed to pass unaltered is a mystery that we shall never solve. Was it due after all to a disagreeable mood of the sculptor whose skill otherwise is beyond reproach? It may be!"

In the relief showing the goddess Nephthys kneeling and mourning for her dead brother Osiris, she would comment: "Her grief-stricken expression is most unusual in Egyptian art and is carved with such delicate artistic feeling that, touching her cheek, one almost expects to find it wet with tears." In the depiction of the little Prince Ramesses in priestly costume and reading from a roll of papyrus, Omm Sety would exult: "This figure of the Prince is perhaps the best rendering of childhood innocence that ancient Egypt ever produced. Here is a real boy, not a miniature man. The body and limbs, though strong and healthy-looking, are softly rounded and have an immature grace. It is, in short, the portrait of a handsome, lively little boy already displaying the charm for which the adult King Ramesses was famous."

When leading her visitors out through the aisled columns near the seven doorways in the western wall, Omm Sety would stop for a moment and say: "At certain times of the day, the light so shines on these normally brown sandstone columns that they seem to become greenish and translucent. Here and there a square patch of sunlight from an opening in the roof spotlights the cheery face of Ramesses or the calm and kindly countenance of one of the deities" . . . at which point, the sun god would, likely as not, graciously produce the desired effect, imbuing the entire temple with that luminous sense of "benevolence, serenity, and love" that Omm Sety's inspired guiding made all the more palpable.

* * *

In 1972, Omm Sety suffered a mild heart attack and spent a few nights at the Balyana hospital. She refused to remain bedridden for long and was soon up and about in her usual fashion and in defiance of the doctor's orders. During this period she decided, seemingly out of the blue, to sell her old house, explaining, "I had no privacy with His Majesty there, and I sometimes felt that we could be overheard by anyone who felt like eavesdropping!"

She then built herself a temporary ramshackle *zareba* (a room made of reeds) at the foot of the village water tower—as primitive a habitation as one could imagine. She eventually had a little mud-brick house constructed for her by the son of Mahmoud Soliman, the onetime Keeper of the Sety Temple who had met her on her first pilgrimage to Abydos. His son Ahmed now looked after her—and she him—and Omm Sety lived like a member of his family in this dwelling that was attached to Ahmed's property just a short walk from the temple.

She called her new dwelling the "Omm Sety Hilton." A high-rise, the structure consisted of two ten-by-ten-foot rooms built one on top of the other—the upper story being, in her words, her "summer residence." The house contained a little sink (an outhouse served for her toilet) and her usual rickety furniture—two wardrobes, a bed made from *guerid* (the hard, woodlike midrib of a palm frond), and a bookshelf; a Bunsen burner and an old teapot; and a battery-run radio, on which she would listen every night to the BBC Overseas Service. (Unusually well informed about world events, Omm Sety would often report to news-starved tourists who were visiting Abydos the latest goings-on in whatever part of the globe they happened to be curious about.) And in the little garden outside—where her animals continually raced about—she planted and grew onions, spinach, thyme, watercress, figs, and grapes.

Shortly after she and her menagerie moved into these quarters in July of 1972, she received her first visit from "His Majesty" in her new habitation. And in her secret diaries she recounted this amazing housewarming appearance:

July 20, 1972

His Majesty came to me last night at about 12:30 past midnight. I was still awake, and had the Butagaz lamp going, and was lying on the outside bed (where I sleep), reading a

*science-fiction book. After our usual affectionate greetings,
Sety asked me if I was comfortable in the new house, to
which I replied that I was. He said, "I will see it with you."
He put his arm round my shoulder and we walked around.
He said, "I will 'Open the Mouth' of each room and make it
Holy." ("Opening the Mouth" was a ceremony performed on
statues, mummies, and temples. It corresponds to the modern Christian consecration.) His idea of the ceremony was to
hold me close to him and kiss me on the mouth, though ever
since I came to Abydos he had only kissed my forehead,
cheek, or hands. When we got to my room, Teti Sheri had
her kittens on the day-bed, and although the poor cat was
screaming with terror, she got between Sety and her kittens
and prepared to attack him. I was about to catch her, but he
said, "Do not fear, Little Mother, I will not swallow your
babies!" The word he used for "babies" was* noonooiu, *the
plural of* noonoo. *(I have heard modern people call a baby*
noonoo.) *He noticed the statues of Osiris and Isis in the
niche in the north wall, and bowed reverently. Teti Sheri was
still cursing and swearing, but he took time to "Open the
Mouth" of this room too; and because we were standing in
front of the statues, he kissed my forehead! Then we went
outside and sat down together, holding hands. Sety said that
it is the best place that I have lived in in Abydos.*

*Presently, I said, "My Beloved Lord, will you tell me some
things about the Gods?" To which he replied, "I will if I am
able to." I said, "Have you ever seen Set [the evil brother of
Osiris]?" He looked at me, and then looked away, with a
very strange expression on his face, but did not reply. I was
afraid I had made him angry and said, "If what I asked has
angered you, Lord, be gracious and pardon me." He said, "I
am not angry, I will tell you. I have seen him once; that was
during my life on earth, when I was a young man. Bentreshy, do you know that I was once a priest of Set?" I
replied that I did, and that a stela still existed, which
Ramesses had made, recording the family history. Sety
smiled and said, "The mouth of Ramesses was always as big
as his nose!" He said that for hundreds of years, all the men
of his family had been military men, and that most of them
were also priests of Set, whom they adored as a God of War
and the patron god of their nome. He said, "This is not a
good thing. One should not serve an evil being, even if it*

*appears to have a good or useful attribute or function. Many
of my companions in the Military School were also training
for the priesthood of Set, but they did not take their studies
to their hearts. Most of them only passed their initiation
('entered the first gate') because the God had too few servants. I took everything to my heart. By day I studied and
exercised in the Military School. At night I did not sit in the
beer-houses or run after women like a dog after a bitch. I
studied the cult of the Lord of Strength and I studied the
magic powers which he offered. It is because of what I
learned at this time that I am now able to come to you in the
form of a living man. But those things I could have learned
in the service of other Gods. After two years had passed, I
asked to be allowed to try and enter the 'First Gate.' The
Chief Priest agreed. For 10 days I ate no meat and drank
only water. On the eleventh day I fasted. One hour after
sunset I was taken to the Chapel of the Great of Strength,
which was lit by a lamp with three wicks. In a niche (serekh)
in the west wall was a statue of the God, a man with the
head of a strange animal. I was told to kneel in front of the
statue and repeat the God's name. I was not to rise from the
floor; I was not to leave the Chapel. I was then left alone. I
did as I was ordered. After some time I felt the earth trem-
ble, there was a terrible noise like thunder, and a bright light
came from the niche. Instead of the painted wooden statue,
there stood the God himself. Bentreshy, he was of a beauty
that cannot be described! His hair was red as new copper, his
eyes were as green as the great ocean, but he seemed to be
the spirit and soul of all that is cruel and evil. His voice was
evil music when he said, 'Come to me, my son and servant.' I
jumped to my feet, I screamed, 'Never will I serve you!' I
opened the door and fled from the chapel. As I did so, I
heard the terrible, mocking laughter of the God. The priests
were waiting in the courtyard. They cried, 'Praised be the
Lord of Strength! He has revealed his face to his servant!'
They guessed what had happened, but they thought that my
flight was caused by religious ecstasy. The next day, the
Chief Priest wrote my name in the records as Wab-priest of
Set; but I swear to you, Beloved, that I refused to enter his
chapel again, and I never served him, even for one hour."*

"Did you ever see him again?" I asked. "No," he replied,
"I have never seen him, but often I have heard his terrible

laughter. I heard it on the day when my eldest son went to his death. I heard it on the night when I learned of your death. I heard it as I left the Court of Our Lord Osiris, after I had been condemned to wait in sorrow and loneliness for your return. How often during those thousands of weary years I have lain sleepless on my bed, my body and soul in agony, longing for you, and have cried your name aloud in the night and have heard, like an echo, that terrible, mocking laughter!"

I burst out crying, and knelt at his feet and hid my face in his lap. He comforted me; and after a while I asked, "Why did you not change your name?" He smiled, "Silly child, the name we are given at our birth cannot be changed before the Gods; it is a part of us, like our ka [a person's vital force, spiritual 'double'] and our glorified spirit. I always hated my name until one night, in the garden of the House-of-Men-maat-Ra [Temple of Sety the First], I told you to call me by it, and then it became like music from my 'Harp-of-Joy.'" "But," I said, "in the House-of-Men-maat-Ra your name is written 'Thety' with the emblem of Our Lady Isis." "O stupid child," he said, "you must go back to the Temple School and learn to write! Do you not remember that the emblem of the blood of Our Lady reads 'set'?" (This is very interesting, since in all the modern books on Egyptian philology that emblem is said to read th or ti! But what His Majesty says makes more sense.)

I apologized to H.M. for asking a question that had clearly pained him to answer, but he said that to talk thus eased the pain in the heart. "I have tried not to tell you things that would cause you sorrow," he said. I answered, "Among the Barbarians is a saying: 'A trouble shared is a troubled halved.'" Then he said, "Put out that beautiful lamp." I did so, and he got up and went to the bed and said, "Come, Beloved, hold me in your arms until I have to leave you." That is how we passed the rest of the night. Before he left, Sety promised to return to me soon.

And return soon he did. "His Majesty" visited Omm Sety the following night and on many other nights during the next several weeks, as her diary entries relate:

July 26, 1972

His Majesty came again last night! This is very unusual. I awoke at about 1:30 A.M. feeling a weight on my shoulder and body. I found H.M. fast asleep beside me, his face resting against my shoulder and one arm across my body. By the light of the night lamp he looked very contented and peaceful, so I did not move or try to wake him up, although I wanted to speak with him. After a while I fell asleep, and he left without waking me. I hope that he can continue to come often. Perhaps the new house is lucky for us, even if it stands in what was once part of the Nif-wer Canal!

July 29, 1972

I don't know what is the matter!!! Last night, at about 11:40 P.M., His Majesty came to me again. *He held me in his arms so tightly that I could hardly breathe, and said, "What have you done to me, Bentreshy? I cannot stay away from you!" I replied (when at last I could breathe!), "I have done nothing, My Lord, except think of you with love, as I always do." He said, "Bentreshy, your bad little heart calls to my heart, and my sad old heart runs to you, it drags me with it. What are we to do?" I said, "We have to be patient and remember that we will have Eternity together." He said, "O wise Little One, beloved Little Sister of my Heart!" I sat on the bed, and he came and lay on his stomach, with his head in my lap. He put one arm around my waist and with the other took my right hand and laid it, palm upwards, under his face.*

For some while he lay very quiet, and I thought that he was asleep. But after a while he said, "Now tell me a story." "What about?" I asked. "Any story," he said. So I told him about Atlantis, explaining that the great ocean with the cold and shining mountains that he had seen was once a great land, full of wise and educated people. I told him that at that time the Western Desert was at the bottom of the sea, and that when Atlantis sank, the Western Desert arose as dry land.

For a while he was very quiet. Then he said, "A Khyti (Cretan) once told me such a story. He said that our ocean (the Mediterranean) was once a great land, but it sunk, and his land and the rest of the Nebu Hamebu *(the Aegean Isles) were once the tops of the mountains of this drowned land." I said, "Some people think that our Lord Osiris was a survivor of the lost land." He replied, "No, our Lord came from Amenti, whence he returned." I said, "I have been thinking that our Lord Osiris is the same as King Mena." "Who is Mena?" he asked. I said, "The king who united the Two Lands" [Upper and Lower Egypt]. He said, "His name is not Mena, it is Meny, and his true name is Narmer." After some silence, "Why do you think then that our Lord and Meny are the same?" I told him the similar points in their story. [Tradition has it that Narmer-Mena—the First Dynasty King—was killed by a hippopotamus; Osiris was murdered by Set, who sometimes took the form of a hippopotamus; the King's son and successor, Hor-aha, was once referred to as "Hor-aha, the Son of Isis."] H.M. said, "I have never heard that Meny was killed by a hippopotamus. I think that Our Lord ruled* Kem *["The Black Land," the ancient name for Egypt] some time before Meny. All that he taught and all that he made was destroyed by Set. Later, our Lord Horus and his followers, of whom Meny was one, seized power. They reunited the lands and restored all the work of Our Lord Osiris. Beloved, your stories give me a pain in my head! Heal the pain with your caresses, and let me sleep in peace in your arms. By the life of Ra, I will be a good man!" That was the end of the matter.*

P.S. On re-reading this account, I am puzzled by His Majesty's statements about Meny and the Pre-dynastic period. If Osiris lived on earth in those days, all traces of his civilization seem to have vanished. This he explains as being due to the destructive malice of Set. But even so, one would expect something to have remained. Of course, as regards buildings, it is possible that they were very simple structures of mud-brick, suited to the unskilled labour available. We do know that very fine pottery was produced at this early date, and some of the painted vases show what seem to be large ships with cabins and many oars. There is also proof that the people believed in a future life, because they buried personal objects and food and drink with their dead. There is nothing in the known stories of Osiris to say that he united Upper and Lower Egypt; rather it suggests that his influence extended over all Egypt, with no geographical boundaries.

The question now is: Where does Horus come into the story? We are told that he was conceived after the death of his father. But how long after? If, as H.M. says, Osiris, and so presumably his brother and sisters, were not deified mortals, Isis may have lived in hiding in Egypt or elsewhere for hundreds of years before Horus was born. Some of the stories concerning Horus, including a dramatic text said to date from the First Dynasty, say that after Horus had finally defeated Set and avenged Osiris, the Great God decreed that Egypt should be divided between them. This accounts for the Two Lands, subsequently united by Meny. The Palermo Stone (late Fifth Dynasty) mentions the "Followers of Horus" and gives some of their names. These are supposed to have ruled Lower Egypt. Personally, I doubt His Majesty's theory. He definitely says that Meny and Narmer are the same person, and we have solid, contemporary evidence that Narmer was succeeded by Hor-aha, who in his tomb at Sakkara is plainly stated to be the Son of Isis. I think that the "Followers of Horus" were the people of Horus the Elder, brother of Osiris and Set. Even before the time of the New Kingdom, Horus the Elder and Horus the son of Isis had become confused in the minds of the people. I will have to try and get more information about this matter. An educated priest would probably know more than H.M., if I can tactfully get him to ask the opinion of such a man. Kha-em-Wast, the fourth son of Ramesses, would probably know, but he is an awful liar and trouble-maker. A few years ago (after I came to Abydos) Kha-em-Wast told Sety that I had got married! There was a hell of a row about that, and H.M. has refused to meet Kha-em-Wast ever since!

August 1, 1972

His Majesty came again last night!!! I woke up, I don't know at what time, and found him lying beside me, holding me in his arms. It was a hot night and the moon was bright. The bed cover was kicked off onto the floor and my night-dress was up above my knees. He saw me looking suspiciously, and laughed. "No, Little One," he said. "I did not do that, I am a good man! They did themselves by themselves." I believe him (though many would not!). I sat up and wanted to start talking, but he pulled me down again, and said in a firm but quiet voice, like a commander speaking to a junior officer, "No talking! A little kissing! Much sleeping!" Then he laughed again and said, "Truly, Bentreshy, I want to sleep, and when I lie beside you, my rest is sweet indeed." Nothing more was said after that, except a few silly names, and he very soon was sound asleep.

I stayed awake for some time, very happy, but puzzled by the sudden frequency of his visits. Maybe it is because the land I now live on has never been inhabited by people. It was once the site of the Nef-wer Canal, and until a few years ago was covered by the Inundation. When a place has been inhabited by people, some of their influence is left behind, and, in the course of time, can build up and form a kind of thick curtain between us and the spirit world, especially if the inhabitants had been of bad character or low mentality. This also may be why H.M. came so seldom when I was living up in the village. On the other hand, he used to come very frequently when I lived in the Pasha's House at the Pyramids. That house was nearly 200 years old, but it had the atmosphere of a house that had been built with love and care. It was haunted by the spirits of the Pasha, his wife, and two servants, and a lovely white donkey. But they were gentle, kindly spirits, and I think it was their love of the house that called them back. According to spiritualists, such an atmosphere makes it easy for other spirits to manifest themselves.

August 9, 1972

His Majesty came again last night! I was asleep, but woke up with my cat Mery screaming and spitting as he ran out of the house. H.M. was standing just beside the night lamp. He looked fed up. I got up quickly and went to him. He kissed me and held me in his arms and said, "Bentreshy, a tired and lonely old man wants to sleep in the place that your cat has just left." I said, "You are not old, my Beloved, and you will not be lonely any more tonight. Come." We lay down side by side. He put his arms round me, and soon we both fell asleep. It must have turned cold before the dawn, because when I woke up I was covered with a blanket that I had left folded up on a box in the house. Apparently, he

*looked for something to cover me, and found it. I am happy
to see him so often.*

* * *

In Abydos, Omm Sety had gotten to know all the leading
Egyptologists of the day. Dr. Lanny Bell and Dr. William Murnane,
who direct the University of Chicago's Epigraphic Survey at Chicago
House in Luxor, would often, in the words of William Murnane, "go
up to Abydos to see Omm Sety, have tea in her place, talk, and see
the temple. Once she accompanied us to Omm El Gaab, the burial
place of the First Dynasty pharaohs, which had been thought of as
being the resting place of Osiris. Omm Sety came out, even though
she'd recently had a heart attack, and said, 'I want to walk over there
with you, but if I fall behind, don't worry; I'll be sitting on a stone,
taking a pill, and I'll be right along!' She was very game, she stuck it
out the whole way, and didn't seem any the worse for it."

"She also took us out on a walk once to the southern and northern
regions that most tourists don't get to," Dr. Bell added, "—from the
Temple of Senwosret the Third in the south, up to the Temple of
Osiris at Kom El Sultan in the north. It was always a pleasure to be
with her and to listen to whatever she said."

"You really couldn't take her anything but seriously," William
Murnane commented, "—even when you would argue with, say, her
notion that the Osirion was a Fourth Dynasty structure, since we
know that Sety built it. [Most Egyptologists agree with Dr. Murnane; several do not.] But there was a certain element of mischie-
vousness about her, and you never knew when she might be pulling
your leg. John Romer [author of *The Valley of the Kings* and *Ancient
Lives: The Story of the Pharaohs' Tombmakers*] told me that he once
went up to see her, and brought along a bottle of vodka, which he
offered to share with her at the rest house. She looked at the bottle
and said curiously, 'Oh, what's *that?*' 'Vodka,' he replied. 'Oh,' she
remarked, 'I've *never* had any!' You knew that she was angling for a
drink. Very charmingly. . . . She also had a great deal of fun with
the slightly more ribald sides of the stories of the gods and goddesses.
Whenever she'd mention Ramesses the Second, she'd exclaim, 'He's
such a *handsome* boy!' While about some other character, she'd declare, 'Oh, that horrible person!' "

Omm Sety would often talk openly about Sety and Ramesses as if
they were close friends or members of her family. "I never think of
Ramesses as a man," she once remarked. "To me, he's always a
teenager. You know, when you meet a child and then don't see him

again, you always remember him as a child. I remember Ramesses as a tall, good-looking boy with a sort of devilish glint in his eye . . . good-natured, but noisy and restless."

As far as Omm Sety was concerned, Ramesses was "the most slandered of all the pharaohs" because of his being identified—incorrectly, according to her (and to other scholars as well)—as the biblical Pharaoh of Oppression. "It's true that he had his little faults (and who among us has not?)," she once commented, "but cruelty and despotism were certainly not among them. Ramesses had a tiresome habit of having his own name carved on other men's monuments, and he was inclined to blow his own trumpet; but that is a far cry from deliberately oppressing a captive people, much less ordering the indiscriminate slaughter of baby boys. On the contrary, the evidence of contemporary monuments shows that Ramesses was a handsome and cheerful and kindly man, an affectionate father, a wise and lenient ruler, a brave warrior, and a lover of animals. Not only did he allow his subjects to call him 'Ramesses'—when, in those days, it was forbidden to anyone but members of his immediate family to refer to the Pharaoh by his personal name—but he also let them use his pet name, 'Sisi'! . . . Now, does this sound like Mr. Cecil B. de Mille's despot?"

She was, however, far less charitable about Ramesses' mother (the "Great Wife" of Sety the First), Queen Tuy, whom she considered "the original Miss Rich Bitch. . . . I don't have anything against her personally. She was an exemplary lady, but she had that snooty look . . . though Ramesses must have liked her since he built the only known monuments to her. Sety never made a single one for this woman. He was fed up with her, I imagine. Purely a marriage of convenience.

"You see, Sety wasn't a royal person. His family were all military people. In his youth he had been married to a lady of nonroyal blood, by whom he had at least one son. She died before her husband's accession and was buried in a fine stone sarcophagus on which was engraved the usual married woman's title, 'Mistress of the House.' An instance of Sety's kindness is that, after he became King, he had her tomb opened and the title 'Mistress of the House' replaced by 'King's Wife,' so that she might take her rightful place in the other world. If she wasn't a queen in life, she was in death. But the King's 'Great Wife' she was not—Mrs. Rich Bitch had *that* title!"

One might imagine that Omm Sety's "familiar" and "familial" approach to the ancient royalty of Abydos might have annoyed many Egyptologists. That seems not to have been the case. Dr. Kenneth Kitchen—the leading authority on the Nineteenth Dynasty and the author of *Pharaoh Triumphant: The Life and Times of Ramesses II* and the compiler of the complete *Ramesside Inscriptions* in seven volumes—knew Omm Sety and considered her to be "a true Ramesside," adding: "You know, there *is* a certain truth to that 'familial' approach of hers, after all. The Temple of Sety is Sety's local Abydos memorial temple, and it commemorates his father, Ramesses the First, in parts. Ramesses the Second appears in it as a prince, and then he himself finishes the work on it as Pharaoh. *His* son, Mer-en-Ptah, completes the Osirion, while adding a few things over there. And *his* son, Sety the Second—who, remember, is a great-grandson of Sety the First—contributes a few inscriptions at the back of the shrine. . . . So there *is* a family thread going right through that temple.

"I remember very well Omm Sety telling me that Ramesses was 'so rambunctious, just like Mohammed Ali, the boxer!' She would always comment about how 'handsome' both Sety and Ramesses were. Of course, *everybody* admires Sety's mummy, not just Omm Sety; it's the most handsome mummy there is. As far as Ramesses is concerned . . . just think of Amelia B. Edwards sailing down the Nile in 1874 and, arriving at Abu Simbel on an 'enchanted' moonlit night, describing [in *A Thousand Miles up the Nile*] how handsome Ramesses seemed to her.[5] When I first read her book, I found myself thinking, 'You know, she's got a point there: Ramesses *does* have a good profile, and Queen Nefertari *was* beautiful'—as the statues show us.

"About the matter of Omm Sety's belief in reincarnation—that was a personal matter, a little bee in the bonnet. She was a charming person, she loved the temple, she was on the side of the ancient Egyptians and cared for their history—which is what Egyptologists are supposed to do. She was so transparent in her character, and had such a curious history herself, when you come to think of it, that you couldn't help liking her. My attitude was: that's how she thinks,

---

[5] "Now, Ramesses the Great, if he was as much like his portraits as his portraits are like each other, must have been one of the handsomest men, not only of his own day, but of all history. . . . The face is oval; the eyes are long, prominent, and heavy-lidded; the nose is slightly aquiline and characteristically depressed at the tip; the nostrils are open and sensitive; the under lip projects; the chin is short and square. . . . A godlike serenity, an almost superhuman pride, an immutable will breathe from the sculptured stone. He has learned to believe his prowess irresistible, and himself almost divine" (Amelia B. Edwards).

well, fair enough, she's entitled to her personal view of life, it's all right. Make that allowance and there was no problem.

"Omm Sety came to all sorts of perfectly sensible conclusions about the actual, objective material of the Sety Temple—which may have *also* coincided with things that she felt she knew some other way—because she had time on the site that ninety-nine percent of us don't have . . . and that paid dividends. So even in a minimal interpretation, she had the opportunity to make many quiet little observations. Never mind the last life . . . *this* one was quite enough!

"Now, concerning Omm Sety's hostility toward Akhen-Aton [the heretic Eighteenth Dynasty Pharaoh (c. 1353–1335 B.C.), husband of the beautiful Nefertiti and possibly the brother or half brother of Tut-ankh-Amon, who changed the religion of Egypt from polytheism to monotheism and the worship of the solar disk, the *Aton*], you have to realize that this Pharaoh not only went against the god Amon-Ra, but he also tried to stamp out the Osirion religion. (Omm Sety would always refer to Akhen-Aton as 'that criminal!' whenever she spoke about him to me.) Of course, Sety came back with a rebound and restored the old gods, dedicating three chapels in his temple at Abydos to Amon-Ra, Ra-Hor-akhty, and Ptah—the three gods of empire."

In 1979 the director Nicholas Kendall came to Egypt to make a film for the National Film Board of Canada entitled *The Lost Pharaoh: The Search for Akhenaten.* This documentary focuses on the archaeological work of Dr. Donald Redford, Professor of Egyptology at the University of Toronto, who in 1975 had unearthed some stones that had originally been part of the foundation of one of Akhen-Aton's temples inside one of the pylons of the Karnak Complex. And Dr. Redford asked Omm Sety to appear in *The Lost Pharaoh,* in which she describes Akhen-Aton as "a very ugly man, almost to the verge of deformity. He had a great long jaw, a long back, and an awful stance. The funny thing about him—he had many female characteristics: a protuberant belly and very wide hips and fat thighs; and below the fat thighs, spindly legs like a chicken's. Some modern doctors, judging by the portraits of his statues, say he suffered from some glandular disease [Fröhlich's syndrome], and that it was progressive. According to these doctors, he would have become impotent and couldn't possibly have produced children. So where his six daughters came from, God knows! Since the daughters all resemble him, however, I should think they're all his. Seeing that he was ruining the country, his wife Nefertiti should have slipped something in his beer and run off with his army commander, Hor-em-heb!"

To people brought up to think of Akhen-Aton as "a gentle and poetic idealist dedicated to a universal god" and author of the great "Hymn to the *Aton*" ("Thou arisest beauteous in the horizon of heaven, O living *Aton*, beginner of life when thou didst shine forth in the eastern horizon, and didst fill every land with thy beauty . . ."), it is curious to discover that not only Omm Sety but also scholars such as Veronica Seton-Williams and even Donald Redford himself all dismiss the heretic Pharaoh as a "one-track-minded, authoritarian iconoclast who impaled captives and deported populations" (Redford) or as a man who "rode around in a chariot just worrying about his nutty religion" (Seton-Williams). To Omm Sety, Akhen-Aton was a "fanatic" (she often compared him to the Ayatollah Khomeini) who "brought shame to our country." As she would remark to a visiting tourist who had asked her about Tut-ankh-Amon (the second successor of Akhen-Aton), "I walked into King Tut's tomb once, and I exited quicker than I entered, for while I was inside, I felt as if someone had got ahold of my back and was pushing me, saying, 'Get out, get out, get out!' . . . I don't like that family."

In one of her diary entries, Omm Sety wrote the following:

December 18, 1973

His Majesty came last night at about 11:30 P.M. I asked him what he knew about Akhen-Aton. He frowned and replied, "Why do you ask about that evil man?" I said that his character, though bad in our eyes, was interesting, and that the "Imy-rawer Hani" [Hanny El Zeini] was interested to know more about him. Then Sety smiled and said, "For the pleasure of the 'Imy-rawer' I will tell you what I know. I myself once asked why Akhen-Aton's guard Ka-Hor deserted from the bodyguard about one year before the Criminal died. They could not endure the conditions of life there, and they said that certainly the curse of Amon [a form of the great creator god whose cult center was at Thebes and whose name signifies 'The Hidden One'] had fallen on the King and driven him mad. Kai-saneb [an old, retired general of Sety's time who, as a young officer, had served under Akhen-Aton] said that a story went round among the soldiers that just before the King died, he said that his God had changed him into a young maiden, and that he had taken poison in order to go as a pure bride to his god. But I, living as I did in the Northland [ancient Memphis], never heard of this, and it

*was generally believed that Hor-em-heb [the great com-
mander of the Egyptian army under Akhen-Aton and Tut-
ankh-Amon] and Ay [the counselor to Akhen-Aton and Tut-
ankh-Amon who assumed the throne on the latter's death]
had him killed in order to save the Black Land [Egypt]." I
asked if H.M. knew whether Akhen-Aton had a sickness
[Fröhlich's syndrome], which modern doctors believe made
him impotent, and whether his daughters (with the exception
of the first) were not really his at all, but were maybe the
children of Amon-Hotep III [the Eighteenth Dynasty Pharaoh who was the father of Akhen-Aton]." He laughed and
said, "No, I never heard of such a story, and I do not think
that it is true. Perhaps the last two girls were not his own, as
by then Nefertiti hated him, and may well have taken a
lover. But if that was so, she covered her secret well, and the
Criminal believed that he had begotten them. If that story
had been true, all Egypt would have known about it, for, as
you know, the* rekhyt *[common people] dearly love to hear of
such scandals in high places! But I will ask Kai-saneb if he
had heard of this matter, and when I come again I will tell
you more of what happened in that accursed city [ancient
Akhetaton, Akhen-Aton's capital], but I am sure you will be
very angry. Now kiss me, for I must leave and go back to my
guests, and your kisses on my lips will make the wine taste
all the sweeter." I duly obeyed the royal command, and he
left.*

And during the next three years His Majesty's visits continued
apace, providing always more amazing stories, comments, explanations, and reflections from the other world:

August 29, 1974

*His Majesty came last night after an absence of more than
20 days. He told me a story that is strange and very terrible;
in fact, if I did not know that he does not tell lies, I would
have thought it a kind of ancient "science fiction"! It happened that we were looking up at the stars, which were very
brilliant and beautiful. Then I asked Sety why the Egyptians
always drew stars like a disk emitting rays of light. He answered, "There is a tradition handed down by the wise men
of the time of the ancestors that the stars are round worlds,*

some large and some small." I said that was the modern idea, and that men are trying to build "metal birds" that will reach them, and that they have already succeeded in reaching the moon. Sety said, "I cannot believe that! Either they lie, or they have gone there as an akh *[astral body], and that is very bad and is forbidden by the Lord of All!" I asked how he knew, and for a while he did not reply. Then he said, "I will tell you something, my Little One, something that I have never told anyone, not even my son Ramesses. You must understand that after my arrival in* Amenti, *I was a man maddened with sorrow. I thought that I would find you, but I did not. I searched, I questioned, but to no avail. My friends among the priests cast pitying eyes upon my grief, but they were forbidden to answer my questions or to give me any word of comfort. In despair I even braved the wrath of the Council, and they replied, 'She whom you seek is not here, nor is she upon earth.' When I tried to ask more, they said one word, 'Begone'!*

"Then I began a search; I reached the skies, and in so doing I found that some, and therefore perhaps all, of the stars were worlds. I ranged among them as an akh, *but they were strange and hateful. One was all covered with swirling water, churned by a strong, ceaseless wind. One had a covering of strange green plants, greener and more fertile than the land of Ta-she (Fayyum) [the largest of the Egyptian oases, located some fifty-six miles southwest of Cairo]." I asked if he saw people or animals there, but he said he saw no living thing except plants. Then he continued, "One was a barren land, covered with gray rocks and from its surface rose thousands and hundreds of thousands of towers, some only as high as your wall there, others as high as Akhet Khufu [the Great Pyramid]. They looked like trumpets standing upright on their wide end. The narrow upper ends were open, and from them came warm air with a most terrible stench." I asked if the towers were the work of hands, and he said, "No, I think they were the work of some evil god, for they were in one piece, and not built up with blocks of stone: and again I saw no living thing.*

"Now, Little One, I will tell you the most horrible thing. I found a world on which people had lived. There were great cities with very tall buildings built of large blocks of red

stone that had glittering particles in it. There were fine, wide streets, and some of them had part of the way paved with a shining metal of bright blue. In fact in the very place where we would have used copper, there was this beautiful blue metal. In the streets lay long metal things with windows and seats inside, but they had neither wings like the metal birds, nor had they wheels. Inside there were people, like us, but much taller, and they were all dead. In the tall houses, in the streets, in the workshops (which had many strange things made of blue metal) were many people, men and women and children, and all were dead. They were not decayed, their flesh had dried like that of a sahu. But none of them had any hair on their heads or bodies, or on their faces. I saw a large, open space like those where the metal birds alight, and there were many of those strange metal things; some of which were full of dead people, some empty, some had some people inside, and others about to enter, when they all died. One lay at a little distance. It was broken, and most of the people in it were broken." I asked what he thought had happened, and he said, "They all seem to have died suddenly, each one in his place. Most of them had a look of horror on their faces. It was terrible to behold. Also I think that they were people of a high culture, and they seem to have had many things that the people of the earth use today. In some houses I saw pictures made with light. The clothes of the people were strange. They were all alike, men and women, long coverings for the legs and short tunics, and they were made of strange material that was not woven, but was like papyrus, but seemingly soft and pliable." I asked how long he thought they had been dead and he replied, "I cannot tell. A terrible thing about the place is that there was no air, not a faint breeze stirred. There was no water. Outside the city were vast fields of cultivated plants, all standing dry and motionless, and tall trees, dead and dry and not a breeze to blow their dry leaves away. There were also some strange looking animals, all dead, and one still had a mouthful of plants partly in its mouth. I was horrified and sick at heart, and I fled back to Amenti. Then the Council summoned me. I was told that I must never go to such places again. They said that I was a man of the earth, and I must never go to any other place. They said the stars were evil places, and their evil influence must not be allowed to contaminate the world of humans." But I said, "If people now go to the stars as they wish, can that harm this world?" He replied that it would seem so, as the Council cannot lie. Then I wondered what terrible thing had happened, and he replied, "Those people seemed to be like us, therefore when they were alive, they must have had air and water. Perhaps one of their gods suddenly removed all the air. I cannot know when that happened, for there was no sign of decay in anything, and yet I felt in my heart that these people had perished many thousands of years before I saw them, but I do not know."

He looked quite troubled as he was thinking about the awful thing he had seen. I asked why he had not told anyone about that adventure. He replied, "Why should I speak of it? If I told Ramesses, surely he would want to go and see for himself." I asked if I might tell Dr. Hani [Hanny El Zeini] about it, and he smiled. "Yes, you may tell him. He is a wise man and will not try to visit the stars, and perhaps he will know how all those people could have died at one time. Tell him also of the words of the Council, that he may warn others of the danger."

I asked when it was that he knew that I had returned again to earth. He said, "After long ages of suffering, Our Lord Osiris had mercy upon me, and the Council summoned me and said that you were 'sleeping in the blackness, and that one day, you would be re-born.' That comforted me a little. Then much later, I was told that you had been re-born on earth in almost the same form as you had before, and I was permitted to search for you as an akh *wandering all over the world, and saw many strange places and things, until at last I found you, and the rest you know."*

He left me soon after ending the story, but I could not sleep for thinking about it. The sudden death of a nation reminded me about the hairy mammoth elephants found in a frozen Siberian bog. They were perfectly preserved, and even their flesh was eatable. One had a mouth full of grass and buttercups, and the latter only grow in a temperate climate. Scientists say that the climate of Siberia was temperate, millions of years ago, and for some reason a sudden icy spell of cold killed the elephants as they were feeding, quick-froze them, and kept them in a natural "cold storage." But

*that cannot be the case with the people that Sety saw, as he
said that they were all dried up like mummies. The queer
thing is that they must have had a very high and complex
civilization. What can those wingless and wheelless vehicles
have been?*[6]

September 5, 1974

*His Majesty came last night but did not stay long. He said,
"Do not forget to go to the House of Men-maat-Ra tomorrow" [the Temple of Sety the First: Men-maat-Ra ("Estab-
lished-is-the-Justice-of-Ra") is the Horus name—a titulary
epithet—of Sety the First]. I replied that I had not forgotten
but said I had a problem as there were now many strange
and impolite men working as guardians in the Temple, and
I was afraid that if I went there with the offerings, they
would crowd around begging and snatching at everything,
and asked his advice. He replied, "You have a statue of Our
Lord Osiris here. Set your offerings before it here, so that
they will not be disturbed and polluted by the ignorant
rekhyt [common people]. Then go to the House of Men-
maat-Ra with some incense. It is enough, and it is acceptable." When he appeared, the two geese made a great
squawking and flapping of wings, which made Sety laugh. I
told him that I had got them as guardians. He said, "In
that, you are right. One goose will make more noise than 10
dogs. Have you given them names?" I said that the male was
Snefru and the female Nebet. He laughed. "The Majesty of
King Snefru has grown wings and a long beak. You are a
funny girl to choose royal names for your animals." I told
him that when I was child I had a pet frog named Pharaoh.
He laughed and said, "If you had called him Pharaoh Ay it
would have been a good name, for that man had a face like
a frog, but the frogs have a better character." I asked where
Ay was now, but he only said, "I do not know where he is,
and I am happy that I do not have to meet him. He was a
very bad man, and brought much harm to the Black Land."
I wanted to talk more, but he said that he must leave me.*

[6] By a curious coincidence, the now accepted acronym for the radio Search for Extra-
terrestrial Intelligence is SETI!

September 7, 1974

His Majesty came very late last night. He was in official costume, and wore the Double Crown [representing Upper and Lower Egypt] which he took off and put on the guerid table. He had just come from the evening service for Osiris in Amenti. He said, "Did you go to the House of Men-maat-Ra, Little One?" I replied that I had done so, and burned incense there. I showed him the little altar that I had made in the east room, with the offerings still in place, grapes, dates, biscuits and beer. He said, "That is very good and acceptable. What a beautiful covering the small cakes are in." He meant the gilt foil on the tea biscuits! I wanted to talk but he said that he could not stay, but would return soon. When he left, the neighbour's dogs and my geese made a big dowsha *[noise].*

September 8, 1974

His Majesty came last night just before midnight. He could not stay long, as he was having a banquet [in Amenti] in honour of the birthday of Isis. I asked who was coming. He replied, "My son Ramesses and the Great Royal Wife Nefertari (he pronounced it Nofert-iry), some commanders of the Army and their wives, the Great Priest Mery and his wife Werni, whom you know, and their son Wen-nofer and his wife. O My Love, I shall be the only lonely man among them. Would that I dared to bring you to join us. But it is too great a risk!" I would have loved to have gone, as I very much want to meet Nofert-iry, who I think must be as nice and intelligent as she is beautiful. Sety asked, "What are you doing, destroying your room?" I explained that it was unsafe, and that I was building a better one. He said, "May it be blessed for you. Surely I shall come to share your nights in it. Now, My Little One, I must go to join my guests. Shall I greet Ramesses for you?" I said, "Please do, and also his lovely lady, and all your guests, and I take the opportunity to wish them a happy opening of the year." I also asked him to greet Ankhsi [a housekeeper and lady-in-waiting in Sety's palace] for me. He seemed pleased that I had remembered her, and after a few kisses and hugs he left.

January 2, 1976

Today is the first day of the Great Feast of Osiris, and His Majesty came last night to remind me to go to the House of Men-maat-Ra [the Temple of Sety]. What a time we had! I thought at one time that we had made enough noise to wake the entire village. When he first appeared, I was still awake, having worked late. All the cats rushed out of the room, except Baby Khufu, who was afraid, but stood staring at H.M. and spitting before she ran. He had noticed her, and after the usual fond greetings he said, "You have a very pretty little cat, she looks like a small lion." I agreed, and asked how were Ramesses' pet lions. He started to laugh, and said, "The last time my son visited me, he brought his favourite lion Amit (the Devourer) with him. I could smell its stink before it came through. Therefore I told Ramesses to take it out to the courtyard, where my men would care for it. This he did. We were seated together in my room, which you, my Little One, know, and after some time we heard a noise from outside, a sound of men laughing and shouting, an unusual thing. Ramesses was not pleased. He went out to see the cause of the noise. Then he came back, and he was laughing loudly. He told me that the husband of Ankhri, who is Overseer of all my horses, and some of the men from the stables, were trying to make his lion Amit eat bread dipped in beer. They told him that the lion had eaten two loaves 'like a true warrior,' but had spit out the third, and refused to eat any more." We both laughed about that. Then H.M. said, "Now, Little One, do you know that in the morning you have to celebrate the Feast of Our Lord Osiris?" I replied that I had remembered, and prepared everything, and I told him that I had forgotten the days of the Feasts for the birthdays of Osiris and Isis until the time had passed. He said, "I know that, you bad girl. Because I could not come and remind you you cannot remember? Oh, bad, bad, bad," and he gently slapped my face. I did not ask how he knew I had forgotten, probably Kha-em-Wast [the fourth son of Ramesses the Second] had found out and told him. Then he gave me a lot of kisses to make up for the slap, and said that he would come and visit me again during the Feast. I asked if he was going to hold his usual banquet for his friends on the first night and he said that he was. Then he said that on the second night he was making a big feast for his soldiers, and that they were all going to dance. I was astonished, I could not imagine him dancing! He said, "You silly girl, do you not know that all of us, officers and soldiers, have a war dance? This we have done since the time of the Ancestors." I said that I'd love to see that dance, and he said, "I will show you, but you must beat on the drum for me." I said that I did not have a drum, but he said that the table would do, and showed me how to beat ten fairly rapid even beats and then one big bang and a pause. I tried it, and at the second go got it right. Then he took off his robe and stood in his pants and said, "Begin!"

What a surprise I had, I had no idea he could dance, and so well! The dance consisted of quick movements and, with the big bang, he suddenly stood still in the position of an archer taking aim, or a spearman about to throw his spear, or a man about to use his war axe or mace. Some of the quick movements consisted of spinning round with arms stretched out sideways ⳨*, jumping up and down with arms raised like the* ka-arms ⳨ *and the fists clenched, raising each knee rapidly (also with the arms raised)* ⳨*, running but standing in one place with one arm stretched out in front and making a chopping motion as though using an axe* ⳨*.*

These movements were repeated over and over again, gradually getting faster, and finally ending in a jump and finishing with a shout! It was a fine dance, but my room is rather small, and I thought that any minute he'd crash into the cupboard! After that, he put on his robe and said, "Now let a poor old man get under your nice warm red cover and have a rest." I praised his dancing, and he seemed pleased but said that Ramesses did it much better, especially the jumps. After a lot of silly talk we went to sleep. He left just before 5 A.M. and set the dog howling and barking.

·V·

Hanny El Zeini

A Chronicle of a Friendship

For the fainting—from his friend—loyalty.

(The Book of Job)

"**D**o you ever get lonely here in Abydos?" Omm Sety was once asked. To which she replied: "I was an only child, and so I was accustomed to playing alone. I only feel lonely if there are no animals around. Of course, what I do miss sometimes are people to talk to about mutual pet subjects." And aside, of course, from "His Majesty," the person Omm Sety spent most of the last twenty-five years of her life talking to about these subjects was Dr. Hanny El Zeini.

In June of 1956 the then thirty-eight-year-old industrial chemist and mechanical engineer was chosen president of the Sugar and Distillery Company of Egypt. Just three months earlier, Omm Sety had moved permanently to Abydos, almost thirty miles north of Nag Hammadi; and, as destiny would have it, Hanny El Zeini happened to be in Abydos in December of that eventful year.

"Seven weeks after my assuming the presidency of the Sugar and Distillery Company," Dr. El Zeini has commented, "Nasser, in a dramatic and quite unprecedented move, nationalized the International Suez Canal Company. Egypt had witnessed very few moments of glory, joy, or real happiness since the Turkish invasion in 1517; and the twenty-third of July 1956 was one of those happy moments. Egyptian national feelings were electrified. The leftovers of colonial imperialism in England and France were now—in the Suez War—fighting their final and losing battle in a land that was never their own.

"The Sugar and Distillery Company at Nag Hammadi was like a mini-United Nations, since most of the staff who worked for me were French, Belgian, Italian, Greek, and British subjects. All of those young people, though, had been born in Egypt and knew little about their countries of origin; and I had no doubt about the sincerity of their true feelings toward their adopted country. What really took me by complete surprise was the violent and unrestrained reaction of an Englishwoman living in a small village thirty miles north of Nag Hammadi, whom I met during the third week of December 1956. This woman, I was later to find out, had led all the village inhabitants in several protest marches against the invasion; and her anger, especially against her own countrymen, was ill concealed. Since she was a newcomer to the village, however, her sincerity was in doubt; and a lot of skeptical-minded villagers told her openly to stop 'showing off,' which she did not. Few realized then that they were dealing with a true-blue Saidy Egyptian woman who felt anguish and wrath for her 'true' country . . . Egypt. For in fact, as I later found out, this woman had had the experience of living for more than twenty years in Egypt, had been married to an Egyptian teacher, and was officially an employee of the Egyptian Antiquities Department.

"When finally the armies of the three countries involved in the Suez War were preparing for a very reluctant withdrawal—and after several weeks of tense, nerve-racking anxiety at work—I felt I had the right to take half a day off from the factory. I went with some friends from Cairo to Abydos to show them around the beautiful Temple of Sety. There I saw an excited, barefooted English lady who was talking Arabic with a strong 'Irish' accent, and saying what she thought of the whole of the Suez affair with unrestrained, Egyptian-style anger. Under such circumstances, all this sounded very strange to my ears. It was partly cloudy that day, and rather dim inside the temple; and the angry muttering seemed to come from far away—the echo giving the woman's voice an uncanny ring, as if it were from another world.

"The inspector, who was kindly volunteering to explain to us the different scenes on the walls, suddenly stopped and mumbled a few words of apology. With a broad grin he went to salute the angry English lady. A few minutes later they both came to meet us. 'This is my colleague, Mrs. Omm Sety,' the inspector said. The lady extended a small, dainty hand. We shook hands, and I remember that I immediately liked her open and frank expression. She was a robust woman in her early fifties with a couple of twinkling blue eyes, a very disarming smile, and very particular golden hair, almost the color of freshly threshed wheat straw, cut in a decidedly ancient-Egyptian style.

"News travels fast in this part of the country, but I was a little surprised when she asked me straightaway about news from the Suez front, where I had recently been. I said that it was generally agreed that the invading armies, in spite of elaborate preparations for withdrawal, were having a hell of a time with the local resistance. They were now restricted to very limited areas in Port Said, and even there they were constantly harassed by the Egyptian population, armed and unarmed. While I was explaining to her in detail the contents of the different news bulletins from Cairo, the BBC, the Voice of America, and so on, she constantly interrupted me with violent remarks about the aggressors. Anthony Eden, in particular, was the primary target of her emotional outburst. She used a very selective Egyptian vocabulary of the choicest insults, half of which would have been enough to make Anthony Eden 'drop dead.' (I remember that she spoke of the invaders as *'Ibu El Kelb'*—'sons of dogs.') I also could not restrain myself from asking her why she was walking about barefooted inside the temple. Her answer was prompt and firm: 'This is a holy shrine built for our lord Osiris. If I were given the authority to do so, I would not allow anybody to visit this holy place with his shoes on, but I am just a poor insignificant employee of the Antiquities Department.'

"My first impression of Omm Sety, then, was that she was 'quite a character.' I was also impressed by her frankness, her very evident sincerity, and her honesty. It took us, however, three years to become real friends, since, in the aftermath of the Suez tragedy, most of my time was taken up with labor problems, mechanical complications, and electrical failures at the sugar factories. I must admit, in all frankness, that it took me several years to understand that we both belonged to two different eras of history. She, to all intents and purposes, was a woman of the Ramesside period and only partly interested in the present; while I belonged entirely to the present, with its problems of pollution, war, rumors of war, population explosion, et cetera."

An inveterate amateur Egyptologist and desert traveler who has systematically collected neolithic rock drawings and inscriptions from the Eastern and Western Deserts of Egypt, Hanny El Zeini— when I first met him in January of 1985—had retired from the Sugar and Distillery Company, for which he had invented the patented Egyptian cane diffusion process. Although he was now a consultant for the United Nations Industrial Development Organization, he was spending much of his time with the principal Bedouin tribes in the Sinai as part of his research on a book he was beginning to write on the Exodus. ("I'm trying to find out the true names of the sites mentioned in the Bible," he told me, "as well as attempting to discover what route the Israelites took, and how and on what they were sustained for forty years.")

One often forgets that the biblical characters of Job and his friends are, in fact, Bedouins themselves . . . and the Book of Job—in the words of one critic—"the product of an international literary elite, the reflection of the highly developed sensibility and intellectual life of empires that stretched from the Crimea to the Indus and the cataracts of the Nile." It is this wide-ranging sensibility and intellectual curiosity that Hanny El Zeini certainly embodies. It was with him that Omm Sety spent twelve years collaborating on several books, the first of which to be published was *Abydos: Holy City of Ancient Egypt,* for which Hanny El Zeini took hundreds of photographs—all with mirror-reflected natural light, "in order," he has stated, "to let the readers see the sculpture and images of the temple in the way they were originally created and observed, with all their soft shadows."[1] It was to Hanny El Zeini alone that Omm Sety confided her most secret thoughts and to whom she told the entire story of her life. No one knew her better than he did; and it is important to find out and say something about her remarkable collaborator and "best friend."

Upon entering Dr. El Zeini's apartment in the Maadi suburb of Cairo, one is immediately confronted by an extraordinary array of treasures: coral, shells, and mounted fish from the Red Sea; two six-foot-tall Buddhist praying horns, made of beaten copper, from Nepal; a forty-four-paneled folkloric mural from Ethiopia; seven glass dwarf statuettes from Czechoslovakia; ivory figurines of elephants, giraffes, and gazelles from various parts of Africa; a jade owl from Chile; stone eggs from the Far East; rock formations from the Sinai; neolithic flint implements from the Egyptian deserts. As displayed on walls and cabinets in the El Zeini residence, these objects from

---

[1] About this almost 300-page book, published in 1981 in Los Angeles by L L Company, the late Professor John A. Wilson, the acknowledged dean of American Egyptologists, wrote: "It is remarkable how Omm Sety gives a comprehensive coverage of every ancient element in Abydos, while maintaining lively interest. . . . She is a responsible scholar . . . and her text should be treated with respect."

four continents comprise a veritable Museum of the World—a reflection not only of their owner's wide-ranging travels but also of a profoundly cosmopolitan view of life.

Born in Cairo in 1918, Hanny El Zeini—a vigorous, broad-faced man with a disarming smile and laugh—was brought up in a "very religious but extremely tolerant" Muslim household. "When I was young," he has stated, "Cairo was an international town. My family lived for a while in a part of Heliopolis where many British, Italian, Greek, Belgian, and French people had their homes; then later in a quarter called Daher where our neighbors included many Jewish families—there was a synagogue, in fact, in front of our house.

"At that time, Egypt consisted of one million Jews, two and a half million Copts, and twenty-five million Muslims; the prevailing atmosphere was one of brotherhood and tolerance. On Coptic, Jewish, and Muslim feast days, we would go over to our friends' houses and say, '*Kol sana wa anta tayab* [We hope you will be happy every year]!' I remember that one of the most famous actors during that period was Naguib El Rihany; and one of his most popular roles was in a play that took place in a pharmacy owned by a Muslim named Hassan, a Jew named Cohen, and a Copt named Marcos. Each one accused the other of being stingy, but in the long run they all found a way—with good-natured self-mockery—to arrange things with mutual concessions. When I was growing up, I was very curious and had an ardent desire to learn (as we say in Egypt, '*Ya'esh El Moualem Wa' Yat'alem* [The learned live to learn]'), so I would ask everybody I met about his or her country. From my earliest years I began to travel as soon as I was allowed to.

"When I was twelve years old I and four of my schoolmates took a twelve-mile hike, without guides, into the Eastern Desert. My young companions, incidentally, included Anwar Sadat and Mohammed Hafiz, who would later become President Sadat's National Security Adviser. Our supplies consisted of sandwiches and water. It was a one-day trip, and we were all so exhilarated by the experience that, during the next four years, we continued our treks into the desert. I remember that when I was sixteen, we were on the road to Suez, and we met our first real Bedouin—and this really excited our imaginations! He showed us what is known as Bir Yusef (Joseph's Well), into which Joseph was supposed to have been thrown by his brothers. All we could see was the outline of a well, quite sandy. And I have to say that it was a bit disappointing, because the story of Joseph was my very favorite tale ever since I was a child.

"My grandmother (my mother's mother) read and wrote very little, but she had a natural genius for telling beautiful stories. Since I was the oldest grandson, I was allowed to sleep over at her house from the time I was four years old. I always insisted that she tell me, just *one* more time, about Joseph. I loved to hear about how he was thrown into the well and then saved. I remember my grandmother becoming very emotional when she described how Jacob felt upon learning that his son was dead. The way she told the story, you could just picture Joseph as a very handsome young man, with the women at the Pharaoh's palace so stunned by his beauty that they distractedly cut their own hands instead of the potatoes and vegetables! It also pleased me to hear about how loyal Joseph was to his brothers and how, in the end, he forgave them.

"My grandmother, I should tell you, had had eight children, and she was like a wild animal tamer at the circus. With one look, she could calm a number of little boys down without ever shouting—just a *look* would suffice . . . and yet she was so kindhearted. She was very tall, very thin, very elegant, and had beautiful long hair. In fact, she was a hundred percent Egyptian woman from Upper Egypt who looked exactly like one of the sculpted dancers I once saw on a wall of a tomb on the West Bank. . . . My other grandmother (my father's mother), I should say, was also very beautiful and a wonderful storyteller, though she died when I was very young. She, however, was a Sherifa—a direct descendent of the family of the Prophet or of his first followers. I've always thought that perhaps the reason why I feel so much at home in the desert is because some of my ancestors were Bedouins.

"Both of my grandmothers, and their stories, influenced me greatly . . . as did a particular history teacher I had in grade school; and he, too, was like a storyteller in the wonderful way he recounted to us, with much love and pride, the history of ancient Egypt.

"Of course, in my early teens I used to go over to Giza on weekends; and one summer afternoon I climbed the Great Pyramid: I started up at 4 P.M. and descended several hours later as the sun was going down. (In those days, everything from the foot of the Great Pyramid to the Nile was lush green; whereas today, I just feel sick when I see those ugly buildings and cabarets in its stead!)

"I also distinctly remember, in the early 1930s, going to Giza and sitting, very timidly and as close as I possibly could, to the late Dr. Selim Hassan, who was then conducting his excavations. (At that time, I now realize, Omm Sety was working as a draftsman at the site, but I don't recall ever seeing her.) Dr. Hassan's authoritative manner commanded the respect of all his subordinates. One day, as I was watching his well-trained workmen clearing the area in front of the Sphinx, he passed by the spot where I was sitting. Instinctively, and out of respect, I stood up. He stopped, fixed me with a very penetrating look, then beckoned to me. Shyly and hesitatingly, I walked toward him; and he laid a kind hand on my shoulder and said in a very quiet voice: 'I see you come here very often. Are you interested in my work, my son? Do you know what I am doing?' 'I read all about it in the daily papers, Your Excellency,' I replied, almost stammering. 'Do you indeed? Well, that's very nice. If you have any questions, do not hesitate, come up and ask me.' Needless to say, I was beside myself with pride and enthusiasm. As a teenager, one wants and hopes to become very different things at different times. At first, I remember, I wanted to be an airline pilot, then the maestro of a symphony orchestra. At that particular moment, though, I desired nothing other than to be an archaeologist like Professor Selim Hassan!

"During my teenage years, I, like most of my friends, had two main pastimes: sports (I played football and ran the 1,500- and 5,000-meter events) and reading. Books were very cheap in those days; and when we had a holiday my friends and I would go to the Azbakia Gardens where there were open-air stalls of secondhand books, in all languages, that sold for a few piasters. We'd spend part of the morning there, buy a number of books, and then later exchange them with each other.

"That period was, in fact, a golden age of Egyptian philosophy and literature, with volumes coming out by writers such as Taha Hussein, Abbas El Akkad, Mahmoud Taimour, Zaky Mubarek, and many others. It was truly a generation of intellectuals, the likes of which we probably won't see again. I read books by many of these authors, at the same time that I was discovering the works of Shakespeare, Lord Byron, H. Rider Haggard, St. Exupéry, and Rabindranath Tagore—all of which I loved. The book that impressed me the most, though, was *All Quiet on the Western Front.* I read it before World War II began, and it made me hate war . . . even the *word* 'war.' . . . You know, some people in Egypt were sympathetic to Hitler because he was 'sticking it' to the British. I hated his guts. His madman's talk of a superior race disgusted me. I mean, coming from a people who, like the rest of the Europeans, were barbarian food-gatherers not so many hundreds of years before—and certainly in the light of Egyptian civilization and cultural accomplishments—it was just completely absurd! In the late 1930s, when Jewish refugees started to come here from Germany, Austria, and Czechoslovakia, I saw first hand the bad shape they were in, and I knew something wrong was going on in Germany.

"I also remember being deeply affected by the murder of the Libyan religious and nationalist leader Omar El Mukhtar, who was killed in cold blood by the Italians; and by the assassination of Gandhi, whom I considered a saint. I also had a friend who was shot by a British soldier, and for a while I was very political and wound up in prison on several occasions. I soon discovered, however, I had no aptitude or taste for politics. I've never, however, let myself become permanently embittered by the horrible events I've witnessed during my lifetime. It's very easy to be indifferent, detached, and uncommitted; but evil can't be fought by being cynical.

"Although I loved literature, the humanities, history, and archaeology, I studied science at Cairo University. After receiving degrees in industrial chemistry and mechanical engineering in the late forties, I began working my way up in the Sugar and Distillery Company, which was then owned by a French/English/Belgian consortium. (I was in favor of Egyptianizing the company and thought Egyptians should 'infiltrate' as chemists, agronomists, and accountants.) I began as an analytical chemist and at the age of thirty became production manager and then, when I was thirty-eight, the president.

"Having at that point to deal with a labor force of almost five thousand workers—and twice this number of cane growers besides— and having later to travel to the seven sugar mills located all over Upper Egypt, as well as to the refinery and distillery that were just seven miles from Giza and Sakkara, I was fortunately, and happily, able to spend a good part of my weekends visiting the pyramids, temples, and tombs of ancient Egypt and witnessing the painstaking work of such giants of Egyptology as Selim Hassan, Ahmed Fakhry, Labib Habachi, Zakaria Ghoneim, Sami Gabra, François Daumas, Jaroslav Černý, and W. B. Emery.

"I think it is also clear that I felt 'destined' to meet Omm Sety—it was 'written' *(Maktub),* as we say in Arabic. Perhaps I should use the word *kesma,* which means 'providentially predetermined/inescapable/the will of God.' A lot of people, of course, wondered about my friendship with Omm Sety, since it was apparent that we belonged to two different worlds—she being 'mystical' and 'spiritual,' while I, by the nature of my profession, was concerned with 'hard facts.' Maybe we attracted each other as opposites, but maybe we had a lot in common and didn't realize that until we really became friends. Both of us respected sentient life—a little bit like Buddhists.

I should say that I really never believed in reincarnation or astral bodies before meeting Omm Sety, perhaps because I never personally witnessed any supernatural or spiritual phenomena. After a long visit to Nepal and India in 1978, however, where I met with Buddhist and Brahman mystics and discussed with them the subjects of *karma* and reincarnation, I grew to realize how very little we know about the realm of the spirit. Experiences very much like those described by Omm Sety were related to me by Buddhist monks and sages high in their Himalayan sanctuaries.

"Being Egyptian to the marrow of my bones, I have always been quite conscious of our own great spiritual heritage. Occult science and metaphysical knowledge seem to have found a natural soil in the fertile land of Egypt since time immemorial. The subject of reincarnation was one of the dogmas of Egyptian religion and philosophy that stirred the imagination and curiosity of the ancient Greeks, many of whose most learned intellectuals—like Thales, Pythagoras, and Plato—once studied here in Egypt. In the absence of a deep-rooted belief in reincarnation, it would have been pointless if, throughout their history, Egyptians should have taken such pains-taking care in the mummification of the bodies of their dead. Even in predynastic times, the earliest inhabitants of the Nile Valley con-served their dead in pottery box coffins, where they were placed in crouching positions—representing the return to the mother's womb —with their heads facing west. Were they, even then, so certain of a rebirth? Of resurrection? Of reincarnation? In what form? There is little room for doubt that they did believe, at the very least, in a second life.

"When Omm Sety first confided to me the story of her reincarnation, she had little suspicion that this was one of my favorite subjects. She *was* an amazing companion to me and occasionally I had to pull the reins in on her because of her volatile Irish temper, for I didn't want her to get into trouble. She was also vulnerable—she was like a child sometimes, and she needed looking after. She was a great, sin-cere, and beloved friend to both my wife and me, but I have to confess that it took me several years to believe her story in its most unusual details. When I became convinced of her honesty and integ-rity, however, I found it difficult not to believe. For it is the story of an extraordinary love—so pathetic and yet so strong as to defy time and place, and so true and unselfish that it transcends many of our most banal and sterile convictions. For those who believe in the exis-tence of an entity inside us that we vaguely call a 'soul,' and for those who believe that love is the light deep within our being that brightens our whole existence and that nobody can extinguish . . . for those people no explanation is necessary. For those who do not believe, no explanation is possible."

* * *

For a quarter of a century Dr. Hanny El Zeini listened to Omm Sety's life story and spent fascinating hours and days in her company. The following section consists of some of his reflections on and conversations with his longtime friend.

* * *

"When I was three years old," Omm Sety told me, "my parents and I lived in a flat in London, and there was a staircase of many steps leading from our flat right down to the bottom. And one day I just fell down these steps . . . rolled down . . . bouncing like a ball."

It was a cool, pleasant evening in July; and after a day of overwhelming heat, Omm Sety and I were sitting in the Osirion. For the first time I had brought with me one of those early Philips cassette recorders, which, compared with today's models, was very large and clumsy. After a tour of the Sety Temple, I thought we would just sit and relax, and listen to the refreshing music of Handel, Mozart, Tchaikovsky, and Delibes.

After a while Omm Sety, having given me permission to record our conversation, began narrating the story of her childhood. It was on one of those evenings that she told me how she had seen the Temple of Sety in a photograph in a magazine that her father had brought home, and how she had excitedly informed him that she *remembered* this temple but wondered where the gardens were. (Her father, of course, had asked her to stop telling lies.)

"But from that moment thereafter," she said, "I always kept on and on asking about this garden . . . even after I came here. Sure enough, when they were making the foundations of the workshop for the restoration of the Sety Temple, they found the garden just where I said it was, with the remnants of the tree roots and the well that watered it and the channels."

Up till then, I had been listening very attentively but also, to tell the truth, with mild astonishment and very well-concealed skepticism. I remained, however, politely silent and made no comments. Eventually I could not refrain from asking her: "Where was that garden supposed to be?" "To the south of the temple," Omm Sety answered without hesitation. "Was anybody from the village present during the discovery of the remnants of the tree roots?" I questioned her. "We recruit most of the labor for our excavations from the village here," she replied. "But the real expert foremen are Kuftis." Kuftis come from a town called Kuft, which is better known to Egyptologists as Koptos. These are skilled, deft diggers who make excellent, reliable foremen for excavation. Koptos still retains the monopoly on such foremen. "The man who unearthed the roots of several trees is here in the village," Omm Sety continued; "we call him 'Abou Eid Mubarka,' meaning 'He with the Blessed or Lucky Hand.'" . . . I remember saying to myself: "It won't do anybody any harm if I personally check with this man about the authenticity of this discovery."

For a few weeks I found myself practically drowned in problems connected with my scientific work, for I had reasons to worry about the upcoming harvest of our sugar cane. I almost forgot about Omm Sety's extinct garden until one day some friends from France came to visit me in Nag Hammadi and expressed their desire to see the Temple of Sety. Suddenly I remembered the story about the garden and thought I had better check the matter out. Omm Sety took my guests around the temple; and with her extremely amusing French, combined with a dash of her irresistible Irish charm and sense of humor, she simply delighted my guests. While they were on the tour I sent for the foreman—a tall, thin, wiry, middle-aged man who had been responsible for clearing the site of the trees—and I asked him about the remnants of Sety's garden. He asked to be excused for a few minutes, and after a short while he returned with a hoe in his hand. "I'll *show* you the remnants of the trees Omm Sety told us about," he said to me with that directness especially characteristic of the Upper Egyptian peasant.

Together, we went outside the courtyard of the temple to the southern wall. This mud-brick wall, which must originally have been of enormous proportions, had probably been constantly quarried: the bricks, which were of excellent quality, were always in demand for the construction of the village houses; they had kept their classical dimensions and had not changed for more than three millennia—some bricks, in fact, still bore the stamp of King Sety the First. I looked carefully at the ground and observed what seemed to be the traces of irrigation channels. The man counted several paces and then started to dig, clearing the sand under his feet. In less than five minutes something black and stunted began to appear. There was no room for doubt—this was definitely the stump of a very old tree deeply rooted in the soil. "There is a whole row of these roots running for at least fifty meters from here. Would you like to see a second one?" the man asked me. Without waiting for an answer, he counted out about ten paces before starting to dig in another place. And a big tortuous stump, with enormous roots all around, fully appeared in front of my eyes like a charred piece of a Henry Moore sculpture. "She is a great woman, Omm Sety!" the man exclaimed. "Yes, sir, she is a very respectable scientist."

A few months later I met the inspector of the Antiquities Department who had been charged with the restoration of the temple, and I asked him if he had known Omm Sety before she came to Abydos. His reply was both surprising and, to my great relief, very gratifying, too. "She was directly responsible for the discovery of those tree roots," he informed me, "and she was also instrumental in the discovery of the tunnel running underneath the northernmost part of the temple. You know," he added, "she worked with Professors Selim Hassan and Ahmed Fakhry in Giza, and both of them spoke very highly of her. She's not just a good 'draftsman,' but she seems to have an uncanny sixth sense about the terrain on which she walks, and she really stunned me with her very deep knowledge of the temple and its surroundings. A friend of hers in Cairo told me that during her sleep she has visions of the past that often prove to be quite accurate. She is, however, rather strange sometimes."

The inspector was silent for a minute, and he looked searchingly at me, as if trying to observe the effect of his words. "I feel very grateful to you, Inspector," I told him. "The problem is, I know so little about her, and I just wanted to be sure that there really was a garden to the south of Sety's temple." "I assure you," he replied, "that if I were ever asked to do any research work or excavations in Abydos I would not even start digging before discussing the whole procedure with Omm Sety. Somehow I feel she knows more about this place than anybody else in the entire Antiquities Department. I would almost venture to say that she would be indispensable for any archaeological mission attempting any serious work in the Abydos area." It was at that point that I felt I owed Omm Sety an apology; and from then on I felt confident about her credibility, integrity, and professional honesty. In the years to come, nothing occurred to shake my trust in her in that regard.

A few months passed, and then one day her confessions continued. She told me about her recurring dream as a teenager in which she saw herself sleeping in a very big room on rush mats, then being in an underground chamber surrounded by a channel of water, and finally being tormented by questions from a high priest.

"Did this high priest resemble anybody you know?" I asked Omm Sety. "Well," she replied, "as a matter of fact, much later in life, I *was* to meet his physical replica in the person of Professor Selim Hassan. Professor Hassan, although he was a severe teacher, wasn't a nasty, vicious old chap like the man I dreamed about. In fact, Professor Selim Hassan was a man whom I very much respected and admired. It was really much later in my life that I knew *exactly* who that man really was. It was after a long visit to the *Au-Delà* [the Beyond] that I recognized the high priest when I met him face to face. I later saw a photograph of the Osirion, and from my dream I remembered it, with that channel of water going round. Only it seemed to be that the room in which I was—in my dream—was in the center of this masonry island. I mean, it could have just been a 'fantazia'—I don't know, I can't prove it because I can't get into the island. The outside channel was exactly as I saw it in the dream, except that it was very dark because it was roofed."

"So at this very early age you already had quite a clear vision of the Osirion," I remarked, adding: "It's evident that it was originally very heavily roofed; and judging by the size of the columns of the Great Hall and of the remnants of the slabs covering the roof, it seems to have been totally covered and sheltered from the sun. It must have been quite an impressive monument by any standards. What really bewilders me is that you had an early and full vision of the intact Osirion and of the Sety Temple without having seen a picture of the Osirion alone or even combined with the Sety Temple!" "Yes," she told me, "that dream came to me very often . . . especially after the first visit of Sety as a mummy when I was fourteen."

Then, to my utter astonishment, she fell into one of those long spells of absent-mindedness that later on I was to become very familiar with. Was she trying to remember something long forgotten, or was she, on the contrary, trying to shake off some unpleasant memory belonging to a very faraway time? I couldn't tell. But during those spells of absent-mindedness I *also* fell into a reverie of one kind or another about this fantastic spot called "El Araba El Madfouna" —the Buried Hamlet . . . Abydos. What a strange irony of fate! The old town that was once the sacred pilgrimage place of many a nation, the old Mecca of the Egyptians and the old Jerusalem of perhaps the whole world of the Middle East, was to have the very modest, perhaps humiliating, name of "Buried Hamlet"! And here we were, sitting in the Osirion, the place that Omm Sety had dreamed about when she was fourteen years old!

Those evenings in the Osirion were always very hard to forget. After an exhausting day's work at the Sugar Company, or after a busy afternoon photographing inside the temple, I just loved to sit on the edge of the Osirion with Omm Sety, watching the sun disappearing behind the western escarpment, enjoying a well-deserved cup of tea, chatting together . . . and sometimes tape-recording important conversations. Although there usually was not a soul around, except for an occasional watchman heading quietly back home, I often heard some strange kind of long booming sound on some of the tapes when I played them back. Sometimes, for no apparent reason, the recording was quite inaudible, like a whisper. I always attributed this to technical faults in the recorder, but Omm Sety said that these were interventions from the *"Au-Delà* (Beyond)"—a sign of disagreement with or disapproval of our conversation.

* * *

Occasionally Omm Sety and I would take short trips to Luxor, Dendera, Aswan, and several other archaeological sites. She was always full of enthusiasm, extremely energetic, tireless, and an inexhaustible source of information to me. I noticed she was particularly elated by our visits to Luxor. There were two very good reasons for this: first, we were visiting mainly New Kingdom temples and monuments built by her "very own people," as she used to tell me enthusiastically. We also used to spend time with the people of Chicago House, one of the oldest institutes devoted to the study of Egyptology. Omm Sety was among real friends and felt happy here, relaxed and full of good humor.

During one of our visits to Medinet Habu—where the mortuary temple of Ramesses the Third is located—I asked her about Ramesses the Third and about the conspiracy that culminated in one of the most famous trials in Egyptian history. Omm Sety told me that, in 1945, she had written a long article about the trial and the judgment of those involved in the case. A few days later she sent me a copy of this clear, vivid, well-balanced, and beautifully written article. A couple of weeks after that I had a chance to ask her about it when I visited Abydos for the day.

"Well, Omm Sety," I said, "I really must congratulate you on that wonderful article about the trial. If that treacherous conspiracy had succeeded it would have been the very untimely end of one of Egypt's most distinguished pharaohs—perhaps the last of the great pharaohs."

"It was all very thoroughly planned," she replied, "and it might have succeeded, but for the loyalty of the King's men, who discovered the conspiracy just in time to foil it at the eleventh hour. As you read in my article, the whole plot was planned by Queen Tuy, who furtively recruited her collaborators, Pebekamen and Mesedsure—the latter being her butler. Pebekamen was the real 'thinking head,' you see, because he was a magician."

"Was it necessary to have magic in a plot like this?" I asked. "I thought that the Queen, with her strong influence, her knowledge of the palace routine and of all the habits of the King, wasn't really in need of a magician."

"No," Omm Sety told me, "she couldn't have dispensed with magic in a plot like this. The King was already advanced in age and, like all the Ramessides, he had a lot of children. Queen Tuy wanted at any price to secure the throne for her own son, Pentawer, because Ramesses the Third had promised the crown to another prince by another of his wives. So the role of the magic in the conspiracy was crucial. The palace was already full of foreigners who could be easily bought for the promise of wealth or a good position; they never really gave a damn who sat on the throne. A plot of such proportions could only be masterminded by an Egyptian court official."

"Preferably versed in the occult science, I suppose?"

"Oh, definitely! You know, since predynastic times, magic was a science; and throughout all periods of Egyptian history it was a venerated science that was to be taught only to the 'elite,' the governing class that formed the privileged aristocracy of Egypt, so to speak, and not to the ordinary scribes of the administration or to the lesser employees of the state."

"You didn't write much in your article about the role of magic in the conspiracy . . . although the details of the trial were very painstakingly mentioned," I commented. "Did you neglect or rather ignore the role of magic in the plot intentionally?"

"I didn't want to bother the reader with so many details because I had already taken pains in telling the full story of the conspiracy itself and those involved in it. It was also evident that, as for being a magician, Pebekamen was a real *abeet* [which means an "idiot" and a "failure" in Arabic]—his magic never really worked. He wanted to bribe two of the judges in charge of the trial; but before the plot was discovered he had also secured the cooperation of some women in the harem, an overseer of the treasury, and, most important of all, a general in the army named Peyes. It was quite a multitude of conspirators. What concerned Pebekamen, above everything else, was how he could fool the harem guard. He was perhaps already aware of the danger of involving so many persons in the conspiracy; and the possibility that some information would leak out and reach the ears of the King was not to be discounted. So, like any astute conspirator, he procured for himself an outfit of magical waxen figures of gods and men, by means of which he imagined he would have the power to disable the harem guard or at least distract their attention—otherwise it was always possible that a guard might have intercepted one of his messengers entering into the quarters of the harem. The waxen figures never worked, information must have leaked to some important officials of the King's suite, and the attempt on his life was foiled."

"But tell me, Omm Sety, do you really believe that if this Pebekamen had been successful with his waxen figurines the plot would have succeeded? I know from your article that the King, who was quite old at the time, was badly shaken by the whole affair. Couldn't he have just ordered the execution of the conspirators, thus bringing the whole conspiracy to a quick end without submitting the whole business to such lengthy procedures? I don't think anybody would have blamed him. By the standards of the time, there would have been nothing unusual about that, and I suppose that as Pharaoh of Egypt he was fully entitled to do so. What do you think?"

"Concerning the failure of the waxen figurines to perform their job," Omm Sety replied, "I would rather think that there were a few mistakes made in the procedures used or in the way the magic texts were employed, thus rendering the whole process absolutely futile and fruitless. . . . Probably there was a lack of precision in the copying of the appropriate verses, or bad timing in the way they were written or recited—all this is very important for the success of the magic formulas.

"As for the second part of your question, let me tell you this: Don't you ever believe a word about a pharaoh's 'inalienable right' to administer justice all by himself! That was never the case. A lot of religious people like to present to us the distorted image of pharaohs as harsh despots who would bend justice according to their caprices and who would indulge in extremes of useless cruelty in judging offenders. I don't know exactly when the goddess Maat came to prominence in ancient Egyptian theology, but she represents an order of things in which truth and justice hold a sacred place—and *maat* represented both. Ramesses the Third, like all the other pharaohs, could never have ignored *maat*—justice and truth—in such a case involving conspiracy against his own person. It's rather fortunate that the full documentation of that memorable trial survived on papyri so that posterity can judge for itself what giants those wonderful pharaohs were . . . not in physical stature but in magnanimity and high moral values."

"When I think of the times when *maat* was absent in Egypt," I said to Omm Sety, "I wonder how our people managed to survive those periods of despotism, oppression, and injustice."

"*Maat* is inborn in the conscience of every Egyptian," she stated. "It's a sort of 'collective conscience.' If you analyze those occasional outbreaks of revolt and violence in Egypt throughout its long history, you always find that such outbursts of anger were always directly connected with social and moral injustice. During periods of oppression you could always find, even among the meekest folk, a giant who would speak out about justice in defiance of the most despotic of rulers. Look at our own Saad Zaghlul Pasha and his outright challenge to Lord Cromer! There were others like him. Maybe you also remember the story of the 'eloquent peasant' of Fayyum Province who, refusing to compromise, insisted on having his rights, which had been abrogated by the governor of the province, fully restored to him; and to this end he addressed himself directly to one of the pharaohs of the Middle Kingdom—all of whom, as you know, were considered to be 'tough guys.' I'm sure Egyptian history must have been full of incidents like this but, unfortunately, papyrus is such a perishable material that probably thousands of such documents must have been destroyed by time."

* * *

After an extended business trip abroad to the United States and Latin America, I returned to Nag Hammadi after eight months; and upon my arrival in Abydos, I found that Omm Sety was in very bad health. She had lost a lot of weight and had aged terribly. I asked her what was the matter, and she said she was suffering from diabetes. Without waiting for her to make any objection, I almost dragged her into my car and took her to the Balyana hospital, where she was thoroughly examined and was told that there was no indication of any signs of diabetes. The specialist who had made the first diagnosis of diabetes was now summoned to the office of the hospital's director. Yes, he remembered that when he had first seen Omm Sety he had very strong doubts about the sample of urine she handed to him; the color looked "funny," and he had asked her to bring another sample of urine, which she never did. (I knew beforehand that she detested seeing physicians; and going to a hospital was, for her, certainly a most unwelcome business.)

On my insistence, the analysis was repeated—and now, no trace of diabetes. Casually, I asked Omm Sety what kind of a container she had used for her previous sample of urine. "An old bottle of Coca-Cola," she told me. "Are you sure it was clean?" "No, I never washed it," she replied. "Are you quite certain it was empty?" I demanded. "Hmmm . . . well, you know four months is a long time. But I can't say for certain if I washed the bottle or not." And the head physician was now quite sure about his new diagnosis: Omm Sety was not a diabetic; and judging by what the first doctor had suspected from the start, the earlier urine sample was colored by the remnants of Coca-Cola. So that was it. I was really very angry.

"Why in God's name didn't you give the analyst another sample of urine when he asked you to?" I asked her furiously.

"I didn't feel like it," she petulantly replied, adding, "Well, *dash* it all, I had none to give him!"

"You could have gone the next day just to make sure," I said to her. "But what on earth did you do to get so thin and lose so much weight?"

"I stopped eating all carbohydrates."

"Meaning what, exactly?"

"No bread, no rice, no biscuits. Plain tea without sugar, just boiled vegetables and meat . . . and no fruits, either."

"Did anybody advise you to do this madness or was it your own idea?" I asked. "Didn't you realize you'd already lost too much weight?"

"No," she said, "and I felt just fine. His Majesty was a very frequent visitor, and he never made any remarks about my getting thin. In fact, he doesn't seem to realize that I'm getting old. He believes I'm still a girl of fourteen."

"And you like that, of course!"

"Indeed I do . . . yes, sir, I most certainly do. . . . But just the same, it seems very funny that His Majesty is so oblivious to the passage of time. Sometimes he stays away for seven or ten days without coming to me, but when I ask him why he hasn't visited for so long, he simply says, 'Oh, but, Little One, I was here only last night, you're becoming very weak of memory, don't you remember that it was just last night when I told you to clean the statue of our lady Isis because it was getting too dusty?' But that was really ten days before, and not 'last night,' as he had said."

"Now that you're back at home," I told her, "you have to regain at least ten of the twenty-five kilos that you've already lost. And then in a week's time we'll go once more to the hospital for a second check on the analysis to see how you are doing, okay?"

"Okay," she grudgingly replied.

                              *   *   *

Having spent nearly a lifetime in Upper Egypt and having lived close to most of the important sites of the major Egyptian temples and monuments, it was almost inevitable that I would meet up with "reincarnations." On and off I came across resuscitations of an Old Kingdom king or a Middle Kingdom pharaoh, occasionally a prominent queen, or, in the most modest case, a New Kingdom vizier. I cannot honestly remember the number of Ramesses, Nefertitis, Cleopatras, Hatshepsuts, et al., I have encountered; and most of the stories they told me were unimaginative, colorless, and stupid. There were only two cases that were really worth listening to, and both of these persons testified that they were reincarnations of people of a humbler origin. Omm Sety, needless to say, was one of these; the other was a quite beautiful American woman.

I met her in the following way: Omm Sety and I were passing the evening on board the *Isis,* a floating hotel that was sailing from Nag Hammadi to Luxor and Aswan, and then back again. When the boat was docked at Nag Hammadi, we were having our dinner and chatting lightheartedly, when suddenly we heard a female voice from behind us saying, "Do you mind if I join you?" Unhesitatingly, Omm Sety said, "Not at all, please have a seat."

This unexpected encounter was destined to be one of the most bewildering and, in a way, delightful incidents I experienced with, and thanks to, Omm Sety. Immediately, the two women started conversing like old friends. I was astonished. Omm Sety, who was usually reserved with people whom she did not know well, was talking with this American woman with a warm, affectionate, even loving familiarity. Each one was telling the other about herself, what she was doing, what their children's business was, et cetera. It was then that this woman mentioned that she was a grandmother. Seeing how incredulous I looked—she seemed to be in her thirties—she went to her cabin, came back with her passport, and when she showed it to me I was quite surprised to discover that in fact she *was* only thirty-seven. While she was away searching for her passport, Omm Sety remarked, "Don't you think she is very beautiful? She looks so Egyptian! I just love her. She looks so familiar to me, I don't know why. I feel I have seen or known her before . . . I don't think she's a total stranger to me."

As we ate our delightful dinner, our guest talked about her life in North Carolina, her married daughter, her two younger sons, and how she and her husband had been separated for the past two years. At last came the most fascinating part of the conversation. She said that some strange power was attracting her to Omm Sety; as soon as she saw her, she felt she had to talk to her about her life. She asked me politely if I would mind if she asked Omm Sety about her private life. I said not at all.

Apparently she had been "told" in a dream that she had had a previous life as a lady-in-waiting at Akhen-Aton's palace in Akhetaton. She described with great precision what life had been like during the reign of the "Heretic Pharaoh." But what really took me by complete surprise was the stunning detail with which she described the palace and the town. She had never been to Egypt before, and her tour group was not planning on visiting Amarna to see the remnants of Akhetaton. Perhaps, I thought, she had read enough books about the "Heresy Period" to enable her to be so well informed!

Omm Sety seemed to be listening to this very beautiful woman with something more than ears. There was a strange, intense look in her eyes. And I noticed, to my great surprise, that this young woman was pronouncing some of the ancient Egyptian names in a very peculiar and particular way—totally different from the pronunciation I was accustomed to from textbooks or from discussions with Egyptologists.

"I am planning to leave the ship tomorrow and take a taxi and go to Amarna to see as much as I can of the remnants of Akhetaton," she told us. "Do you know if there is any hotel close by where I could stay? I would just love to spend a few days there," she said, addressing me.

"In the village itself there's nothing," I informed her. "But in Minieh, twenty miles north, you can find two or three sufficiently comfortable hotels . . . nothing luxurious, but a clean bedroom, and the food really is quite good." "That's it, then," she said. "That's exactly what I will need. Nothing more."

Omm Sety was keeping silent, and the other woman was doing all the talking. I had known for a long time that the subject of Akhen-Aton was not exactly a favorite one with Omm Sety. As a matter of fact, whenever I felt like teasing her, I would somehow bring up the subject of Akhen-Aton and then would invariably follow one of our amusing quarrels. This time, however, there was a total lack of anger, an absolute absence of that strange sense of discomfort that

Omm Sety would feel whenever the name of Akhen-Aton was mentioned. Suddenly, silence fell on our little group as we were eating our dessert. And then came the inevitable question: "Do you believe in reincarnation, Omm Sety?"

"Yes, my dear . . . indeed I do," Omm Sety replied.

"Well, that's a relief because I was afraid you would find the question absurd or crazy. My problem is, I feel such an irresistible desire to go to Akhetaton that I'm quite willing to give up the rest of my trip to be able to see this city. You see, I have some kind of connection with Akhen-Aton. He fills me with disgust, and yet I feel terribly and irresistibly attracted to him—I mean to his very own person, as well as to his wife. Does this make any sense to you, Omm Sety?"

"It does make sense to me, don't you worry about that, my dear."

"You don't mind listening to my story, do you? . . . I don't want to spoil your evening. . . . I hope I haven't already spoiled your dinner. . . . You see, this is a God-given occasion for me to find someone to talk to. Are you sure I won't bore you?" She was addressing me with a charming, almost childish enthusiasm. "I'm sure I will be listening very carefully," I said to her, "and I'm equally sure that Omm Sety will be too," I added.

"I was born into a fairly rich family," the woman began, "the only girl among four brothers. My father was a career diplomat, and so we naturally traveled quite a lot, most of the time in the Far East. Later, when my father was about to retire, we spent most of our time in Western Europe where I met my husband—who worked as an engineer—and my plans to go to college in the States were just dropped. At the age of nineteen, I had a daughter.

"When I was about twelve, my oldest brother bought me a book about Akhen-Aton and his period as a birthday present. We were both terribly fond of Egypt, and we kept hoping our father would get an assignment in this country. While we were in Italy, Father responded to our entreaties and agreed to pass a week in Egypt before leaving Italy for Denmark. Unfortunately, Mother came down with pneumonia, and the trip to Egypt was canceled.

"In the book about Akhen-Aton there were several pictures of Amarna . . . a few very beautiful scenes of the tombs. Whenever I saw those pictures I almost automatically closed my eyes and saw myself walking very briskly in a palace, followed by two women about my age. Somewhere at the end of the palace there was a large room with a very beautiful lady waiting for us to give her a few things from a small box of cosmetics and a larger one containing some very beautiful jewelry. This vision often came to me whenever Egypt was mentioned.

"When I was fifteen I woke up one morning and to my utter astonishment I found a few written pages in my notebook which I immediately recognized as mine . . . but the handwriting was rather sketchy, as if I had scribbled the lines in a great hurry. I have never been a somnambulant, and if ever I was, this wouldn't have remained a secret to the six other members of my family or to the staff of the house. So I was intrigued . . . and scared, too!

"This went on for a week, at the end of which it dawned upon me that my previous life was being dictated and revealed to me very clearly by someone who spoke English with a very strange accent— an accent I could never make out. Occasionally that person, dressed almost like a Jesuit monk, mumbled a few words in a language that sounded a little like Spanish, but I was never sure. He was always reserved, rather aloof, and reticent. Just before I got married, I was quite convinced that a long, long time ago I had had a previous life in Egypt. I felt quite sure I would recognize the place where I had lived if I ever set my eyes on it in this country.

"I'm the third child in my family, and you may be surprised if I tell you that my eldest and my youngest brothers were the only two in the family who believed me. The others, including my parents, thought this was all a kind of hallucination, and my mother was scared stiff. She vaguely suspected I had become addicted to some kind of drug, but I assure you, I've never even tried any and I don't even enjoy drinking. I've never smoked cigarettes. I just feel that my life was and, perhaps still is, associated in one way or another with Akhen-Aton and Nefertiti—especially the latter—and the urge to visit the palace in Akhetaton is much too strong for me to resist!"

She went on giving minute details of her life as a lady-in-waiting to Queen Nefertiti. She said that the Queen was very much in love with her husband. She also said he was moody and extremely temperamental, that he was not as terribly deformed as he appears in his sculpted representations, and that his eyes were irresistible to any woman. His look was dreamy, tender, passionate, and at times so fiery that nobody could meet that look for long. She said that he yearned for a son—a prince to inherit the throne—who would continue his teachings on monotheism; but he was, nevertheless, a very loving father to his daughters. She banished as rubbish all thought of his being a homosexual—something that finds favor in the eyes of some extravagant modern writers. She was so precise in her description of Akhen-Aton and Nefertiti, and of incidents that had occurred in the royal household, that even Omm Sety, with her profound, sometimes unreasonable hatred of him, listened intently without uttering one single comment. This fact alone surprised me very much. Even I, with my skepticism about people who pretended to be reincarnations of one figure or the other, was really quite impressed.

We did not realize how quickly time had passed until, looking around, I saw that all the other tourists had gone to bed and that there were just two yawning waiters talking in undertones in a corner of the dining room. Glancing at my wristwatch, I was alarmed to find that it was already half past two in the morning and that the American woman had been talking for more than four hours! Omm Sety had to be driven back to Abydos, having flatly refused to pass the night—or the few hours remaining of it—in our place at Nag Hammadi. When we were all just about to say good-bye a heavy silence fell upon the three of us for a few minutes. Omm Sety had always been unpredictable; the only extreme emotion she ever expressed in my presence was anger, especially when she heard somebody talking in a high-pitched voice inside the Sety Temple or making some disdainful remark about ancient Egypt. Even when she was suffering from an extremely painful varicose ulcer, she never indulged in a good cry. What happened at our departure was quite staggering.

We shook hands with the American woman, who quite spontaneously kissed each one of us. We wished her a safe trip to Akhetaton. She continued waving as we descended the stairs of the ship; and then suddenly Omm Sety stopped, turned around, and started to walk back, and the American woman ran quickly down to meet her. In an almost choking voice she was saying, "Oh, my dear Omm Sety!" The two women fell into each other's arms, crying and sobbing as if they were mother and daughter saying good-bye forever. I just stood speechless.

Three weeks later I received a short letter from our American friend, who had already returned home, sending her best wishes to Omm Sety and myself. She was elated by her visit to Amarna, although very little remains of Akhen-Aton's palace or the city itself. The tombs are very badly dilapidated. She had spent four days visiting every one she was allowed to enter, and she had lingered for a long time in the ruins of the palace. When I showed her letter to Omm Sety she started to sob, kissing the letter and murmuring, "Poor child, my poor darling baby . . . I wish to Isis I might be able to see her again!"

I was quite moved. It was the very first time I had seen her crying;

and for me, it was so strange to see such a strong, courageous woman like Omm Sety sobbing over the departure of a woman she had met only once. When she had regained her composure I said, "Omm Sety, it's now more than eight years that we've known each other and we've both met all kinds of reincarnations. Why did you feel so strongly about this one?" "Oh, she's different," Omm Sety replied, "quite different from all those we have seen before. This is a real one like myself."

"How did you know?" I asked. "Though I don't myself deny that I was quite impressed by her innocent candor and her apparent honesty."

"To say nothing of her beauty!" Omm Sety commented, smiling.

"That too. She looked such a normal, healthy woman—not the type to be subject to hallucinations."

"All she said was perfectly true," Omm Sety said. "You can't find such consummately precise information in any book. I'm so sorry you didn't have your tape recorder with you. You would have recorded so much knowledge about the man you admire so much. This was a unique opportunity, and she is perfectly honest."

"Do you believe that this whole story was revealed to her in her dream?"

"Precisely. It could not be otherwise. The same thing happened to me. The only difference is the period of time during which each of us was told her own story. The circumstances are quite similar, though. And I have rarely felt the same way toward anybody else. I felt she was what we call 'a kindred spirit'—although it seemed to me that you were quite the thoroughgoing skeptic, at least in the beginning! Later your attitude changed. Am I right?"

"You don't know how right you are! Indeed, when she started off by saying that she was a grandmother, I began to doubt her. You know, as she proceeded with her story, I felt . . . I can hardly describe it, but I believe I became aware of a spiritual dimension to her story, and your apparent and quite willing acceptance of it made it seem credible. I must admit that she had an innocence about her that, for me, was quite disarming."

"Her end was, of course, sad," Omm Sety said. "For you know that all those who followed Akhen-Aton were despised and roughly handled when he died. But at least she enjoyed her stay-over in Akhetaton after her mistress, Nefertiti, left her to go pass her last days in Thebes. I *know* Nefertiti died in Thebes, and I know *where* she was buried—if I tell you, you'll never believe me! When it was time for our friend to join her folks in Memphis—because apparently she came from an upper-middle-class family, and her father was chief of works in the Temple of Hor-em-heb in Sakkara, as she told us—she was quite hesitant. The poor girl, she could guess what fate was preparing for her! She was stamped for the rest of her life as a follower of the heretic King, the criminal of Akhetaton, as the priests of Amon deservedly called him. Poor, darling girl . . . she must have been an ardent believer in the *Aton* religion, since she clung firmly to it to the last breath. She must have been an extremely courageous woman. You know how the priests of Amon wreaked their vengeance on all the poor followers of Akhen-Aton!"

"Yes, I have an idea, may they be damned anyway!" I exclaimed. "They put the whole country in an awful mess just to take their revenge on a dead king. They must have been quite an uncouth lot. Maybe they never really quite understood the fact that the *Aton* religion, in spite of all its failings, transcended all the petty mediocre trash they were preaching!"

"They were *not* preaching trash," Omm Sety replied angrily, "and Akhen-Aton never came out with something new or unknown to the Egyptian intellectuals. You must not blame the priesthood for the mess in which Egypt found itself after Akhen-Aton's death. The mess was already there . . . all over the Empire!"

"What about our friend's story being dictated to her by some spiritual entity, speaking English with an accent? Does it not sound a little bizarre?"

"Oh no, not at all. The man who appeared to her as a Jesuit monk was himself a reincarnation of someone who had known her well in her previous life. . . . But concerning Akhen-Aton, I don't want to be unfair to this heretic fool. What I *really* question are his motives rather than the way he went about preaching his new faith. And, to me, it is *extremely* annoying to see so much time and attention still being devoted to this man and his damned family and so very little spent on, say, the glorious period of Thotmes III [Akhen-Aton's great-great-grandfather, often called Egypt's Napoleon]!"

* * *

When talking about Omm Sety's Abydos, one must inevitably pay homage to the great Egyptologist Auguste Mariette (the first director of the Egyptian Antiquities Department, who lived between 1821 and 1881), who began the first systematic excavations at Abydos. Upon his arrival there, he made a few strokes with a hoe, and immediately uncovered an unknown painted wall. Thus, to the wonder of the good peasants of the "Buried Hamlet," he discovered the first vestiges of the Ramesses Temple, which was entirely covered with sand—as were all the other temples and tombs in the area. (The name of the village was evidently well deserved.)

One of the elderly local people told Mariette that he had always lived in the village and had never been told about any ancient wall in El Araba El Madfouna. "How old are you that you can remember where it was?" he asked Mariette.

"I am three thousand years old," the Egyptologist replied nonchalantly. "Well, then," said the old peasant after a long pause, "if you are so old and you still appear so young, you must really be a holy man. Let me take a look at you!"

Almost a hundred years after this memorable day, Omm Sety came to Abydos to live in the Holy City. I am sure that, had she been there at the same time as Mariette, she would have told *him* where to dig, having also remembered where things had once stood. I asked her if she wasn't concerned about the neglect of the temples there, since no great attention had been paid to the area since the time of Flinders Petrie (1853–1942) in the early part of this century.

"I really started to worry about this in 1967," she told me, "especially about the possible damage that might be done to the temples by the supersonic flights over the area. The roofing of the Sety Temple, although it was constructed with concrete, was, of course, a great protection. As for the Ramesses Temple—you know what happened to it. Its pillaging by the British was one of the most disgraceful and monumental robberies in history! But, you know, I *am* still very much worried about what might now happen to the temples and tombs . . . especially the Osirion. People in the village keep telling me about the ever rising subsoil water."

"I, too, am terribly worried about all this," I said to her. "I hope I will be able to raise the whole question at the International Congress on Egyptology, this year [1976], and will get the opportunity to raise hell about what is happening to our temples. Maybe somebody will be able to ask for funds from UNESCO in order to save Sety's Temple for your sake!"

"I hope my lady Isis will be kind enough to me and save me from seeing it crumble down," she said plaintively. "You know, I fought so hard to have it roofed, and now I don't know how we can stop this damned subsoil water from seeping up all the time."

"Tell me, Omm Sety," I said—trying to change the subject—"was the land around here as lush during your previous life as it is now?"

"I've told you," she replied, "that Hor-Ra, who dictated to me the story of Bentreshyt, revealed to me that my mother was a vegetable

seller—beautiful ancestry!—and I can vaguely recollect that the let-
tuce and onions produced in this area were very special . . . and
very tasty indeed! But at least the Sety Temple, in spite of the ravages
of time and the madness of fanaticism, is still as majestic and as awe-
inspiring as it was when Ramesses was finishing it . . . and for that
I am very grateful to the gods.

"You know, when I came back here in 1956, I only missed the
garden where I had first met His Majesty. And I sometimes liked to
imagine that at any moment the houses on the northern side of the
temple would crumble down and the palace where His Majesty used
to pass his days here in Abydos would pop up and shine in its full
glory!"

"Apart from your meetings with His Majesty," I inquired, "you
must have had several spiritual encounters or experiences here. Did
you ever meet any of your gods or goddesses inside the temple?"

"No, never," she said. "But once on the birthday of my lord Osiris
—and after having presented the usual offerings of beer and incense
—I heard quite distinctly the beating of sistrums and some beautiful
heavenly music that filled the whole temple. I felt spellbound and
couldn't move from where I was praying in the small Cult Chapel
inside the Osiris Complex."

"If the music filled the temple, as you say, then I suppose somebody else must have heard it," I surmised.

"Indeed there was a new watchman there that day—a nice young
chap named Mohammed, who felt obliged to escort me inside because it was just after sunset and the temple was completely dark
. . . though I found my way without even having to use a torch."

"And did your young guardian angel also hear the music?"

"I really fell into something like a trance," she explained. "The
music was very beautiful, very melodious, and quite out of this world
. . . reminiscent of Bach. But I wasn't even conscious of Mohammed's presence. I remember, very vaguely, hearing footsteps, as if
somebody were running in a great hurry, but the music never
stopped. The next day I asked Mohammed if he had heard anything
and he said he had but was scared to death; so he ran out of the
temple and swore that he would never enter it again except in broad
daylight. But he was ashamed to tell anybody that he had left me
alone inside."

"Did you ever experience any spiritual presence there," I asked
her, "as if you felt that some spiritual entity were trying to communicate with you—as His Majesty does?"

"Yes, two or three times," she told me. "The last time was when I was standing before the enigmatic inscription in the Soker Hall [on the northern inner jamb of the doorway of the Chapel of Nefer-tem], and wondering, perhaps for the hundredth time, what the hell it was all about. You see, it was like a standing challenge, and I always felt what a shame it was to have known and read every inscription in the temple except this one. And I stood there, racking my brain. Then I sat down on the ground, bending my knees and putting my head between the palms of my hands and my elbows resting on my knees; and I heard a voice behind my back saying in the ancient language, 'Read it. . . . Read it.' I looked around . . . there was nobody there . . . but the same voice repeated the same order. So I looked at the enigmatic inscription and found myself, for the first time in years, able to read aloud the whole text, but somehow I wasn't able to recognize my own voice. This was definitely not my own voice."

"Do the women here and in the surrounding villages visit the temple when they are barren and long for a child?" I inquired.

"Oh yes . . . very much so. But I always advise them to make an offering to Hathor [the goddess of love and beauty], either by the ninth pillar of the second portico [which shows Ramesses embraced by Hathor] or in the Chapel of Nefer-tem, where the goddess is represented as a falcon with a woman's head."

"Does it work? I know that at the Temple of Dendera practically all the women in the village make this kind of offering to Hathor."

"Oh, it works!" she exclaimed. "It always works, except in very rare cases. And if it doesn't work, it's not Hathor's fault but most probably a case of *cherchez l'homme* and not *cherchez la femme!*

"But, you know, I have always loved to help the women here during childbirths. I've never been of very much use as an obstetrician, but the miracle of birth had always a strong grip over me; and we didn't have any sort of medical care until the village hospital was opened a few years ago. I used to notice, to my great astonishment, that the women did not lie in bed on their backs, as women do everywhere else, but sat upright on a special chair and held a long knife in their right hand like the goddess Tawert [the female hippo goddess, protector of children]. Do you remember the incised relief of Tawert in the Hall of Soker?"

"Indeed I do," I said. "Traditions die hard in this part of Egypt. . . . But is this upright position suitable for an easy childbirth?"

"I haven't tried it myself," Omm Sety said with a chuckle, "but apparently it's extremely helpful."

"I can understand why the chair is necessary," I commented, "but what on earth is the point of a knife in the hand of a woman delivering a baby?"

"It's not for cutting the umbilical cord, as I once thought," she said, "but rather for warding off evil spirits so that the child will be of sound body and soul."

"I've recently come across a new theory that speculates that, in ancient Egypt, delivery was done under water," I mentioned, "and that *that* is the real meaning for the choice of the hippopotamus as a protector of children. Some obstetricians believe that, if the mother is immersed in water, this alleviates the labor pains. I wonder if it really works?"

"Why not?" she declared. "I've seen mummies with very neatly cut parts of the skull, indicating a highly advanced level of brain surgery. If the ancient Egyptians arrived that far with regard to one of the most complex of major surgical operations, I don't see why they couldn't have discovered the easiest and least painful method for the delivery of a child. We really know very little about our ancient Egyptian science. What escaped the holocaust of the Alexandria Library and what was not taken away by the Persians when they left Egypt is quite insignificant."

"But Egyptian medicine and surgery depended very much on magic, amulets, secret formulas, et cetera," I interjected.

"Not always," she replied. "We know very little about their knowledge of medicinal herbs. The papers that have survived are, in my view, quite inadequate, and perhaps a little misleading, too. . . .

"But speaking of magical texts, what possible harm is there if they fulfill a beneficent purpose? Take, for example, the case of the scorpion stela. A few years ago there was a small piece of inscribed stone at the head of the field . . . just beyond the rest house on the other side of the canal. And there was a spell on that stela which kept scorpions away. You know, occasionally during the summer, a few scorpions show up and become a real nuisance to the children, who don't pay attention to them. Now, while that stela remained at the head of the field, everybody noticed that the scorpions never appeared either in the field or in the village. Then one day an inspector saw the stela and thought it was his duty to take it to the Department's storehouses in Sohag. Believe it or not, that very next day a child had to be sent to the hospital to be treated for a scorpion bite; fortunately, he was saved by our local doctor."

"I know that a few Rosicrucians and some Shriners have visited here during the past few years," I mentioned, "and that some of them have passed the night inside the temple with you. What does the temple offer them?"

"Peace, serenity, sometimes real happiness," Omm Sety replied. "A couple of years ago there was an American woman, an extremely well-bred lady, who had lost her son in Vietnam. Some influential members of the Rosicrucians told her to come to Egypt and make a pilgrimage to Abydos. So she left her group in Luxor and traveled here; and she spent the day and night with me. First of all, I made her fast and perform an ablution for purification. Then she told me that she was hoping that Lady Isis would be kind enough to put her in touch with her son. So I prayed fervently to my lady Isis, perhaps as I have never prayed before in all my life, for her sake. A little after midnight in the temple we both heard very beautiful music—then it stopped, and we both slept. Strange as it may seem to you, *I* had a dreamless night, but the American lady rose up the next day quite happy and rested. Gone was the tense, miserable look of someone who has endured great pain. She told me she had seen her son in a dream that was almost like reality. He appeared in his T-shirt, smiling and relaxed, and he told her that he had died instantly without suffering—a bullet had gone right through his head one week before the end of the hostilities—and said that she shouldn't worry because he was quite happy where he was. And when the woman left, she cried quite uncontrollably for a few minutes as she was saying goodbye. . . . A lot of people can be relieved of their agony if they trust themselves to the loving-kindness of my lady Isis."

"Do you intend to make this temple a palace of worship as it was in Sety's time?" I asked her.

"I wish I could," she said. "Today, Abydos is easy to reach. You may remember that when Kissinger came to Egypt during his shuttle diplomacy in 1973 some of his companions expressed the desire to visit Abydos, but they couldn't do so because the road between here and Balyana was in such an awful state. So I, in my turn, made my own shuttle diplomacy between the governor of Sohag and the director of the Roads and Bridges Administration, and convinced them that, now that peace was coming, it would be worthwhile to macadamize the road and cover it with bitumen. The governor, who was really a remarkably intelligent and energetic man, gave orders for this to be done . . . and now we're in touch with the outside world."

* * *

Omm Sety often told me that underneath the majestic Sety Temple are a temple treasury waiting to be discovered and a unique document waiting to be mended and reconstructed. The document in question—the diary of Sety the First—was written on papyri; and with the passage of more than three thousand years it must by now have crumbled into fragments or even minute particles. With the aid of special computers, such papyri can be pieced together by competent specialists. (I have seen miracles and marvels of restoration.) What makes this document unique is that it apparently is the only diary known to be written by a king himself, and not by his scribes.

Omm Sety's remarks about the existence of this diary and of this treasury cannot be doubted because on the temple walls themselves inscriptions say that both are hidden somewhere inside it. Excavations have now become much more sophisticated—what with the introduction of electromagnetic equipment, electronic devices, infrared photography, and metal detectors. Perhaps among all of those people who have seen, admired, and loved Sety's Temple there will soon be someone who will not hesitate to finance this important excavation project.

How important? I once asked Omm Sety. And she replied:

"I think that the discovery of the annals will be the biggest find in Egyptian history, since in them would be a recording of events at a very critical period in Egypt's history. These annals were probably hidden during the reign of Ptolemy the Third [c. 246–221 B.C.], when he ordered all the temples in Egypt to turn in their books to the great library of Alexandria. No doubt the books that were turned in— probably a few odes to Ptolemaic gods, several *Books of the Dead,* a number of books of hymns—were quite unessential. Anything of real importance would have been hidden.

"And I also believe," she continued, "that the secret treasury has not yet been discovered. In the set of rooms that we call the Archives or the Library, there is a mention of such a treasury; and so far no part of the building has been discovered that could reasonably have been used as a treasury. There is another peculiar thing: the height of the floor in these Archives contrasted with the height of the floor of the halls—particularly of the Hall of Boats and the Butchers' Hall, which lie immediately to its east—reveals a difference of nearly four meters. . . . So what is under there? Perhaps there is another set of rooms!"

Omm Sety discussed with me the best way to investigate this question without endangering the safety of the temple itself, which was already threatened by the rise of the subsoil water and by the very alarming signs of a gradual sinking of the pavement in the center of the Hypostyle Halls. Omm Sety and I had both become extremely worried and concerned about this threat. There is no denying the considerable efforts undertaken by the Antiquities Department to deal with this problem. Now, in the 1980s, the problem has reached such magnitude that it is clear that a concerted international cooperative effort to save this precious heritage of all mankind has become an absolute necessity—like the salvaging of the temples of Nubia many years ago. As Omm Sety once told me: "The Sety Temple and others like it have weathered many a storm and man's wanton destruction for more than three thousand years. I think they can defy the challenge from below for tens of years to come. But I *do* hope I will go to Amenti before anything happens to Abydos!"

* * *

During the early 1970s, I would spend my holidays at the Sety Temple in order to take photos for the book Omm Sety and I had decided to collaborate on; and she would help me choose the best time of the day to photograph every part of the temple. I was always surprised to see how the expressions of the gods and goddesses would change from hour to hour, depending on the degree and angle of the light—it was rather uncanny. I never saw a scowl or a look of contempt or anger or dissatisfaction on any of the faces. I also once remarked to Omm Sety that there seemed to me to be some kind of resemblance between the goddesses and King Sety himself. She smiled and said that this was not the first time I had made that remark to her and that, indeed, the resemblance was there. Sety, she said, just adored his mother and wanted to immortalize her image in the faces of those extremely elegant, slim, and beautiful goddesses. And Omm Sety told me that he looked very much like his mother.

"Tell me about his mother," I said to her.

"Oh, she must have been a remarkable beauty," she informed me. "You only have to look at the face of the goddesses Renpet or Maat to see how beautiful she must have been. And you have only to look at the reconstitution of *his* face, done by that ingenious woman Anni Quibell [the Scottish excavator and draftsman, 1862–1927], to see how handsome and manly His Majesty was."

"Did he ever talk to you about her?" I asked.

"Of course he did, but not as often as you might think. I have always avoided dragging him into speaking about his family life. You know, it was not a very happy one, and he always shunned talking about it."

"But I suppose he had a happy childhood," I hazarded. "In a way, nobody expected his father, Ramesses the First, to become king, and we know so little about his short-lived reign."

"That's quite true," she said. "But when he was young his father was 'playing the military' even in his own house. That is what His Majesty told me. Ramesses the First was a career soldier, and as tough as they make them. If you see a film of either the First or Second World War, just watch any NCO to see how he bellows his orders and how he tries to scare the wits out of the new recruits, and you'll have a sense of the behavior of Ramesses the First."

"Did His Majesty ever demonstrate this to you? I mean, did he try to imitate his father?" I wondered.

"One night," Omm Sety replied, "His Majesty appeared unusually early, and he was quite gloomy and depressed. I was really quite upset. When I asked him what was the matter, he said that it was the anniversary of the execution of his eldest son, the black sheep of the family, who tried to overthrow his father in the early years of his reign. He was judged by a court, found guilty, and executed. As you know, people who met their death in this way were never properly buried but were wrapped in the most common draping material, usually made of woven palm cloth like *maktaf,* and the body was then unceremoniously thrown into a pit and the person's name was hacked out of all inscriptions.

"So it was a particularly sad evening for His Majesty. I tried very hard to think of something to divert him from dwelling on this appalling incident. Suddenly I thought I would ask him about King Ramesses the Second—his beloved son—and about his own mother. I already knew that he was always on very bad terms with both his wife, Queen Tuy, and his daughter, and I always carefully avoided mentioning their names to him. To my relief, he chose to talk about his mother and about how she used to mimic his father when he was shouting orders in the palace, and his mother was always responding good-naturedly, 'Yes, my commandant!' 'Sure, my commandant!' . . . And gradually His Majesty became more relaxed."

* * *

Whenever I found Omm Sety physically fit to endure a long trip, I would invite her to go to such important sites as Kom Ombo, Edfu, Esna, and Luxor. She was never particularly enthusiastic about the Ptolemaic temples . . . and, in fact, neither was I. The sculpture in these temples is quite elaborate but not very inspiring. Omm Sety used to gaze very casually at the scenes; then, smiling quizzically, she would say:

"Look at those women. They appear to be like neither goddesses nor queens; they may be beautiful, but in a coarse and vulgar way."

"I think I agree with you there, Omm Sety. I find nothing divine or majestic about these personalities. Also, the systematic hacking up of the limbs and faces of the gods is terrible. It's really fortunate that the early Copts of Egypt didn't have ladders high enough to reach to the upper sections of the sculpture, thus saving them from destruction."

"But still," she declared, "even the intact scenes are not so beautiful. The women have got very spectacular endowments, but they don't look naturalistic. Look at those big busts! They'd create turmoil inside an overcrowded bus in Cairo or London, don't you think?"

"Yes," I said, laughing, "they're really quite unnatural, but maybe that was the influence of the Greek school of sculpture."

"I'm not so sure about that," she remarked. "Greek sculpture was always very aware of the harmony of lines in the human body. But these awful creatures have absolutely *nothing* of that!"

"At least the architecture is quite impressive," I added, "although its creators added very little stylistically to the ancient Egyptian school."

"They did not and could not," Omm Sety stated, "because everything they learned had already been done in On, Memphis, or Thebes. There is, however, one new style that we can say they did introduce into our country."

"And what may that be?"

"Bosom-ology and Bottom-ology!" she told me, laughing. "There are enough shapes of bosoms and buttocks to represent the entire size range of English, French, and German women's underwear!"

* * *

On another occasion, when the late Professor John A. Wilson of the Oriental Institute in Chicago—an old and dear friend of Omm Sety's—was a guest at Chicago House in Luxor, we were both invited to spend Christmas Eve with him. As usual, Omm Sety was the center of attention and was full of wit and good humor; and, for the first and last time in her life, she agreed to stay over at Chicago House that night. Early the next morning, however, she insisted on returning to Abydos as quickly as possible. I wanted her to be checked out by a cardiologist before going home, but she wouldn't

Sety the First offering a golden *usekh* collar to Osiris in the Cult Chapel of Osiris, Temple of Sety. *(Hanny El Zeini)*

Isis and Osiris as they appear on the northern wall of the Second Hypostyle Hall, Temple of Sety. *(Hanny El Zeini)*

Omm Sety sitting on the floor of the "island" of the Osirion, March 1958. Since this photograph was taken, the Nile river bed has risen, leaving the "island"—as well as the Central Hall of the Osirion—permanently underwater and entirely covered with reeds. *(Hanny El Zeini)*

The Sarcophagus Chamber of the Osirion, on whose walls are depicted astral bodies (here called *akhu* or "glorified spirits") leaving their earthly bodies. Omm Sety, who herself claimed to "travel" in such a manner, once said about this depicted scene: "As you can see, the astral bodies are clothed, but there are none of the 'silver cords' that the Theosophists, among others, believed were attached to the earthly bodies during out-of-the-body experiences." *(Hanny El Zeini)*

Omm Sety and her friend and collaborator of twenty-five years, Hanny El Zeini.
(Randa El Zeini)

Omm Sety at Chicago House—home of the University of Chicago's Epigraphic Survey—in Luxor, December 1975. Seated with her are the Egyptologists the late Dr. John A. Wilson, the late Dr. Labib Habachi (left) and Dr. William Murnane (far right). *(Hanny El Zeini)*

Omm Sety telling a "saucy" joke to M. Tracey and to Nagi, a guide from Luxor, 1977. M. Tracey, an English tour guide and author, was one of Omm Sety's closest friends and a frequent house guest at her home in Abydos. "At night," M. Tracey recalls, "we'd sit up in our dressing gowns, drink some beer, and chat about this and that for hours and hours." *(Collection of M. Tracey)*

Omm Sety "at home" in 1980, shortly after having broken her right hip. In the niche behind her are some of the clay figurines of ancient Egyptian deities that she had made herself. *(Hanny El Zeini)*

In keeping with ancient Egyptian tradition, Omm Sety prepared her "House of Eternity" in the garden behind her home. Below the rectangular white patch, she built, as she once described it, "a lovely underground room made of red brick, lined with cement, and covered with slabs of concrete. On the west wall I carved a nice little false door, just as they did in ancient tombs . . . and an offering prayer . . . and a figure of Isis with her wings outspread." After Omm Sety's death, however, the local health department refused permission for her to be buried here; and her body was interred in the desert just northwest of the Sety and Ramesses temples. *(Hanny El Zeini)*

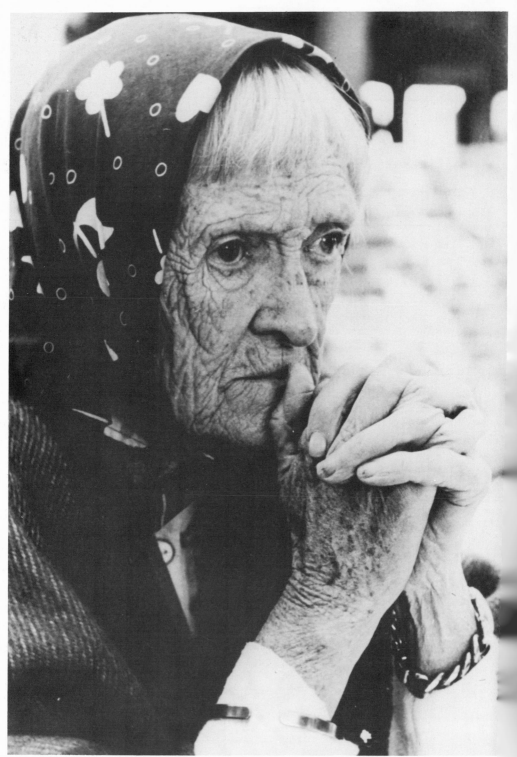

A portrait of Omm Sety taken shortly after she had prayed in the Temple of Sety on the Great Feast of Osiris, January 2, 1979. *(Hanny El Zeini)*

have anything to do with a medical examination. We quarreled, but I finally got her to agree to the necessary checkup. She was doing quite well for her age.

On our way back to Abydos we passed by an old cemetery in the desert just outside a village named Sheikh Aly. I quickly noticed what looked like a fresh painting on a tomb—something quite unusual in Muslim cemeteries. Our curiosity was aroused, and she said that the matter was worth closer scrutiny. I had previously passed by this very cemetery on hundreds of occasions, but this was the first time I had noticed such unusual paintings on the tombs. On closer inspection we found, to our great surprise, that *all* the tombs, without exception, were painted; but the desert dust and the sun had made them fade to the point that even the colors had disappeared. Every tomb had some painting connected to the job or profession of the buried person: one for a baker showed variously shaped loaves of bread, while a butcher's tomb was decorated with choice pieces of slaughtered oxen. Omm Sety, with her amazing powers of observation, was able to decipher many painted scenes. . . . But all of a sudden she became quite panicky, exclaiming:

"Oh, my goodness, the cats!"

"Don't worry, Omm Sety," I tried to assure her. "They're born thieves, and I very much doubt that they'll starve."

"I'm not sure I left them all the food they need for breakfast and lunch," she said nervously.

"The butcher's shop is not far from your house," I reminded her, "and *I* am quite sure they will make themselves his guests, whether he likes it or not."

"I'm worried about Hatshepsut," she told me. "That cat is as pitiless and as cruel as her namesake. I'm certain that by now she is swearing and spitting and calling me names!"

"Names? Like what?" I asked her, smiling.

"Most probably '*Ya bint Sittin Kalb, Fen El Akl* [Daughter of sixty dogs, where is our food?].' "

When my driver returned to Nag Hammadi, after having driven Omm Sety to her house, he told me, with a look of utter bewilderment: "All the cats, dogs, geese, and rabbits were waiting for her outside the front door, and they were making a hell of a din, loud enough to wake up the dead. But what was quite strange, sir, is that all the dishes were full of food for those awful beasts. They sure enough were not hungry . . . but why that awful noise?"

·VI·

Omm Sety
The Final Years

Now I direct my eyes into the west,
Which at this moment is in sunbeams drest;
Why westward turn? 'Twas but to say adieu!

(John Keats)

Having lived in hardly the most sanitary or luxurious environment for almost a quarter of a century, Omm Sety—now a septuagenarian—was showing signs of her age. A heart attack, a broken knee, phlebitis, flus, dysentery, eye catarrhs, and chronic appendicitis had all taken their toll. No longer the vigorous, heavyset woman of the past, Omm Sety was now thin and quite frail. Not one to complain openly about her condition, she would simply apply whatever medications or remedies were at hand—Osirion water, a cup of mint tea, scorpion bites, a prayer to Isis—and go about her business. "I have my own built-in antibiotics," she once told her tour-leader friend Maureen Tracey. When Tracey was staying one night at Omm Sety's house, she was astonished to see her hostess fill up a glass with water and gulp down several dog vitamins (Bob Martin's Conditioning Tablets) that Tracey herself had brought from London for one of Omm Sety's canine pets. "If they're all right for the dog, they're all right for me!" was her only comment.

"One day in 1978 or '79," Tracey would later recall, "Omm Sety said to me, 'Oh, I don't know, Tracey, I've been a bit fed up lately, and I've finally arranged for a plot of earth to be buried in.' She asked if I could somehow arrange to get her one of those green plastic body pouches that the Americans used to bury their dead soldiers in during the Vietnam War. 'What a laugh for Osiris,' she said to me, 'when I come to the other end and he thinks I've come prepackaged!' [On Egyptian bas-reliefs, Osiris' skin was painted green as a sign of his resurrection.] . . . Well, I finally *was* able to obtain one of those body pouches through a friend of mine in the American military. Omm Sety then told me that she planned to be buried in the white dress that she had worn on her first pilgrimage to Abydos."

"It was sort of assumed," Omm Sety later explained, "that I would be buried in the tomb plot belonging to Ahmed's family. You see, the Muslims make two tombs—one for the women in the family and one for the men—and they look rather like vaulted underground air raid shelters. One day, one of the religious leaders belonging to the mosque here happened to ask Ahmed where he was planning on burying me. 'In the family tomb,' he replied. 'Oh no,' the leader exclaimed, 'we can't have that evil woman in our Muslim cemetery!' So, some time later, the head priest of the Coptic monastery of Sitt Dimiana—which dates back to the seventh century—asked Ahmed the same question, and he, too, said to Ahmed, 'Well, don't think we're going to bury that awful heathen woman in our Christian cemetery!' (Incidentally, both the Christians and the Muslims have pinched parts of the ancient cemetery for their own burial grounds!) So I told Ahmed what to tell all of them to do with their cemeteries and decided to build a tomb on the western side of my garden.

"It's a lovely underground room made of red brick, lined with cement, and covered with slabs of concrete. On the west wall I carved a nice little false door, just as they did in ancient tombs [a door connecting the world of the living to the world of the dead, and through which the *ka* was believed to pass freely]. Then I also carved an offering prayer asking for '1,000 jars of beer, 1,000 loaves of bread, 1,000 oxen, 1,000 geese, 1,000 jars of wine, perfume, and every good and pure thing.' At the head of the tomb I finally carved a figure of Isis with her wings outspread. One of the men working for the Antiquities Department made me a stone headrest, the staff of Chicago House gave me an imitation *shawabti* [a magical servant statue that, when the deceased was called upon to do work, would answer for her and perform the required task], and my friend Tracey sent me a plastic sarcophagus, which fits very well. (I've already tried it out.) . . . So now, when I pop off, all they have to do is scrape a bit of dirt away, lift up one of the concrete slabs, shove me in, give me a kick, and I'm all set!"

* * *

At the end of 1979, Omm Sety was working in the temple one day and, having caught a dose of the Asiatic flu, took a couple of aspirins, lay down on the floor of one of the rooms, and fell asleep. "After a while," she later recalled, "I felt something licking my face. I looked up, and there I saw a great big black dog with long legs and a tucked-up belly and prickly ears—and I thought it was Wepwawat come to fetch me. [A jackal-like deity whose name means "Opener of the Ways," Wepwawat guided the souls of the dead to the Other World.] So I said, 'All right, I'm ready, but can we just go and get my cat?' Then I looked more closely, and came to, and I realized that this creature was only a dog belonging to the rest house by the name of Nico. But I had been quite sure it was Wepwawat!"

In early 1980, Omm Sety had gotten noticeably thinner and weaker; and her abbreviated diary entries of this period give a picture of a struggling but indomitable woman who was undergoing constant pain.

Wednesday, January 2
First day of the Great Feast. Went to the Temple with incense and beer. Feel very ill again. Dr. Hani [Hanny El Zeini] sent a friend with some multivitamins and Asmac.

Sunday, January 6
Feel a bit better. Went and sat in the Rest House. Foukay treated me to a *koufta* lunch. Sold pictures for 18 pounds.

Monday, January 7
My grandson, Mohammed, came to see me, he had some friends with him. He spent the day here, and will stay the night. He has come back from Kuwait especially to join the army. It's the first time I've seen him, and he looks typically Irish, like my uncle Wilfred [Reuben Eady's brother]! Seems to be a nice, polite boy.

Tuesday, January 8
Stayed home all day. Mohammed left for Alexandria to join the army.

Thursday, January 10
Swan's group came with two friends. Went to the Temple with them. Later coughed up a funny lump of very thick phlegm coloured black, white, and red (like our flag!); it was followed by a pink lump and then a white one. After that I can breathe easily. Think it was an old blood-clot that got stuck in my left lung around 1942!

Wednesday, February 13
At Rest House fell down and broke my right leg. Am in terrible pain.

An ambulance was called to take Omm Sety to the Balyana hospital, where she was given an X ray and informed that the head of her right femur had an impacted fracture. She remained in the hospital for about two months. Restless and in pain, she slowly began to recuperate and, little by little, started to walk again with the aid of crutches. But no longer would Omm Sety be able to move and get about as freely as she had once done.

In October of 1980, Julia Cave, a producer and director for the BBC, arrived in Abydos with a film crew to begin shooting scenes for a movie entitled *Omm Sety and Her Egypt.* This wonderful fifty-minute documentary presented the history of Abydos, described the excavations that had taken place there, and featured interviews with T.G.H. James of the British Museum and Dr. Rosalie David, the author of *A Guide to Religious Ritual at Abydos*—a brilliant scholarly analysis of the Sety Temple and the cult of Osiris. The "star" of the film is, of course, Omm Sety, who talks at length about her life and who, though in great pain, managed to rise to the occasion and walk haltingly on crutches to the temple. As the camera shows her entering the building, we see this drawn and exhausted woman's face turn suddenly radiant before our eyes, her body and spirit mysteriously transformed and rejuvenated. As Omm Sety's diary entry for October 20 states:

Went walking to the Temple for the first time in 9 months, thanks to the mercy of Lady Isis. Julia Cave and Co. came, and made some photos and recordings in the Temple. They sent for my chair, as it's a long business standing around while they adjust lights and cameras. They invited me to lunch at the Rest House, carried me there in the chair, and then back home. Leg aching badly, but so very glad to have been to the Temple.

And when the documentary was shown on BBC 2 in May 1981

the television critic for *The Times* of London wrote: "An incredulous smile froze on my lips as I watched the Chronicle film *Omm Sety and Her Egypt.* Could I be absolutely positive it was all a lot of eyewash? Of course I couldn't. And neither will you be able to. In any case, it makes marvellous television."

The same week that Omm Sety was working with the BBC, she received a visit from the American producer Miriam Birch, who was writing and producing a one-hour documentary entitled *Egypt: Quest for Eternity* for National Geographic Films. This beautifully photographed movie concentrates on the life, work, and times of Sety's son and successor—perhaps the most famous pharaoh of all time—Ramesses the Second. Appearing in this movie were Dr. Kent Weeks and Dr. Lanny Bell; and Miriam Birch had come to Abydos to find out whether Omm Sety might also be willing to participate in it. She agreed, but the shooting of her scenes did not take place until the middle of March 1981. At that time the staff of Chicago House traveled up to Abydos, where they were filmed belatedly celebrating Omm Sety's seventy-seventh birthday. "To Omm Sety and her seventy-seventh on her way to one hundred and ten!" Dr. Bell says as we see him raising his glass. To which Omm Sety, with her irrepressible charm and wit, replies, "And let us drink to our dear old friend, Ramesses the Second . . . a nice fellow and a very good son!" Then the producer and her crew carried this valiant woman to the Sety Temple. ("She was in a lot of pain, but she ignored that," Miriam Birch recalled.) It was March 21, 1981; and this was to be Omm Sety's final visit to her beloved shrine.

* * *

On April 8, Omm Sety, while lying in bed, happened to pick up a copy of an old issue of an English magazine called *The Lady,* given to her some time back by a visiting tourist. Browsing through it, she came across an article on the subject of "The East Sussex Coast and Downs," which included a photograph of the Polegate Mill, where, as a twelve-year-old living on her granny's farm, she had played and caused so much havoc to its owner, Mr. Katz. "I found this picture in *The Lady* magazine," she wrote in her diary—pasting the photograph on the page opposite—and added: "Never expected to see 'the Cat Mill' again. Glad it's still standing and in use once more. Who rides the sails now?"

On April 10 she gave away two of her cats, Ankhsi and Ahmes. ("Hope they will be happy.") On April 11 she complained of having a bad cold and a sore throat; and, on April 12, of losing her voice.

On April 13, however, she was much better—in fact, well enough to meet the visiting Bob Brier, with whom she had a "long and interesting talk."

Dr. Bob Brier, philosophy chairman at C. W. Post College on Long Island, in New York, and a parapsychologist and Egyptologist who wrote the book *Ancient Egyptian Magic,* has stated: "Omm Sety had the best feeling of anybody I've ever met for what ancient Egypt was really like. When you conversed with her you felt that there was no distance between her and life as it was lived in the olden days. You really felt: yes, this is what it must have been like. . . . I would have viewed temple ceremonies in a certain way, but she'd say, 'No, *this* is how you did it, you brought beer there, you did this or that, sometimes people got drunk.' It just rang true. You'd see her getting together some offerings for the temple, and it wasn't anything fancy or super-duper—simply a loaf of bread, a jug of wine . . . and that's the way people must have done it. . . . The last time I saw Omm Sety, by the way, she told me that she would love to see the movie *Star Wars,* since she'd heard and read about it and thought it sounded wonderful! When I said good-bye to her and mentioned that I'd be back to visit her in June, she said, 'If you don't find me here, I'll be out back in the garden.' "

Later that day a tourist, whom Omm Sety had never met before and who had apparently heard some "rumors" about her, came by her house and brashly asked: "From your memories of a previous life, what was your relationship to Sety the First?" To which Omm Sety, feigning ignorance, replied: "Oh, none! I'm not one of those reincarnated royalty. I must have seen him when he came to Abydos for the great feast, when the King was supposed to play the part of Horus. The excellence of the work in the temple rather suggests that he kept popping in unannounced to see how the work on it was going. . . . Yes, I must have seen him once or twice."

Even with persons she did know, like, and respect, Omm Sety would rarely discuss her "secret" relationship with Sety. As Dr. William Murnane once remarked: "As for Sety having been her 'paramour,' we never talked about that. She never volunteered any information, and I never pushed. But I remember that once, very early in our relationship, I sort of brought up the subject indirectly; and she didn't either quite pretend ignorance or tell me directly to mind my own business, but she answered in a way that made it clear that she wondered what made me bring it up. And so I never did again. I hadn't, incidentally, been referring to any sexual aspect, but rather to some particular point about daily life in ancient Egypt—the inference of my remark being that, even though certain things were to remain unspoken, surely she must be familiar with the particular point I had raised. Her answer to me could have been taken to mean, 'You're being impertinent.' I guess I deserved it. Unlike most people who were deemed to be eccentrics, Omm Sety was not anxious to ram her private beliefs and feelings down your throat. They were her personal affair, and that was all."

Her past *and* present "involvement" with "His Majesty" was something she revealed in detail to only one person—Dr. Hanny El Zeini. She occasionally *would* say something about her previous "liaison" with Sety to somebody with whom she felt an affinity. One of these persons was Olivia Robertson, a cofounder of the Fellowship of Isis, whose headquarters are in Ireland, and who met Omm Sety in 1975.

As Olivia Robertson recently commented: "In 1976 at the vernal equinox, my brother, Baron Robertson of Strathloch (registered as such by the Chief Herald of Ireland), his wife Pamela, and I founded the Fellowship of Isis. To date [August 1985], we have 5,654 members in fifty-five countries—a large number of them in Nigeria—and centers in twenty-seven of these countries. Our priesthood consists of fifty-one priestesses and fifty-five priests. We are multireligious, multicultural, and multiracial; and our members belong to many of the world's major religions and follow many spiritual and occult paths.

"Omm Sety was enrolled as a member—Number 2,089—on March 23, 1981. She was a latter-day Isis, enacting in everyday life the time-honored Mystery of the search for and finding of the dead Osiris and his awakening by a loyal wife. The dead Pharaoh Sety the First was brought to life for thousands of pilgrims and visitors by this twentieth-century priestess of the mysteries, Dorothy Eady. Her love and devotion for the Temple of the Heart of Osiris in Abydos revitalized the religion of ancient Egypt in our day.

"I met Omm Sety in October of 1975 and liked and admired her, and believed in the wonderful account she gave me of her psychic discovery of her long-lost lover, Sety the First. What Omm Sety contributed to the Fellowship of Isis was her example of the continuity of priesthood in the person of woman with a six-thousand-year-old tradition. Through her life she brought the truth of reincarnation and the Mystery of Isis and Osiris into living reality. So she acted as a bridge—a rainbow bridge—that connects the world of the terrible wars of the twentieth century and a new age when the ancient verities are, and will be, coming to life. She was a latter-day Isis, demonstrating that any woman who truly loves her husband *is*

Isis, and has the power of awakening him into greater life as Horus.
Father Vann, S.J., draws a comparison to the awakening of Christ by
Mary Magdalene when he emerges from the tomb. I hope that the
story of Dorothy Eady reaches many receptive hearts!" (And on
April 15, 1981, Omm Sety noted in her diary that she was happy to
receive the March 23 letter from Ireland, admitting her officially as a
member of the Fellowship of Isis.)

It is clear that Omm Sety—who, as a girl, had, of course, once
played the role of Isis in a small theatrical production in Plymouth,
England—was truly a daughter and follower of the goddess. Healing
and protecting, faithful and righteous, loving and restoring, Omm
Sety, like the tutelary deity she worshiped, was also giving and generous to a fault. When Bob Brier, on his visit to her house on April 13,
happened to express his admiration for a needlepoint embroidery of
Osiris hanging on her wall, she simply took it down and presented it
to him.

Another Egyptologist and tour guide (who prefers to remain
nameless) recently stated: "I used to encourage the cruise passengers
to buy Omm Sety's embroideries and to contribute to a bag of 'bits
and pieces'—old novels and magazines, sewing materials—at the end
of a cruise. (The bag would be kept on board and given to Omm Sety
on the following trip.) And every year I would bring her a little
present—packets of good tea, for instance, and one year, at her request, a broom head ('these palm switches are useless!' she used to
say).

"On my last visit to Abydos, we arranged that the tour manager
should visit Omm Sety while I took the party first to the Ramesses
Temple, and I would then see her when I returned to the Sety Temple. And when I finally got back there, I was met by the tour manager, who explained that there was something we had to do. A few
weeks previously, Ahmed had had a very serious car accident on the
way back from Cairo. Fortunately, though others were killed, he had
survived with only minor injuries. Omm Sety now wanted to say
thank you to the goddess Isis for preserving him. In the ancient
Egyptian way, it must be a votive offering of the most precious thing
she had. So she took off the necklace of blue amulets she always wore
and gave it to my friend, asking her to place it in the niche of Isis in
the great Hypostyle Hall of the temple, on the stone floor under the
figure of the goddess. 'But,' said my friend to Omm Sety, 'the temple
is full of tourists: one of them will take it.' 'No matter,' she replied.
'Once made, the offering may pass to anyone, as it used to do to the
priests' (who ate the offered food, et cetera). But she would like me

to have the necklace, Omm Sety had told the tour manager. And if I accompanied her when she placed the offering at the feet of Isis, I could pick it up and keep it. So this, solemnly—and rather overcome, I must admit—we did; and I have a treasure—the little string of blue faience (palpable fakes, fortunately!), together with a little slip of paper with a prayer to *Isis the Great, Lady of Heaven* written on it in (very clumsy) hieroglyphs. . . . And I mention this incident because some people have said that Omm Sety was bogus . . . but in fact she *really believed* in the power of the ancient gods."

* * *

"Death holds no terror for me," Omm Sety once said. "I'll just do my best to get through the Judgment. I'm going to come before Osiris, who'll probably give me a few dirty looks because I know I've committed some things I shouldn't have—I've already been through the 'Negative Confession' and I've counted seventeen things I shouldn't have done—but in fact they've mostly been for the sake of animals. When I was a kid on my granny's farm, for instance, we had a neighbor—an awful man—who mistreated his animals: he drove his horses and constantly beat them. Well, I let salt water onto his land and completely flooded it, after which he packed up and left. But I think I was justified in doing it. . . . I also cursed the King, but it was Farouk, so maybe that won't count. I've caused people to weep, but usually there was good cause for it. I must say I never was an obedient daughter to my parents, and that may go against me. On the other hand, they were always making me do things I didn't want to do, and making me not do things that I wanted to do. If they had had their way, I never would have come to Egypt! . . . But I'm hoping that I will get through the Judgment."

As a young girl studying with Dr. Budge in the British Museum, Dorothy Eady had come across and translated the one hundred and twenty-fifth chapter of the *Book of the Dead.* In it she read how the deceased, after having had his heart weighed on the scales of justice against a feather of truth, had to enter the Hall of the Double Truth. And standing in front of forty-two different gods, the deceased— shod in white leather sandals, his eyes painted with antimony, his body anointed with unguents—separated himself from his evildoings by turning to each god and reciting a series of denials:

> Hail, thou whose eyes are of fire, who comest
> forth from Saut, I have not plundered the god.

Hail, thou Flame, which comest and goest, I
have spoken no lies.

Hail, crusher of bones, who comest forth from
Suten-henen, I have not snatched away food.

Hail, thou whose face is turned back, who
comest forth from thy hiding place, I have not
caused shedding of tears.

Hail, Bast, who comest forth from the secret
place, I have not dealt deceitfully.

Hail, Sertiu, who comest forth from Annu, I
have not been angry and wrathful except for
a just cause.

Hail, Lord of faces, who comest forth from
Netchfet, I have not judged hastily.

Hail, Nefer-Tmu, who comest forth from Het-
Ptah-ka, I have done neither harm nor ill.

Hail, thou who makest mankind to flourish,
who comest forth from Sais, I have never cursed God.

"I *do* think I will go to Amenti when I die," Omm Sety once stated,
"and I bet I'll see King Sety again, even if I have to sit all day outside
the palace and scream and faint when he comes out—you know, just
like the teenagers with the pop stars. I'd do the same for Ramesses.
'Oh, Your Majesty, *please* tell me the story of the Battle of Kadesh!'
I'd beg him. And he'd have no hesitation doing so. He's had three
thousand years to improve it. It'll really be some tale!"

* * *

On April 21, 1981, Dorothy Eady/Bulbul Abdel Meguid/Omm
Sety died in the holy city of Abydos, thereby fulfilling the second half
of her lifetime goal. "I consider myself to be a very lucky woman,"
she had commented two years previously, "and give heartfelt thanks
to the ancient gods who heard my prayers and brought me home."

The local health department refused to allow her to be buried in
her garden tomb. Instead, her body, facing west, was interred in the
desert on the fringe of the Coptic cemetery, just northwest of the
Sety and Ramesses temples. A gravestone has still to be erected . . .
and the burial site is marked only by a few limestone flakes, on which

offering prayers have been written in hieroglyphs, and by a broken teacup—placed there by unknown friends.

* * *

"For those who love her," Omm Sety once wrote, "Abydos still has a mysterious life. Other ears than mine have heard music at night in the Hypostyle Halls of the Temple of Sety. The tinkle of sistrums, the beat of a tambourine, and the wail of a reed pipe have been heard. I have seen the golden glow of a lamp in the Cult Chapel of Osiris when no lamp was lit; and I have stood alone at night in Pega-the-Gap, on the first evening of the Great Feast of Osiris, listening to the howling of the jackals. But when midnight came, the cries of the jackals were hushed, a deep silence fell, and then suddenly I felt as though I were surrounded by a great multitude of people. I could see nothing but the starlit desert, but all around me I could hear the breathing of many people and the soft whisper of sandaled feet upon the sand. I walked in the midst of this unseen crowd right up to the walls of Kom El Sultan. Then it seemed as though all the people went through the gateway and vanished into the past, and I was left outside, cold and lonely in the present."

But, surely, she has by now made her journey through the gateway to the West, where she has undoubtedly met up with all her beloved friends, and, in the words of the *Pyramid Texts,* is "sleeping that she may wake, dying that she may live."

·VII·

A Dream of the Past

(Text and Drawings by Dorothy Eady)

*T*his fantasy is based on a study of the bas-reliefs in the wonder-fully well-preserved Tomb of Ti, at Sakkara. Ti was a man of humble birth, who by sheer ability gained the favor of King Nefer-ir-ka-Ra, of the Fifth Dynasty [c. 2446–2426 B.C.]. This monarch, noted for his kindly and democratic character, promoted Ti to successive posts of honor and responsibility, until he became one of the most powerful nobles in the land. Furthermore, King Nefer-ir-ka-Ra bestowed upon him in marriage one of the ladies of the royal family, the gracious Nefer-hetep-es, and their sons were accorded the rank of princes.

—Dorothy Eady, 1949

A DREAM OF THE PAST

It was one of those real scorching hot days at Sakkara, when the glare of the sun on the sand is almost blinding and the view of the fertile Nile Valley is a blur of pink, blue and green haze. It was almost two o'clock in the afternoon and even the little breeze that blew fitfully over the sand dunes seemed to have got that "after lunch" feeling and had degenerated into a mere feeble sigh.

The entrance to the Tomb of Ti, a huge, rectangular blotch of indigo shadow in that dazzling glare, seemed cool and inviting, so I entered. I had come to Sakkara especially to study tombs, and that of Ti was one of the best of its period; it was at hand and it was a blessed refuge from the heat, so I entered and found the reality as good as the promise. It was cool and peaceful, and the subdued light, bright enough to reveal the beauty of the sculptured walls and dim enough to rest the eyes, was a welcome respite from the glare outside. But I was in no mood for study, idly I wandered from chamber to chamber, admiring the beauty of the painted reliefs, until at length I found myself in the innermost chapel. I rested for a minute on the steps of the altar before the false door, then crossed over to peer into the small, rectangular "spy-hole" of the serdab, the dim, doorless statue-chamber that lay beyond. I wanted to see once more the life-sized statue of Ti that stood within, a splendid thing, beautifully modeled. It represented him in the prime of life, well developed, clad in a white kilt that left his legs and torso bare. A curled wig was set upon his proudly carried head, and his face, with its large, intelligent eyes, wore a dignified but kindly expression.

To my surprise, the statue was not to be seen. I was about to return to the entrance of the tomb and ask the ghaffir in charge what had become of it, when a slight sound made me spin round. There before my very eyes was the missing statue! But no, this figure moved; it was the living reality of the statue and it stood between me and the door of the chapel! The Apparition frowned upon me and in a melodious voice, pitched, however, in a commanding tone, enquired sternly:

"Who are you? And what are you doing in my chapel?" I made a great, but certainly unsuccessful effort to appear unconcerned, and replied in a shaky voice, that I was a student of Egyptology.

"I came here only to study." I faltered; and added: "Have I the honour to address Ti?"

This answer did not seem to have quite the effect I hoped it would.

"You are addressing the Sole Companion of the King, the Overseer of All the Works of the King, the Overseer of the Scribes of the King's Book, the Director of the Palace, the Superintendent of the Canal-Banks, the Overseer of the Schools, the Director of the Court-Wigmakers, Overseer of the Pyramid of King Nefer-ir-ka-Ra, Overseer of the Pyramid of King Ni-user-Ra, the Honoured One Before His Lord, Ti."

I stood corrected!

"Moreover," he continued, "I do *not* approve of Egyptologists; are they not those ill-mannered wretches who turn us inoffending persons out of our sarcophagi, steal our funerary equipment and offer it as a sacrifice to their false god who is called, I believe, Science and whose temple is museum?"

I tried to explain that the Sole Companion of the King [et cetera] Ti, was labouring under an error, but somehow, he did not seem to be convinced. So I started to point out to him how vastly better he was being treated by his despised Egyptologists than by his poor, illiterate descendants, who only wanted to enter the ancient tombs in order to steal and sell all the portable goods and destroy the immovable objects.

"Look at your case, sir," I urged. "Has not your tomb been restored and strengthened; haven't you got a nice, sound roof over your head and a good iron door to protect your property, a better door than the wooden affair you yourself installed? And is not your tomb once more swept and garnished and visited by pilgrims coming from the far ends of the earth to admire your masterly artistic taste? Now, who is responsible for all this? The Egyptologists."

He seemed to see my point and he grudgingly admitted that I was right to a certain extent. We had a little more argument, and finding that he had no apparent homicidal tendencies, I urged my case with renewed courage.

In the end, I think he was more or less convinced, but being a man, and a proud man at that, of course he wouldn't admit it directly.

"Well," he said at length, "as you have spent many years studying us, tell me what knowledge you have gained."

And he asked me a few questions concerning life in ancient Egypt. I answered as best I could, putting forward some of my own pet theories. Some of my answers must have sadly misfired, for once or twice he looked most annoyed; other replies frankly amused him. Presently he held up his hand.

"Enough!" he cried. "Stop groping in the darkness. I was just about to make a little journey of inspection around my estates, when I found you loitering in my chapel; you had better accompany me, and see what one phase of our life is *really* like."

Gratefully I thanked him.

"Come then, follow me," he cried and strode on ahead of me. I followed dutifully in the august footsteps, on and on. It seemed a long way that we were walking, I had not realized that the tomb was so large. Suddenly, I realized that there was no tomb, we were out under the open sky, walking briskly along the banks of a canal. I say walking, for I was progressing in that manner, but Ti was being carried along in a cage-like palanquin borne upon the shoulders of ten sturdy servants. He sat with his knees drawn up against his chest, his back supported by a fat cushion. Underneath the palanquin walked a little pigmy named Pepi, leading Ti's tame ape and his favourite hound.

Very soon we arrived at a farmyard, where men were busy fattening a flock of tame cranes. Two men were at work preparing the rolls of paste on which the birds were to be forcibly fed, while another fellow was cooking a pot of stew for himself and his mates. The pot was set upon a charcoal fire, and his greatest difficulty seemed to be in keeping the embers of the fire fanned to a glow, and at the same time to stir the contents of the pot. Three other men were catching the cranes by their necks and forcing the paste rolls down their long beaks.

Ti did not linger long here, but made his way to a nearby pen where men were scattering an ample feed of grain to a large flock of ducks and geese, fine, fat birds that were fit to grace a King's table.

From there we passed on to an open shelter where Ti had to attend

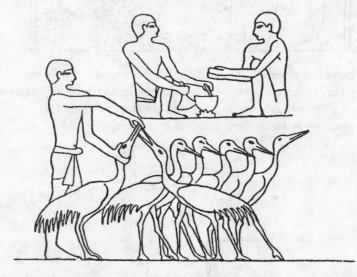

to his accounts. His scribes came before him, one at a time, and each read out the items for which he was responsible. As these accounts were written on rolls of papyrus, it was an imposing ceremony as each scribe unrolled his screed with a flourish and held it out at arm's length to read. They looked as though they ought to be declaiming epic verse, instead of merely reading out accounts of farmhands' wages and quantities of cattle fodder!

The next part of our journey was made by boat, the prow of which

was carved to represent the head of a shrew-mouse. We were rowed along the canal, past flocks of geese and cranes, and herds of domesticated antelope and gazelles. Some of these were allowed to roam free, but the majority were tethered by a rope, one end of which

passed around their necks, while the other end was attached to a stout peg driven into the ground.

In the fields, the fellaheen were ploughing the rich, black earth, using the selfsame wooden ploughs that we see in use beside the Nile today. The motive power was supplied by pairs of oxen, red, red and black, and wonderful spotted creatures that recalled the half-forgotten "Noah's Ark" of my extreme youth.

On the land already ploughed, industrious husbandsmen were scattering grain, and after them came a gang of noisy lads driving a herd of long-horned rams, whose duty it was to trample the seed into the good earth. With shouts and light blows the boys drove the bleating, nimble-footed herd hither and thither, raising such a commotion of noise and dust that we were glad to pass on.

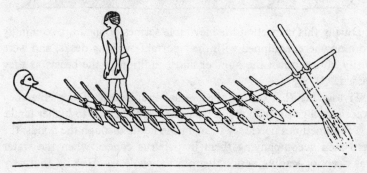

We had not gone far, however, before we met some men approaching with a vast herd of cattle. These were a great source of pride to the heart of Ti, and he left the boat and went ashore, leaning upon his staff, to watch the kine go by. And fine beasts they were, to be sure!

Some of them had their necks adorned with fancy collars of woven straw or grass and were led individually, each beast by its own attendant; but some of the bulls were rather lively and two men were sometimes needed to restrain their spirited capering. They passed by us slowly, long-horned and poll cattle, gentle-eyed, swollen-uddered milk-cows and plump yearling steers. In their wake followed a bevy of boys carrying the very young calves; and after them again, yet another herd, this time of tame gazelles and oryx, ready fattened for the slaughter. The former were as docile as a flock of sheep, but I noticed that the men preferred to keep a firm hold upon the long, curving horns of the latter.

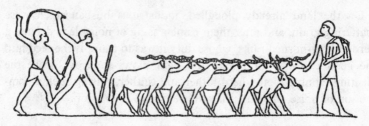

During this inspection the inevitable scribes popped up, seemingly from nowhere, equipped with their portable writing desks, and were busily noting down the number and condition of the beasts as they passed.

Ti told me that during the annual inundation of the Nile they experienced great difficulty in transporting the cattle to higher lands. It was sometimes necessary to swim the herds through the floods, the herdsmen accompanying them in papyrus canoes when the water was deep, or wading beside them in the shallows. He said that very often a kindhearted fellow would carry a young calf upon his shoulders to save it from fright and fatigue.

"Of course," he added gravely, "we always take a magician with us on these occasions, in order to recite the crocodile spell, otherwise those creatures would take deadly toll of man and beast."

I looked to see if he was "pulling my leg," but his handsome face was gravely serious.

We left the scribes to their work and walked on through the fields to where the full-eared yellow corn stood breast high. We watched the harvesters reaping with their wooden sickles set with sharp-

edged flints; as they worked they sang, keeping time with the rhythmic strokes.

The cut corn was bound into sheaves and loaded onto the backs of donkeys, to be taken to the threshing floor. As usual, the stubborn

beasts gave trouble, and one unruly fellow was eventually grasped firmly by one leg and ear, while a sturdy youth gave him a few well-deserved blows with a stout stick. A pretty sight was the dainty young she-ass, trotting away with her golden burden piled high upon her back, her woolly foal cantering along beside her.

We followed her to the threshing floor, where more asses were being employed in trampling the corn, which was spread almost knee deep upon the hard ground. Shouting boys, naked but for a girdle, urged the beasts round and round in a packed mass. Sticks whistled through the air, imprecations on the unruly asses were yelled with vigour, and dense clouds of dust arose. But in spite of all the commotion, some of the wily beasts managed to snatch a mouthful of corn here and there, for they were all unmuzzled.

Nearly the same operation was being carried out by oxen, and as these creatures were more docile, there was less noise and confusion; indeed, the men sang to the oxen as they trampled round and round, an endless, monotonous song that was, however, very fascinating. The oft-repeated refrain ran:

"Thresh for yourselves, O oxen, thresh for yourselves.
The straw for yourselves, the grain for your masters.
Rest not, for the air is cool today."

Our next stop was at a place where a group of women and girls were winnowing the threshed grain, throwing it up into the air on their broad wooden winnowing fans. The women wore a single short garment of white linen. It was not a very practical garment, as its narrowness prevented any free movement on the part of the wearer, so most of the younger girls had removed it and were going about their work clad only in narrow girdles, in which, however, no one seemed to see anything amiss. Their heads were bound up with white cloths in order to protect their black hair from the dust. The separated grain and husks were piled up into two large heaps to await transport to Ti's huge, conical granaries.

To avoid the dust of the winnowing we returned once more to the canal and reembarked. We soon found ourselves in a swampy region, where a gang of fishermen were hauling in a large net full of strug-

gling fish. Some of this silver harvest was sent directly to Ti's house, to be eaten fresh; while the greater part was gutted, sun-dried, and stored away in salt for future use. Ti said that such dried fish formed the staple diet of the poorer classes and, judging by their fine physiques, it did not seem to hurt them.

The water was now too shallow and reedy for our rowing boat, so we left it moored to the bank and continued our journey in a light canoe that was really nothing more or less than a large bundle of reeds skillfully bound together in a graceful shape, and possessed of a minute wooden deck. I was loath to trust myself to so frail a craft, especially in waters that were known to be the haunt of crocodiles and hippopotami, but Ti assured me that it was perfectly safe. I was indeed surprised to find that the boat safely carried not only Ti and myself, but a servant and two men who propelled the craft along by means of long poles. We glided smoothly along through the dense papyrus swamps, the nesting place of thousands of wild birds, and the hunting ground of weasles and ichneumons, who preyed upon the eggs and the nestlings.

The surface of the water around us was glorious with the gleaming white cups of the lotus, some of which grew high out of the water on long, fleshy stems. The feathery, bell-like heads of the papyrus reeds were also a beautiful sight, and as we glided by, Ti plucked a couple of these, which he courteously handed to me.

Suddenly, a loud commotion broke the peace of the scene. Ti urged the men forward, and we glided swiftly in the direction of the uproar. Upon a wide lagoon some men were engaged in a hippopotamus hunt. Despite the imminent danger, they were conducting operations from two small canoes, smaller even than the one in which we were travelling! They were armed with harpoons and strong ropes, and their method of procedure was for one man to skillfully cast his noose over the brute's great, ungainly head, and immediately pay out the line, which was wound upon a reel. At the same moment the harpoonist drove his weapon into the thick hide. Now this harpoon consisted of a heavy, barbed head, fitting loosely onto a stout wooden shaft. Attached to the butt of the head was a strong line, also wound

upon a reel. As the harpoon pierced the flesh of the creature the now useless shaft dropped off, leaving the barbed head embedded fast in the wound. Maddened by pain, the hippopotamus made for deep water, towing the frail canoe after it. When forced to rise to the surface for air, the creature was again attacked in the same manner, until, weakened by loss of blood, it was unresistingly towed ashore and given its death blow.

Ti explained that hippopotamus hunting was a sport in which he often indulged, and that he only refrained from taking a harpoon on the present occasion because he thought that perhaps I might feel a little nervous. (He thought quite correctly!)

Anyone would imagine that the successful pursuit of two full-grown hippopotami would have afforded sufficient exercise for one day, but the huntsmen, after a whispered consultation, came forward and begged to be allowed to give us a display of quarterstaff fighting. Ti readily gave permission and the men, laying aside their harpoons, armed themselves with long, light staves. They manoeuvered the canoes apart, then, at a given signal, drove furiously to meet each other. Blows were delivered and parried with the staves, the idea apparently being to knock one's opponent into the water. Humorous

imprecations, couched in unparliamentary language, were bandied about.

"Crack him on his box!" yelled one fellow. "Split his back open!" shouted another. Suddenly, a lucky blow tumbled one combatant into the water; he vanished with a loud splash, but came up laughing and spluttering on the other side of the canoe.

At this, Ti called out to them to desist, awarding the victory to the crew that had succeeded in "drowning" their man. Victor and vanquished, laughing fraternally together, made for the land, and we continued our journey.

On arriving back at the farmhouse, we found a great activity afoot, for before setting out Ti had ordered a feast to be prepared for me.

"Quite a modest affair," he assured me. If this was modest, I should like to know what happened when he gave an official banquet! Gangs of butchers were slaughtering oxen and gazelles in the courtyard; the beasts were thrown down, bound, and their throats cut with large, razor-sharp flint knives. In less than no time the tasty joints were sizzling over huge charcoal braziers, in company with fat geese and ducks. A constant procession of comely servant girls entered the house, each bearing upon her head a large basket of foodstuffs, fresh fruit and vegetables from the garden, and newly baked bread and cakes from the oven. Some led young kids with their free hands, or carried live fowls, or cheeses neatly packed up in little reed cases.

In the meanwhile, Ti had introduced me to his wife, Nefer-hetep-es, a dignified and handsome lady, who was a member of the royal family. She wore the same simple, tight-fitting garment as her maidservants wore, but in her case it was adorned by a wide "dog-collar" necklet, a circular collar, and wide bracelets and anklets, all of brightly coloured beadwork, interspersed with rigid golden bars. Her hair was entirely hidden by a long, plaited wig

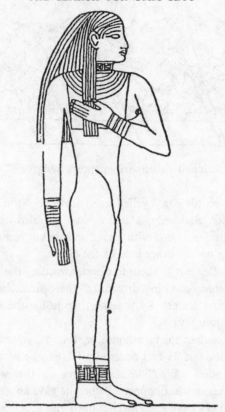

which was divided into three tresses, one hanging down her back, and one over each shoulder.

With her were her two sons, Demege and Ti junior.

While we were talking, menservants, deftly moving, brought in the meal.

The food was served on separate tables set before each diner, who sat upon finely carved ebony chairs with high, padded backs, and legs formed to represent the fore and hind limbs of a bull. Before the meal commenced, a serving lad brought a copper basin and ewer of water for each of us to wash our hands, as the larger part of the meal was to be eaten with the fingers, though small knives, spoons and prongs of copper were provided to cope with the more difficult dishes. There was no stinting of good wine and beer, all of which was brewed on Ti's own estates.

To further add to our enjoyment, two male singers, accompanied by an orchestra composed of two harpists and a flautist, struck up a lively drinking song.

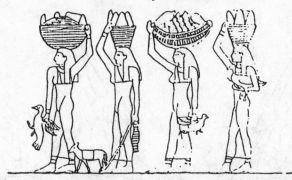

Hardly had they finished when a bevy of graceful girls entered the room, and accompanied by the orchestra, supplemented by other damsels, who clapped their hands in unison, performed a dance which I was amazed to recognize as "Raksi Baladi," so dear to the

heart of the modern Egyptians. It seems that tradition dies hardly in Egypt.

The dancers wore short kilts similar to those of the men, and over them a wide, transparent garment bound around the torso with broad, white ribbons. "Dog-collar" necklets encircled their throats, and their hair was cut short like that of a man.

When the dance was ended, the flautist struck up a solo. At first the music was sweet and soft, but as he warmed to the work the strains became strident and metallic; I was forcibly reminded of unoiled iron hinges! The squeal and groan of iron hinges, coupled with the jangling of keys! The banqueting room grew dim and hazy; Ti and his family, the performers and servants, all vanished.

With a start I awoke—I had been dozing as I leaned against the serdab wall, and the *ghaffir,* reopening the outer iron gate of the

tomb, had awakened me. I looked in the serdab; there stood the statue of Ti in its accustomed place, but, was it my imagination, or did the eyes really crinkle up in a smile and the head nod a gesture of farewell?

Anyhow, I had spent a pleasant time on his estate, and if anyone should doubt the sights I saw, let him go straightway to the Tomb of Ti, at Sakkara, and he will see it all pictured in still vivid colours on the limestone walls.

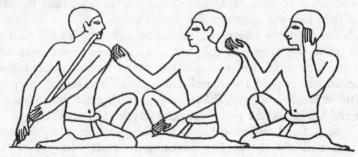

·VIII·

Epilogue:
In Search
of Omm Sety
Some Reflections and
Conversations

which was the veil?
which was the dream?

(from *Helen in Egypt*
by H.D.)

O n April 17, 1979, I came across an article on page 8 of the New York *Times* entitled "A Long Life (How Long?) Given to Pharaohs' Ruins." Datelined *Araba El Madfuna, Egypt,* and written by the paper's Cairo bureau chief, Christopher S. Wren, this 1,200-word report began:

> Om Seti may or may not have lived 3,200 years ago as a temple waif in the 19th Dynasty under Seti I and Ramses II. It is certain, however, that the elderly Englishwoman feels at home only among the renowned pharaonic ruins that she began seeking as a child.

In his profile of this transplanted English lady who lived alone with her cats and rabbits in a mud-brick house in an Upper Egyptian village, Christopher Wren explained that, having fallen down a flight of stairs when she was three years old, the little girl named Dorothy Eady had been pronounced dead by a local doctor.

"When he came back with the death certificate," Omm Sety had informed the journalist, "the body was sitting on the bed playing. They asked why I was crying and I said, 'I want to go home.' They assured me I was home."

I finished reading Christopher Wren's fascinating and haunting account of Omm Sety's life, cut the article out of the paper, put it in one of my files, and thought that one of these days I would really like to meet that unusual woman.

Days and months passed. Then, in April of 1981, I happened to be rereading *The Wonderful Wizard of Oz,* and came across the following scene:

> Dorothy began to sob . . . for she felt lonely among all these strange people. Her tears seemed to grieve the kind-hearted Munchkins, for they immediately took out their handkerchiefs and began to weep also. As for [the Witch of the North], she took off her cap and balanced the point on the end of her nose, while she counted, "one, two, three" in a solemn voice. At once the cap changed to a slate, on which was written in big, white chalk marks: "LET DORO-THY GO TO THE CITY OF EMERALDS."
> The little old woman took the slate from her nose, and, having read the words on it, asked,
> "Is your name Dorothy, my dear?"
> "Yes," answered the child, drying her tears.
> "Then you must go to the City of Emeralds."

For some reason, my mind was drawn back to the article about that *other* Dorothy who had also undertaken an extraordinary journey in order to get back home again. Like L. Frank Baum's little orphan girl who wanted to return to her aunt and uncle's farm in Kansas after she had been blown by a cyclone to the land of Oz, Dorothy Eady's destination was, in a manner of speaking, Oz itself—the "antique land" of Egypt referred to by Percy Bysshe Shelley in his famous sonnet "Ozymandias." (Strange that I had never previously paid attention to the first two letters of that title!) It further dawned on me that Dorothy Eady's "Wizard"—whom, I later discovered, she imagined herself in some mysterious way to have known and loved—was, in fact, the *father* of the "king of kings" (Ramesses the Second) of Shelley's poem—the Pharaoh Sety the First. Growing up in England, Dorothy Eady had apparently never been able to forget that there really was "no place like home." Early on, she made an irrevocable vow to summon up her courage, use her brains, and follow her heart in order to travel to the "City of Emeralds"—the village of Arabet Abydos—where she knew she belonged. Finally, according to Christopher Wren, she had gotten there. And I became curious to find out the whole story of how she had managed to do so.

To this end, in mid-April of 1981 I decided to call the Egyptian Embassy in Washington, D.C., and wound up talking to an extremely gracious cultural attaché who informed me that he had met Omm Sety several times, that she was a truly remarkable woman, and that he would send a wire to the Egyptian Antiquities Department in Cairo to see whether an interview might be arranged. A week later the attaché telephoned to say that Omm Sety had died on April 21, 1981 . . . two years after I had first read about her in Christopher Wren's moving report.

"I was based in Cairo for the New York *Times* from 1977 to 1980," Christopher Wren has recalled. "Also in Cairo at that time was a friend of mine named Don Schanche, who was a writer for the Los Angeles *Times* and who had run into Omm Sety in Abydos and had done an article on her in 1977. I was planning on driving down to Upper Egypt in 1979 to cover a story in Asyut, so Don suggested that if I got to Abydos I should make it a point to look up Omm Sety. He told me a bit about her.

"Now, Don is a hard-nosed reporter, kind of an agnostic, and very suspicious. Being very suspicious myself, I thought that Omm Sety sounded a bit harebrained. But since Don thought she was fascinating, I thought, 'Well, if *he* was interested in her story, I should certainly try to meet her.' So when my wife and I finally got to the village, we asked someone where she lived, went and knocked on her door, and were greeted by a woman with wispy white hair and bright blue eyes. We asked if she were Omm Sety, she said yes, and we then spent four hours sitting in her little garden and talking and drinking tea with her until it got dark.

"She told us about her life, and after speaking a bit about her previous incarnation she said, laughing, 'You know, this story really *does* make it sound as if I'm crazy!' But the more I got into it, the more I realized how remarkable it really was. I thought that she was a terrific person with a marvelous sense of humor. I remember she had a donkey that kept poking its head into her mud-brick house— she lived in extreme poverty—and she told me that she had nicknamed it Idi Amin. Later, I spoke to several scholars about her, and they all said that, leaving aside whether her 'story' was legitimate or not, she really knew as much about Abydos as any other Egyptologist. James P. Allen of the American Research Center in Egypt described her as a patron saint of the profession. What intrigued me most of all was how lucid and rational she seemed . . . especially considering the bizarre nature of her story. At the end of our visit, Omm Sety said of her life, 'It's been more than worth it. I wouldn't want to change anything.' She pointed to the edge of the garden where she had prepared her grave and commented, 'When I die, they just have to lift up the concrete slabs and push me in.' "

* * *

On a dry, sunny afternoon in late January of 1985—nearly four years after Omm Sety's death—I found myself sitting in the little garden where she had once conversed with Christopher Wren and his wife. Omm Sety's tomb was empty, since the local health department had refused permission to allow her to be buried in an inhabitable area. (Her gravesite is located in the desert just northwest of the Sety and Ramesses temples.) I sat amid the onions, spinach, watercress, and thyme that Omm Sety had once planted, watching the shadows of the orange trees moving slowly on the ground and listening to the sounds of braying donkeys, barking dogs, and shouting children in the dusty village roadway outside.

Determined to search out the mystery of Omm Sety's life, I had decided to visit her home in Abydos—which now belonged to her adopted son Ahmed, whose father was the night watchman who first met Omm Sety at the Balyana train station on her 1952 pilgrimage. A lizard was running out of the mud-brick house when I approached it. Inside the disused ten-by-ten-foot main room a few of its former occupant's dilapidated possessions remained: a bed and an empty wardrobe (Omm Sety's clothes were buried with her); a Bunsen burner with a broken teapot; two primitive-looking clay figurines of Isis and Horus that she had made herself, both resting in a niche on one of the walls—above which were an incense burner in its holder and a large poster-photograph displaying a close-up of a cat's face with enormous eyes, above whose head was emblazoned the words: EVERY CAT HAS A RIGHT TO EAT FISH. I also noticed a small, rough-hewn bookshelf filled with an odd assortment of paperbacks that had been given to Omm Sety by visiting tourists. But one book, in particular, caught my eye—*Pilgrimage to the Rebirth* by Erlo van Waveren. Curiously, I myself had come across this little-known but remarkable reincarnation chronicle just a few weeks before my trip to Egypt; and, having been unsettled but moved by the strange and dramatic confession—a kind of allegory of the soul—of this author-therapist's "previous lives" (as the archbishop François de Fénelon, St. Asterius, and the prophet Judas Barsabas), I had, out of the blue, called Van Waveren's office in New York City and made an appointment to see him upon my return to the United States in order to discuss the subject of reincarnation. Now here, in a broken-down bookshelf in a mud hut in a village in Upper Egypt I had again come across a copy of a book that, since its publication by Samuel Weiser, Inc., in 1978, had sold only about five hundred copies.

"I'm so pleased, and *very* surprised, that you found *Pilgrimage to the Rebirth* in that woman's home in Egypt," Erlo van Waveren told me when I finally visited him in New York City several months later. "Maybe your reading the book and then finding it again was a sign of your own interest in reincarnation."

"I'm not sure that I believe in reincarnation," I said to him.

"Ah, that's because you haven't experienced it yet. . . . But maybe you will," he commented, smiling.

A distinguished-looking and elegantly dressed man (he was eighty-two years old when I met him), Erlo van Waveren greeted me in his beautiful New York City brownstone, which contained an extraordinary array of ancient and modern paintings and religious artifacts from all over the world—the centerpiece of his collection being a rare, anonymous sixteenth-century German portrait in oil of the great Swiss physician, philosopher, and alchemist Paracelsus. Himself the scion of a Dutch family that controlled an international flower consortium, Van Waveren dropped out of the family business in order to become, in his words, "a Jungian-directed therapist. . . . I say *directed* because I'm afraid I'm considered a 'black sheep' in the official Jungian circles." He met Jung in 1935, had therapy with him, and later attended his private seminars and lectures in Zurich, before beginning to practice in New York City.

In *Memories, Dreams, Reflections,* Carl Jung wrote: "A man should be able to say he has done his best to form a conception of life after death, or to create some image of it—even if he must confess his failure. Not to have done so is a vital loss. For the question that is posed to him is the age-old heritage of humanity: an archetype rich in secret life, which seeks to add itself to our own individual life in order to make it whole. . . . To this end, he ought to have a myth about death, for reason shows him nothing but the dark pit into which he is descending. . . . While the man who despairs marches towards nothingness, the one who has placed his faith in the archetype follows the tracks of life and lives right into his death. Both, to be sure, remain in uncertainty, but the one lives against his instincts, the other with them."

In this beautiful autobiography Jung approaches but ultimately skirts around the possibility of reincarnation: "I could well imagine that I might have lived in former centuries and there encountered questions I was not yet able to answer; that I had to be born again because I had not fulfilled the task that was given to me. . . . I know no answer to the question of whether the karma which I live is the outcome of my past lives, or whether it is not rather the achievement of my ancestors, whose heritage comes together in me. Am I a combination of the lives of these ancestors and do I embody these lives again? Have I lived before in the past as a specific personality, and did I progress so far in that life that I am now able to seek a solution? I do not know. Buddha left the question open, and I like to assume that he himself did not know with certainty."

According to Erlo van Waveren, Jung *did* in fact believe in reincarnation. "I once spoke to Professor Jung about this subject, and later his wife came to me and said, 'Don't talk to anyone about this, the time isn't right for it.' That was in 1950, and I also had a warning dream that told me not to speak openly about this. In that dream I was talking to a priest about reincarnation, and I tore my clothes on an iron spike. So I kept quiet, because the world to which Professor Jung wanted to prove that there *was* such a thing as the psyche wouldn't have gone along with the notion of reincarnation. Today many people—especially young people—are interested in the subject —they're interested in the roots of life. To paraphrase St. Paul, as I did in my book: 'The trumpet shall sound, and the dead shall be raised, incorruptible; we shall not die.' St. Paul said that twenty centuries ago; but today, once again, we can say that the dead can return, incorruptible, to the state of consciousness that they had in past centuries and continue their psychic awarenesses both now and in the future. Now that I *myself* am in my eighties, I can tell you that Professor Jung informed me that he had come back every hundred years since the thirteenth century. I told him that I'd only had two incarnations during that period, and he looked at me and said, 'You're lazy!' I asked him, 'Don't you ever rest?' And he replied, 'Oh yes, I rested for a thousand years.' Jung recounted several of his dreams—I wrote them down—that revealed to me a number of his incarnations."

"In his writings, however," I said to Mr. van Waveren, "Jung, like the Buddha, left the question of reincarnation open. It is the Buddha himself who appears in that astonishing first paragraph of your *Pilgrimage to the Rebirth*:

> In 1955 I dreamed that the Buddha appeared through a round hole—the Breathing Hole of Eternity—stepped on the foot of my bed and then onto the floor, where he seated himself in the Lotus position. He communicated the

thought that I was to seat myself in his lap and spray my
semen in the form of a peacock's tail on his chest.

What is that about?"

"The Buddha is the world-spirit, the world-teacher," Mr. van
Waveren told me. "When he asked me in my dream to spray semen
in the form of a peacock's tail, it meant: give of your innermost and
of your eternal side. Because the peacock's tail is the sign of rebirth
and of eternal return. The peacock comes back every spring—it's a
sign of the soul reincarnating . . . and it was used in that sense in
ancient Egypt, too. The important point, though, is that the power of
that particular dream was the driving force behind my revelations of
my previous lives. I didn't *dare* to go against the wish of the Buddha!

"You see, the only way to check up about the truth of reincarnation is through dreams—they're the only proof we have. The dream
is the taproot. Professor Jung had a dream in which he entered a
tomb and came across a group of knights and noticed that the finger
of one of them was moving back and forth . . . which meant that
there was still life in his thirteenth-century incarnation. . . . From
there you start.

"Omm Sety, from what you tell me, found out about her previous
life in her dreams—and that's exactly right. It was in *my* dreams that
I discovered that I had been the French archbishop Fénelon, a controversial figure at the court of Louis XIV. I had to accept it on
account of the power and the emotional content of the dreams. It
was all so foreign to me . . . and then I suddenly remembered
things out of that life, with great pain, and I was transported . . .
sobbing, sobbing. Then suddenly I knew who I was in my life before
Fénelon's."

"How far back do you go?" I asked him.

"I came here for the first time in 700 B.C."

"And when do you think you first met your wife [Ann van
Waveren, also a Jungian therapist]?"

"I hadn't seen her for twenty-five hundred years. I was in love
with her in 500 B.C., but I couldn't marry her. For twenty-five hundred years she went her way and I went mine. Then we met again,
and it has been a terribly important marriage, because without her I
couldn't have developed . . . and vice versa. She's always pulled
my psyche in the right direction. . . . And I have an idea that I
knew my mother in my former life as Fénelon—I wrote an essay on
how to educate my mother's daughters.

"But in the beginning I resisted all of this. You see, in the kind of

dreams I'm talking about, the remembrance of one's past originates
in what Jung called the 'shadow' of the former life: that which has
not been comprehended or suffered comes back . . . the shadow
continues to exist. Professor Jung used to say that eighty percent of
the gold is in the shadow—it's our storehouse. People are afraid of
the shadow, of the unknown. So am I. But it's not what I decide, it's
what my dreams tell me. We only remember that which was not
digested in our previous life—and that's the shadow. That which was
digested falls away from us. So when people say: 'I was Nefertiti' or
'I was Napoleon,' you have to ask them, 'How difficult was it?' If
they haven't suffered their shadow, then you can be sure that there's
only an indirect connection. I was overwhelmed by the darkness of
Fénelon's life. I walked the streets by myself for a week . . . I
couldn't accept it. But when the Big Dreams come forth, then we
have our great struggles. There's an unwillingness to go with the
unconscious—it's the fearsome grace of God."

Erlo van Waveren died on November 16, 1985. His wife, Ann, died
thirty-five days later, on December 21. It was the year of their fiftieth
wedding anniversary—this time around.

* * *

"If a man die, shall he live again?" was Job's anguished question.
It is one that nobody has ever conclusively answered. The notion of
reincarnation is also such a hypothesis—neither refutable nor irrefutable—since it has never been unequivocally shown that it does not
occur nor that it does. Fraud, shared fantasies, memory errors such
as paramnesia (false memory) or cryptomnesia (hidden memory),
genetic memories, retrocognition (extrasensory perception of the
past), and "possession" are all possible explanations of specific cases
such as those of Erlo van Waveren or even Omm Sety herself. As
Lyall Watson, in his book *Lifetide,* has interestingly commented:
"The gap between the known capacity of the brain and the demonstration of unusual skill narrows with every new discovery in the life
sciences. The existence of vast untapped information in the genes,
the pressure of alternative memories in the rival systems of every
cell, and the growing appreciation of the powers inherent in the
unconscious make it more and more reasonable to assume that even
a three-year-old child could, given the right circumstances, inherit or
acquire, and then organize, an elaborate second personality. The
very scarcity of those with unusual knowledge or skill tends, I suggest, to support this biological explanation rather than that of reincarnation."

And after reviewing the story of the life of Dorothy Eady, the astronomer Dr. Carl Sagan—author of *The Dragons of Eden, Cosmos,* and *Contact,* and a member of the Committee for the Scientific Investigation of Claims of the Paranormal—commented to me personally: "Dorothy Eady was a lively, intelligent, dedicated woman who made real contributions to Egyptology. This is true whether her belief in reincarnation is fact or fantasy. In assessing the evidence, such as it is, we must recognize that many of us have a powerful predisposition to want to believe in life after death and in reincarnation. The notion that death is a dark, dreamless sleep is as appalling to many of us today as it was to many in Pharaohic Egypt, and in both epochs humans have taken certain steps to reassure ourselves. Recognizing that our hopes may make us vulnerable to self-deception, the burden of proof must clearly fall on the shoulders of those who claim that there is evidence for reincarnation.

"In Dorothy Eady's case, it is striking how many of the supposed corroboratory stories and anecdotes flow through Dorothy Eady herself—in her diaries, and in her stories told to Egyptologists, journalists, and friends. There is, for example, no independent record—a letter written by her father, say—even about her early conviction that ancient Egypt was "home," much less that she correctly "remembered" the original state of the Temple of Abydos. There is nothing in her knowledge of ancient Egypt that requires more than a quick and insightful mind devoted to the subject, and there is certainly no evidence presented, other than Dorothy Eady's own accounts, of friends and relatives walking in on her encounters with some manifestation of the Pharaoh Sety.

"The most economical explanation of her remarkable story is that Dorothy Eady, while functioning soundly and constructively in most aspects of her adult life, nevertheless carried strong childhood and, especially, adolescent fantasies about a past life in ancient Egypt over into adulthood without sufficiently scrupulous attention to the boundary between fact and fantasy. I don't think we should be too hard on her for it; clearly what resulted was a far richer life than she might otherwise have had."

Those of us brought up in the mainstream Judeo-Christian-Islamic tradition, which has denied—often vehemently—the possibility of reincarnation, however, often forget that almost half of the world's peoples *do* believe in it. (According to recent polls and studies, so too does almost a quarter of the population of the United States and Great Britain.) Hindus, Buddhists, Jains, Druses, Alevis, and many African, North American Indian, and Pacific island tribes all take reincarnation—in one form or another—for granted. As the Dalai Lama has stated: "Fundamentally, we believe that a child's consciousness cannot come from his or her parents in the same way the body does. The mind is formless, mere illumination and knowing. Because of this, matter cannot act as its substantial cause. Only a previous moment of consciousness can serve as the first cause of a mind—in this case, that of a former life."

Throughout Western history, we also find an acceptance of reincarnation among the Druids, Orphics, and Cathars; in the speculations of Greek philosophers such as Pythagoras and Plato; as part of the hidden teachings of the Gnostics, Jewish Kabbalists, and certain Sufi mystics; and in the writings of innumerable poets, novelists, and artists. "Some of us have in a prior existence been in love with an Antigone," Percy Bysshe Shelley once declared to a friend, "and that makes us find no full content in any mortal tie." To his sister Wilhelmina, Van Gogh wrote: "I have little confidence in the correctness of our human concepts of a future life. We are as little able to judge of our own metamorphoses without bias and prematureness as the white salad grubs can of theirs, for the very cogent reason that the salad worms ought to eat salad roots in the very interest of their higher development. In the same way I think that a painter ought to paint pictures; possibly something else may come after that." Even the skeptical, tough-minded Voltaire once laconically stated: "After all, it is no more surprising to be born twice than it is to be born once." And recently there has been a good deal of serious speculative and investigative work done on the subject of reincarnation by a number of scientists, psychologists, parapsychologists, and doctors.

One of the most interesting of these is the Cambridge-trained English biochemist Rupert Sheldrake, whose controversial book, *A New Science of Life,* was praised by *New Scientist* magazine as "an important scientific inquiry into the nature of biological and physical reality." In a 1983 BBC radio program entitled "Living Memories," Sheldrake summarized his views about reincarnation, focusing first on the idea of "a pooled or collective memory of the experiences of past human beings, which would act as a kind of substratum or basis for our collective activity. Now, the thing that comes closest to this notion in existing theory is Jung's idea of the collective unconscious. This would provide a common basis, a common memory pool on which we all draw. But when it comes to *particular* memories of *particular* people, we are then going a bit beyond Jung's idea, and it wouldn't be consistent with that.

"What I'm proposing is something that *any* member of the species could tune in on. My theory suggests that conscious memories can be carried from past conscious states to the present simply [by a] similarity with the present state by the process I call *morphic resonance.* If we, and all animals, can tune in to the experience of the past—not just of that of our ancestors but of others of the species—then this influence is *not* going through the genes but is rather something communicated through time and space.

"By the same token, it should be possible to tune in to our *own* past states. The whole theory that memory is stored inside the brain in chemical and physical form—the commonly accepted theory— turns out . . . to have very little evidence in its favor. Most people assume that memories are stored inside the brain, and the usual evidence for that is that damage to the brain can result in loss of memory. This doesn't actually prove anything one way or the other. If you cut out a bit of the circuitry of a TV set—remove the wires and transistors—the pictures on the screen will disappear. Now, that doesn't prove that all the people you see on the screen and the events that are going on there are stored inside the bits you've cut out. It merely proves that you're no longer able to tune in to them. Similarly, if you cut out a bit of the brain and lose the ability to have certain memories, it doesn't prove that those memories are stored there. It merely shows that what you've cut out is necessary in some way for recovering or retrieving or tuning in to those memories.

"I'd rather say that the life of memory is derived from other people in the past, leaving open the question of whether they are the same person reincarnated. If they're simply tuning in to someone else's memories, it doesn't prove that they are that particular person. One has to bear in mind, however, that certain Indian yogis can recall their past lives—it's one of the things the Buddha was supposed to have done. So it's possible that a highly developed kind of consciousness would enable these to be recalled.

"If one picks up the memories of some past life by what's called 'retrocognitive telepathy' (telepathy backwards in time, picking things up from the past), the question whether one *is* that other person or not really boils down to a discussion of what it is that makes us who we are. Is it merely the possession of memories, or is it something else as well?"

Also appearing on this "Living Memories" program was Dr. Ian Stevenson, a professor of psychiatry and director of the Department of Parapsychology at the University of Virginia, Charlottesville, whose landmark books—in particular, *Twenty Cases Suggestive of*

Reincarnation—have been praised by no less than the *Journal of the American Medical Association.*

In his scholarly and objective investigations of almost two thousand cases, Stevenson's findings—the data of which derive mainly from interviews with firsthand informants—seem to present certain recurring features. Most of the subjects are children who, between the ages of two and four, begin to describe events and people from their previous lives. Usually ninety percent of these subjects' statements turn out to be correct. In a high percentage of cases, the previous personality met a violent and often early death. Reported cases were most common in parts of the world where reincarnation is widely accepted—India, Sri Lanka, Southeast Asia, and southeastern Alaska. As Stevenson points out, most Western subjects have no framework of beliefs that might make the notion of reincarnation intelligible to them. "Accepting strange experiences," he states, "means finding a place to put them within our conceptual system, and if we cannot do this comfortably it is easier to get rid of them by denial." (The three-year-old Dorothy Eady, of course, refused to deny them.)

One might also consider some further remarks by Stephan A. Schwartz, the chairman and research director of the Los Angeles-based Mobius Group that devotes itself to research in "psychic archaeology," which attempts to pinpoint and uncover ancient sites by means of "remote viewing" (wherein a "percipient" tries to describe the surroundings of a geographically distant "agent"). In 1979 and 1980, Schwartz and his Mobius team, assisted by a group of Egyptian archaeologists, claimed to discover—as Schwartz recounts in his book *The Alexandria Project*—the ruins both of Marc Antony's palace and of what might have been the palace of Cleopatra—claims, it should be noted, that have been fiercely contested.[1] And while in Alexandria, Stephan Schwartz made two trips to Abydos, where he met and talked at length to Omm Sety.

"I think that a lot of Dr. Ian Stevenson's work is very interesting and compelling," Schwartz recently remarked to me, "but it doesn't *prove* the case for reincarnation because you could also explain his

---

[1] Those not impressed by these particular claims might still wish to investigate the highly regarded research into the possibility of remote viewing done by Robert Jahn, Dean of the School of Engineering and Applied Science at Princeton University, who has used machines that have randomly generated electronic signals or a mechanical cascade of marbles around wooden pegs, and has found that certain subjects have successfully influenced the manner in which the marbles fall or the signals light up solely by means of these subjects' minds.

subjects' experiences in the light of (a) the collective unconscious and (b) remote viewing, which is what the Mobius project is researching and what Omm Sety herself was practicing when she discovered the garden of Sety's Temple in Abydos.

"What seems to be going on is that some aspect of human consciousness apparently has the ability—in *appearance* at least—to move in time and space. Now, it may not, in fact, be any kind of movement at all. There are strong reasons to support the idea that all of these phenomena—out-of-the-body experiences included—are not a function of consciousness moving. That is to say, nothing goes *out* of you, but rather that we all, as an inherent part of our being, walk around with an access channel to a collective—what Rupert Sheldrake calls a 'morphogenetic field'—and that we have an always functioning information channel that allows people, with certain limitations, to describe persons, places, and events that they are physically separated from and that they couldn't know about either from intellectual sources or by means of any normal sensory cuing. We've done a lot of experiments in which, say, a person can tell you that if you go four thousand miles away and look for the hill with the big oak tree, you will then find next to it a rock that looks like a skull; and that if you dig down four feet, you'll then come to the carbon zone, and there you'll discover a bifacial ax head . . . and it will be there!

"Now, when I talked to Omm Sety, I had a very clear presentiment that her story may well have provided a good case for the possibility of reincarnation . . . though certainly for the possibility of an individual's being able to access to what Jung called the collective unconscious—what in the East would be called the *akashic records* [constituting a kind of cosmic library in which is stored everything that has been felt, said, thought, or done from the beginning of time]. When we strip away all the weirdness and occultism and ritualization that has gone on around these phenomena, what we've got is a quite straightforward, albeit not very well-understood, information source. We've tested around 23,000 people now, and this is a broadly distributed talent—though some people are better at it than others . . . Omm Sety being an especially extraordinary case. Almost anybody, though, has the ability to describe something that he *knows* that he doesn't know, and that he *couldn't* know, because it's perhaps an event that hasn't taken place yet.

"Omm Sety knew where the temple garden was. She said, 'If you dig over here, you'll find the tree roots and the canals and so on.' They did, and they found them. Now, as I've said, the information source may have had its origins in reincarnation or in the collective unconscious or in remote viewing. It could have been one or a mix of all three of these since we don't understand this aspect of human consciousness very well. But if you just examine the data—and strip away all of the ideological passion and bias—then the argument is very compelling.

"Omm Sety was a very controversial character because she did things and knew things that she ought not to have been able to do or know . . . and it's much more comfortable to act as if it isn't happening. She was an extraordinary person. I met her at the suggestion of the late Hugh Lynn Cayce, who was the son of Edgar Cayce and who had been interested in finding out whether the information that his father had provided about a new Egyptian chronology was correct or not. It doesn't appear to be . . . and to the ARE's credit, they published the fact that it didn't seem to work. [The Association for Research and Enlightenment, with headquarters at Virginia Beach, Virginia, is dedicated to the study and analysis of Edgar Cayce's more than fifteen thousand transcripts.] He said to me that I had to go to Abydos to meet Omm Sety since he had spent many days with her and thought she was amazing. So at his suggestion I spent several hours with her in 1979, and again in 1980; and I, too, found her an extraordinary person. I'm always fascinated when somebody is consumed by a dream—there aren't many people who are willing to sacrifice everything for a driving dream—and she had been willing to do that. It had worked . . . she succeeded. The quality of her work made people at least accept the *possibility* of what she believed. You just couldn't overlook her concrete accomplishments."

* * *

In a paper entitled "The Evidence of Man's Survival after Death," Dr. Ian Stevenson states that "evidence indicative of survival comes from not just one type of experience, but from several: apparitions, out-of-the-body experiences, deathbed visions, certain kinds of mediumistic communications, and cases of the reincarnation type." It is interesting to observe that Omm Sety herself seems to have experienced all of the above phenomena. Perhaps the most bizarre of these concerns what she believed to be her nighttime astral body travels. In one of her 1972 diary entries, Omm Sety wrote:

> I once discussed the subject of the astral body with a well-educated, intelligent American woman, Mrs. Edyth Mal-

lory, who used to live in Cairo. She was well up in occult science, having studied with the Theosophists. She says that some people can send forth their astral bodies at will. She did not say specifically what they looked like, but insisted that they were *always* attached to the earthly body by a long silver cord. Dr. Albert Doss said the same thing. They did not mention if the astral body was clothed or naked.

In my case the body, which is always naked, is quite young and healthy-looking—no scars and no varicose veins! I haven't seen the face, and there is definitely no silver cord. The hair is golden as it was when I was young, but curiously enough the hair style changes in accordance with that of the earthly body. For example, from 1955 to 1957 I let my earthly hair grow long, and plaited it. During this time also, the astral hair was long; and on one visit I was sitting on the ground by Sety's feet, and he was playing with my hair, and pulling my head about with it. Suddenly, he said, "Get up, Little One." I tried to get up, but found that he had tied my hair to his chair! He and Ramesses and I had a good laugh about this!

As you may remember, the scene in the Sarcophagus chamber of the Osirion shows the astral bodies (here called *Akhu* or "Glorified Spirits") leaving their earthly bodies. In each case, the astral body is clothed, but there are no silver cords. In *Isis Unveiled,* Vol. I, pp. 179–80, Helena Blavatsky quotes Paracelsus as saying that some people's astral bodies leave their bodies during sleep, and visit near or distant places. On waking, the person does not know what has happened, and thinks that he has been dreaming. In the same book (I, p. 226), she speaks of ever-burning lamps, and says that the "astral soul" lingered near the mummy for 3,000 years. It was attached to the body "by a magnetic thread which could be broken but by its own exertions."

But in one of her conversations with Hanny El Zeini, Omm Sety remarked, with a laugh, that "in my case there was no silver cord, because if there had been, I most probably would have tripped over it!"

In the opinion of Stephan A. Schwartz, "A lot of what people subjectively experience as astral travel is probably a form of remote viewing. A genuine OBE [out-of-the-body experience], where there is a detachment of the locus of consciousness from the physical body, usually is accompanied by the ability to turn around and see yourself —as in reports of near-death experiences in which people look down at their bodies and observe what the doctors are doing—your point of reference changes." Omm Sety's experiences seem to have been of both types. Just think of Omm Sety's woman friend who had to open her overnight guest's bedroom window in order to let the astral body return to Omm Sety's seemingly comatose physical body! If nothing "left" the body, what was it that was trying to get through the closed window?

Whatever the explanation for them—remote viewing, lucid dreaming, imagination plus ESP, an altered state of consciousness—out-of-the-body experiences have been reported throughout human history. In tribal societies shamans and medicine men were expected to "travel" in this manner (as well as to communicate spontaneously with and understand the language of animals—another of Omm Sety's gifts). The ancient Chinese shamans and shamanesses (the latter known as *wu)* were supposed, according to Edward H. Schafer, to have had amorous relations with the divine beings they encountered in their astral voyages. Reports of entranced saints journeying to and encountering angels in the Beyond are widespread. We also find the innumerable descriptions of night-traveling witches and hags (from the word *hagazussa,* "the one riding on the fence"), which are the focus of Hans Peter Duerr's recent book *Dreamtime.* Duerr, like others, has pointed out that it was the application to the body of salves prepared from "flight plants" such as thorn apple, henbane, and belladonna that resulted in testimonies of unimaginable flights "over hill and dale." (Similar experiences have been induced by dissociative anesthetics such as the ketamines.) Rogan Taylor, furthermore, has interestingly suggested that the tradition of Father Christmas and his flying reindeer may have evolved from the use of red- and white-colored fly agaric mushrooms by tribes in northern Siberia. Hans Peter Duerr writes in *Dreamtime:* "It is not so much that we fly. What happens instead is that our ordinary 'ego boundaries' evaporate, and so it is entirely possible that *we* suddenly encounter ourselves at places where our 'everyday body,' whose boundaries are no longer identical with our person, is *not* to be found. . . . Such an expansion of our person can easily be described as 'flying.' "

Carlos Castaneda rubbed his body with a variety of thorn apple, then took off on *his* flight, under the watchful eye of his *nagual*—the shamanic teacher Don Juan. "The *nagual,"* says Don Juan, "is the part of us for which there is no description—no words, no names, no feelings, no knowledge." That ecstatic feeling of out-of-the-body soaring has, in fact, been powerfully suggested in Castaneda's own *The Teachings of Don Juan,* as well as in such diverse works as the Omaha Indian "Song of Two Ghosts" ("My friend/This is a wide world/We're traveling over/Walking on the moonlight"); in the Talking Heads' song "And She Was," which describes a suburban housewife, lying on the grass near a factory, who begins to levitate and drift across her backyard, as she removes her dress and slowly rises above the earth out into the universe ("She was glad about it . . . no doubt about it/She isn't sure about where she's gone/No time to think about what to tell them/No time to think about what she's done"); and, perhaps most beautiful of all, in Nancy Willard's remarkable novel, *Things Invisible to See* (1984), in which a girl named Clare, paralyzed after having been struck on her head by a baseball, lies at night in a hospital bed in Ann Arbor, Michigan, on the eve of World War II, and suddenly notices a stranger:

> The old woman hovered over the foot of Clare's bed, and into the room crept the fragrance of laundry drying outside and of leeks and clover and tall grass mowed early in the morning. A faded blue sunbonnet hid her face.
>
> *You see me with your spirit-eyes, daughter,* said the woman. *Now run to me on your spirit-legs.*
>
> The forget-me-nots on her skirt nodded, and in its pleated shadows flashed ferrets and mallards and owls.
>
> She sank close to Clare and touched the girl's side. A wind swept through Clare, as if the bars of her rib cage were parting. Her own breath carried her out.
>
> Out of her body.
>
> Weightless and fleshless, Clare hung in the air beside the old woman and stared down at the slender body that had housed her so faithfully for seventeen years. The long brown hair fell like water down both sides of the pillow. The wide green eyes stared past her, empty. Only the bruise on her forehead was new.
>
> *I can't believe it! I can't believe time has run out!*
>
> *You are not dead, my daughter,* said the woman.
>
> In the chair, Clare's mother slept on, still as a snowbank. Through the carnations on the nightstand flowed streams of light, the spawning grounds of a million tiny stars.
>
> *Molecules,* said the old woman.
>
> The steel vessels on the nightstand hummed; swarms of diamonds kept the shape of basin and pitcher.

> *Everything alive looks dead and everything dead looks alive,* said the old woman and floated to the door, where she paused, glancing over her shoulder, and nodded for Clare to follow.

One thinks, too, of Omm Sety's astonishing account of rising, "stark naked" and "gloriously light," out of her body, and flying with her messenger-guide, Ptah-mes, through a patch of black fog high above the Giza pyramids, and finally arriving at "His Majesty's" palace in Amenti.

In both Clare's and Omm Sety's experiences,[2] of course, there is the presence of a helping spirit that guides each woman on her journey. As anthropologists have often pointed out, shamans and shamanesses draw on a special and personal power that is generally supplied by a guardian spirit, known variously as a *"nagual,"* a "familiar," or, simply, a "friend" or "companion."

In Omm Sety's case, Ptah-mes is really only a "spirit helper," for her true guardian spirit was, of course, Sety the First, who first appeared to Dorothy Eady as a mummy when she was fourteen years old. He did so in a shamanic Big Dream—a dream so vivid that one experiences it as if awake—which, in her case, had an uncanny similarity to one described by the Spanish poet Antonio Machado (as translated by Robert Bly):

> And he was the demon of my dreams, the most handsome
> of all angels. His victorious eyes
> blazed like steel,
> and the flames that fell
> from his torch like drops
> lit up the deep dungeon of the soul.

> "Will you go with me?" "No, never! Tombs
> and dead bodies frighten me."
> But his iron hand
> took mine.

> "You will go with me."

As did the poet, Dorothy Eady went with him.

The word "demon" is derived from the Greek *daimon,* which, before Christian theology "demonized" the concept, was in ancient

---

[2] According to the psychologist Dr. Alan O. Gauld, "OBEs are most frequent during sleep, during unconsciousness following anaesthesia or a bang on the head, and during stress" *(Mediumship and Survival).*

times used to denote a person's "good spirit." It was Plato who said that every human being had a divine *daimon* that was the noblest component of his psyche. Apuleius—the author of the great allegory of the soul known as *The Golden Ass*—described Socrates' *daimonion* as "a private patron and individual guide, an observer of what takes place in the inner person, guardian of one's welfare, he who knows one most intimately, one's most alert and constant observer, individual judge, irrefutable and inescapable witness, who frowns on evil and exalts what is good." To the person who seeks to know and honor him, Apuleius says, the *daimon* will communicate, "now through a dream and now through a sign, or he can even step in by appearing personally in order to fend off evil, to reinforce the good, to lift up the soul in defeat, to steady our inconstancy, to lighten our darkness, to direct what is favorable toward us and to compensate what is evil." It is interesting to note that it was Apuleius himself—an initiate of the later Egyptian mysteries—who thought that the greatest of the *daimons* were none other than Isis and Osiris.

In Keats's "Ode to Psyche," the poet dreams he sees (or sees in a lucid dream) Cupid and Psyche embowered in a forest. (The Jungian analyst Marie-Louise von Franz, incidentally, suggests that Cupid and Psyche—as described in Apuleius' great fairy tale—are structurally "identical" with Osiris and Isis.) In Keats's world the gods are dead—they have no temples, altars, or virgin choirs ("No voice, no lute, no pipe, no incense sweet/From chain-swung censer teeming;/ No shrine, no grove, no oracle, no heat/Of pale-mouth'd prophet dreaming"). So, "too late for antique vows," the poet takes upon himself the restoration of the cult and bower of Psyche by promising to build her shrine "in some untrodden region of my mind/. . . . And there shall be for thee all soft delight/That shadowy thought can win,/A bright torch, and a casement ope at night,/To let the warm Love in!"

Keats's restoration of the antique world is, of course, an interior one. And as André Malraux has reflected in his *Anti-Memoirs:*

> What did our successive interpretations of Horus and Osiris matter? The gods have no meaning if Olympus no longer has one; Anubis the embalmer has no meaning if the world of the dead no longer has one. Each of the gods had belonged to the impenetrable world of Truth that men adored. Egypt had called Osiris back to life through its prayers, and we called him back through his form and his legend—through everything except prayer. He was born

again not in Truth or in the unknown, but in the splendid
halls of the world of art which was to inherit this cargo of
centuries from a ship of pharaohs wrecked among the pa-
shas. The metamorphosis of the doubles of the Egyptian
dynasts descended the melancholy staircase of the Cairo
Museum, between the priestly wigs and the panther skins
studded with golden stars, through a cemetery of gods.

Omm Sety, inspired by the truth of her visions of her *daimon*-lover
and of her tutelary gods, actually decided as a child to return to that
antique world—where she felt she had been born before—in order to
live with and pray to her gods . . . not just in the world of muse-
ums or in the sanctuary of her mind (though, of course, there too),
but in the temple that still housed their images and their spirit. Just
as the historical Sety and his priests once ministered to, cared for,
and paid service to the gods—thereby making the deities a living
presence—so Omm Sety brought both these gods and Sety himself
back to life because of her total, irrevocable, and unconditional belief
in them. She did so not just with prayer but by means of the scholarship she engaged in, the books and articles she wrote, the tours
through the temple that she led, and, above all, by the unequivocal
commitment and devotion to the religion that she professed—a "pagan" worship that would have had her ostracized or stoned or
burned at the stake in more intolerant times (and perhaps even today
in certain parts of the world).

Along with Omm Sety's polytheistic beliefs went her cultivation
and practice of ancient Egyptian magic. Isis, of course, was the goddess of magic; and it was by its means that she protected her growing
son Horus against his enemies, wrested the "sacred name" from the
god Ra (thus taking for herself his magic power), and destroyed the
serpent Apopis by depriving him of his senses.

According to Professor Erik Hornung, the ancient Egyptians considered magic to be a "force"—one that Hornung terms "the nuclear
energy of early civilizations" because of its "dangerousness and its
power to transform the world."[3] Originally given to human beings as
a weapon for self-defense, the force of magic—as Hornung tells us in
Conceptions of God in Ancient Egypt—eventually "comes to serve

---

[3] It is ironical that in a recent U. S. Department of Energy study concerning the
problems of disposing of spent nuclear fuel, it is actually suggested that a kind of
"atomic priesthood"—modeled after the ancient Egyptian protectors of the pharaonic
tombs—be developed to maintain an ongoing security (with attendant taboos and
curses) against unwarranted and unintended entry into the radioactive burial sites!

highly egoistic and aggressive purposes, especially in love charms; and the magician thinks nothing of threatening the powers that are invoked with the ultimate and most dire of events, the destruction of the world. In human hands the force of 'magic,' which had originally been value-free, becomes perverted."

Omm Sety well understood the dangers of such "perversion." And in a diary entry for 1972 she wrote:

> "O my King," I said to His Majesty, "will you please answer me one more question?" He nodded. "Why," I asked, "in the pictures of the Solar Boat in the *Book of Gates* [a funerary text of the Eighteenth Dynasty that depicted the nightly passage of the sun god] are there always the figures of Heka and Sia, Magic and Wisdom?" He answered, "Remember that I told you that there is no Solar Boat, and that Ra, Iwf, and Ra-Hor-akhty [solar gods] are only manifestations of the Lord of All? So too there are no beings called Heka and Sia. In our time there were some true magicians, and magic was a real thing. Magic is represented symbolically as Heka, and as you know, Sia means 'wisdom' or 'understanding.' They are shown together to remind all beholders that those who have and use Heka must also have Sia, or else they make a bad use of Heka. Do you understand now?" "Yes, I understand and will remember," I replied.

As mentioned previously, Omm Sety used the power of Heka—which she derived from ancient Egyptian spells—in order to protect herself and her position in Abydos, to cure the local people who asked for her help, and to make sure that those who abused and tortured animals were dealt with in kind.

Indeed, Omm Sety's use of this "force" can be seen as an aspect of her role as a devoted pagan priestess of Isis and not as a perverse manipulator of "black magic" for satanic, extortionary, or sexually exploitative purposes. For Omm Sety—as for the ancient Egyptians —Osiris was still alive in the rising Nile waters, the sprouting grain, and the waxing moon. Geb and Nut—the god of the earth and the goddess of the sky—were conversing with each other in the gurgling of the Osirion water. The dead and the gods—just like the living— required food and drink, rest and recreation. At sunset the sun god sank below the western horizon, sailed for the twelve hours of the night in his night bark through the twelve divisions of the underworld, where he brought light and sustenance to the blessed dead, and was then reborn at the break of the new day, sailing in his day bark across the heavens in triumph once again.

The former head of the American Research Center in Egypt, Dr. James P. Allen, recently commented: "There is a childlike aspect to those ancient Egyptian descriptions of the journey through the Netherworld, and I think it's common to a certain stage of human development. It's just that the Egyptians concretized it much better and much more fully than anyone else. I'm sure that the aborigines in Australia had an equally developed system, but we don't know that much about it because they never wrote anything down, unlike the Egyptians.

"Omm Sety looked at the world almost the way the ancient Egyptians did. I say 'almost' because she was a product of modern times and couldn't escape that, no matter how much she wanted to. She believed so *powerfully*, though, that she was able to convince herself. If an ancient Egyptian fell asleep and dreamed about Anubis or Wepwawat, and upon awaking saw a dog . . . well, that *was* Anubis or Wepwawat, there was no question about it. The same was true for Omm Sety."

It was with the eyes and vision of a child that Omm Sety could, whenever she wished (and perhaps in spite of herself), behold her ancient Egyptian world. When she entered the tomb of Ti at Sakkara or the Temple of Sety, the images on the walls—as in a children's book—would come to life. (*A Dream of the Past* is, in fact, a kind of children's book.) Osiris and Isis were her protecting father and mother. Sety and Ramesses were her loving friends. The chief priest Antef was her tormenting teacher. . . . For this was her world, and it was only when she was in it that she felt truly at home.

* * *

Although he had gotten to know Omm Sety well and had been made her confidant about her night travels to the Beyond to see "His Majesty," Hanny El Zeini was unable at first to accept dispassionately his friend's confessions. "And one day I decided to visit an old friend of mine in Cairo who was a psychiatrist and ask him his opinion about some of the taped conversations I had had with Omm Sety. He listened to the tapes very attentively and then, choosing his words carefully, said to me: 'I would like to meet this Omm Sety; she is a very interesting case. I cannot come to any definite conclusions about her, however, without examining her closely. But certainly she is not "normal." '

"Now, I knew that Omm Sety would never consent to come to

Cairo, though I really wanted to help her. Then I thought, did she really need my or anyone else's help? After all, to all intents and purposes she was satisfied with her life. Soon afterward, when I went to speak to some members of a spiritualist society in Cairo called Al Ahram [the Pyramid Society], they saw things differently from my psychiatrist friend. A learned Rosicrucian told me I should take everything Omm Sety said very seriously, that she was not living in a fool's paradise. So I returned to Nag Hammadi more perplexed, unsure, and bewildered than before."

Having myself learned about Omm Sety's many lives, I, like Dr. El Zeini, felt bewildered about this extraordinarily complex person. And I, too, would have liked to have answers to a number of questions: Was there, for example, a neurological correlate for Omm Sety's story? I knew that cerebral mishaps—such as what occurred to the three-year-old Dorothy Eady when she fell down the stairs—could produce astonishing anamneses and activate fossilized memory sequences in the brain; but could they reawaken memories of a "former life"? Was Omm Sety simply a case of someone suffering from oneirophrenia (a kind of dream madness) or mythomania (a kind of hysterical acting out of a self-created drama), as Dr. Carl Sagan, among others, has suggested?[4]

From the point of view of the still existing traditional life of the Egyptian peasants and villagers, there was nothing unusual about coming across people who were supposed to be "possessed" by sheikhs who were said to live underneath the earth. "For instance," W. S. Blackman writes in *The Fellahin of Upper Egypt,* "I was told that a woman coming after dark down the stairs which lead from the roof of a house to the ground floor, and carrying no light with her, may become frightened and fall, in which case a sheikh will come into her at once. She will realize what has happened and will ask the sheikh to tell her his name, whereupon he is believed to reply, 'I am

---

[4] Several neurologists to whom I spoke about Dorothy Eady's childhood fall suggested that there were too many unknown factors and variables to make any deductions about any possible neurological causality of her constitutional makeup. In the words of one neurologist: "Three-year-olds will sometimes imagine all kinds of things without falling down the stairs. There are, for instance, popular fantasies in which children imagine they are not really the children of their own parents." But a psychiatrist specializing in adolescent behavior informed me that Dorothy Eady's fall down the stairs might have resulted in early damage to the locus ceruleus (a bluish-tinted eminence on the floor of the fourth ventricle of the brain). And this, in turn, may well have resulted in a long-term characterological discomfiture that manifested itself in Dorothy's feeling out of synch with, or not suited to, her environment. And the amelioration of such a state often occurred with the embracing of an obsession—in Dorothy Eady's case, an obsession with Egypt.

Sheikh so and so.' " This was a world where someone would throw dust after a person who was suspected of having cast the "evil eye"; where every vessel of water was thought to possess a guardian angel; where it was considered unsafe to wake anyone suddenly for fear that the sleeper's soul would not have time to return to its body; where the dead would appear to the living and speak and issue commands to them; where *afareet* [ghosts] haunted wells, springs, and houses, and were often blamed for phenomena such as nightmares and sleepwalking; and where some magicians claimed to be married to *afareet*-brides.

Even closer to home, William James—in his 1896 lectures on "Exceptional Mental States"—said: "We make a common distinction between healthy and morbid, but the true fact is that we cannot make it sharp. No one symptom by itself is a morbid one—it depends rather on the part that it plays. . . . Sleep," he continued, "would be a dreadful disease but for its familiarity. Likewise we do not regard dreaming as morbid because it is customary, but if it were not, it would be the subject of much medical wonder."

James pointed out that each person has within him a "simultaneous double consciousness . . . a secondary subconscious self." He mentioned the case of an eight-year-old boy who had fallen out of a tree and suffered a severe concussion, after which he seemed to drift in and out of several identities. He also talked about a woman who had suffered from attacks of somnambulism since the age of three and "whose life sounds more like an improbable romance than a genuine history."

To James, health was basically an affair of balance. And he concluded his lectures by stating:

> There is no purely objective standard of sound health. Any peculiarity that is of use to a man is a point of soundness in him, and what makes a man sound for one function may make him unsound for another. Moreover, we are all instruments for social use, and if sensibilities, obsessions, and other psychopathic peculiarities can so combine with the rest of our constitution as to make us the more useful to our kind, why, then, we should not call them in that context points of unhealthiness, but rather the reverse.
>
> The trouble is that such writers as Nordau use the descriptive names of symptoms merely as an artifice for giving objective authority to their personal dislikes. The medi-

cal terms become mere appreciative clubs to knock a man down with. . . .

We should welcome sensibilities, impulses, and obsessions if we have them, so long as by their means the field of our experience grows deeper and we contribute the better to the race's stores; that we should broaden our notion of health instead of narrowing it; that we should regard no single element of weakness as fatal—in short, that we should *not be afraid of life.*

It was in the context of these remarks that I therefore decided to pay visits to two psychologists who understand that to know oneself is to know and discern one's own *daimons*—and not simply brush them aside by calling them products of a delusional mind. As the psychologist Dr. James Hillman has written: "To go to the root of human ontology, its truth, essence, and nature, one must move in the fictional mode and use poetic tools. . . . Poetic, dramatic fictions are what actually people our psychic life. Our life in soul is a life in imagination." And it was to James Hillman (who currently lives and practices in northeastern Connecticut) that I first paid a visit in order to interview him and to discuss such subjects as *daimons,* polytheism, the fiction of case history, and the dream world as the Underworld, about which he has written in such extraordinary books as *The Myth of Analysis, The Dream and the Underworld, Inter Views,* and *Healing Fiction.* The following is part of our discussion:

Dr. Hillman, you once commented that "The first community are the dead, the ancestors, the community of souls." And this is something that I felt very strongly in Egypt, with its more than five-thousand-year-old necropolises.

I think that the whole question of commemorating the dead may actually have something to do with our trying not to lose the love of the departed. On All Souls' Day, for example, one dutifully places a wreath on a grave. And perhaps one does it to keep the dead from turning mean and for fear of losing their love. Why is it, for instance, that the beginning of culture is the making of things to put the dead in—clay vessels, sarcophagi, canopic jars, coffins? Maybe we need to understand that the reason why culture is built on the dead—who may be the ground of love, an underworld ground—has something to do with *feeling.*

In ancient Egypt, relatives of the deceased used to bring offerings of food and drink for the ka.

Our dead are dead, but I don't think that the ancient Egyptian dead were dead—and that's why they still ate and had to have their cosmetic boxes and servant statues and so on. Their *souls* weren't dead. Moreover, you don't find that idea of "I live alone, I die alone"— that whole "ego" view, which is a lonely, isolated view. In ancient Egypt you get the sense of your joining the community of the dead who are already there, like presences, waiting for you.

When visiting the tombs in Egypt, I had the experience of thinking: the Egyptian underworld is the psyche.

I felt exactly the same thing. In the tombs of the Valley of the Kings I thought: "My God, it's all *right here,* we're *in* it!"—that was the experience. It was as if I were walking into the unconscious—that ridiculous term we use for the kingdom of Hades/Pluto.

You've stated that at one time you thought that one could do analysis sitting on a park bench but later changed your mind, saying, "You can have a good psychological conversation on a park bench, but the sanctuary of the tomb *is constellated by the analytical room." Can you imagine doing therapy in one of the tombs of the Valley of the Gods? That would be amazing.*

It would be great! Boy, you'd certainly knock off an awful lot of shit right away! [Laughing.] I mean, what would be the use of talking about what she-said-to-him or he-said-to-her-yesterday? Instead, you'd be into the power of whatever images were really moving you —like the power of the images depicted on the walls—and they would be the images of *right now.*

In The Dream and the Underworld *you state: "Underworld is psyche. When we use the word* underworld, *we are referring to a wholly psychic perspective, where one's entire mode of being has been desubstantialized, killed of natural life, and yet is in every shape and sense and size the exact replica of natural life. . . . It is in the light of psyche that we must read all underworld descriptions."*

And the tombs give a depiction of how the whole psyche works. The ancient Egyptians were much more psychological than we are—they lived in the psyche, and their paintings and poetry reveal that . . . they're metaphors of how human existence really is. But you can also find this in American Indian mythology and the dreamtime of the Australian aborigines. Those people didn't do anything unless they were in touch with that psychic reality.

In Ancient Egyptian Religion, *Henri Frankfort writes: "We have seen that the Egyptian explained the daily appearance of the sun as its birth; the moon waned because it was the ailing eye of Horus. When barley was made into beer and bread, it was Osiris—manifested in the grain—who died. We shall meet such images at every turn, and we must not interpret them as allegories, for we cannot abstract a meaning from them without falsifying the beliefs which they express. Images are not ornaments or adjuncts of ancient thought. They are inseparable from it because the ancients reached their insight in a manner which was intuitive and imaginative as much as intellectual."*

It's marvelous. And, you see, the same thing happens in dreams. People dream again and again about the fading of the light or about driving home at five or six o'clock. Now, those are cosmic events in the dream—they have to do with vesperal consciousness. These moments of time that have to do with the descent of the light are places on the goddess Nut's body; but we, in our language, insist on saying that they are only metaphors for the decline of our powers, of our getting older. . . . "Watchman, what of the night?" We have to *describe* all of that. But anybody with that cosmic-clock sense doesn't have to say: "Sunset *means* dying-of-the-light," because it's contained in the image. (Even certain laws get "sunsetted," and old people live in communities named "Sunset Hills.") A poet would just mention "sunset," and a whole mood gets constellated by that. But *we* need to interpret it intellectually, and it's a shame that we have to do that. I, personally, try *not* to do that when I'm talking to patients. I just use the word "sunset" again and again until the person feels the impact of it—as one does viewing a scene in a movie.

Again, the ancient Egyptians were living in a world in which everything around them was alive. And that's *psyche.* If the wind was blowing, they paid attention to it—it was mythical, it was natural, it affected their health—nothing could be separated out. And it seems to me that the real question is: how did we lose this sense? Where did it go?

Omm Sety seems to have lived in the world of the psyche in much the same way as did the ancient Egyptians. But it's difficult to know what to believe about her experiences.

You don't have to "believe" anything. You're just presenting what unique things she did. She lived uniquely and saw uniquely, and that's worth something.

In your book Healing Fiction, *when referring to the Platonic idea of memory, you say:* "This remembering-what-never-happened must rightly be called imagining, and this sort of memory is imagination. Memoria *was the old term for both. It referred to an activity and a place that today we call variously memory, imagination, and the unconscious.*"

We like to say that someone "just imagined it," and that's a mistake. What used to be said about memory was that it was simply a kind of "imagining" to which a sense of time was attached. So that whether you were *remembering* something or were "just" *imagining* something was different only because in the former case you were putting past time onto it, and therefore thought: "It happened at such-and-such a time." But there are cultures that don't have a way of expressing past perfected time in their languages . . . so whether something happened or not doesn't matter. The very speaking keeps it present, keeps it happening. *We,* however, think a thing really occurred if one adds a sense of past time to it. If you add that sense of time to Freud's case studies, for example, then they actually happened; but if you remove the time factor, then it was "merely" imagination. I think that Freud removed the time factor, and everything was occurring right now. But Jeffrey Masson and the other new literalists and fundamentalists are all trying to get it back to *what really happened*—like the search for the historical Jesus. I, personally, don't think that it matters.

Now, with regard to Omm Sety: she was completely in the Nineteenth Dynasty in her imagination. But whether she was or wasn't *really* there seems to me irrelevant. . . . I mean, if a writer works on a biography of Tolstoy for six years, he will get so involved with his subject through a kind of *participation mystique* that he will start having dreams about the village Tolstoy lived in or about his daughter. Maybe there's a "Tolstoy complex" running around out there and the writer bumps into it . . . or maybe everything's right there in the libraries. But I don't think that this kind of thing is that unusual. Writers get into this condition all the time. And so, of course, do actors who, after they've played a role, sometimes don't remember a thing about how they did it.

As far as the subject of reincarnation is concerned, I would look at that simply in light of how it worked and what it did for Omm Sety . . . but I wouldn't ever quarrel about whether or not such a thing is possible. That's the way this woman understood her life, and it was *psychologically* true. She was kept alive by her story, and I think it's wrong to doubt it. But it should be taken as a *story*—the story she told herself in order to live the life she lived.

* * *

Finally, I went to see Dr. Michael Gruber, a brilliant New York City-based psychologist who has a special interest in the energetics, dreams, and imagery of the psyche, and who teaches classes in the alchemy of psychological change. On seeing him in his office, I first quoted to him the statement made by James Hillman that "therapists are the new historians" and that "case histories are fundamental to depth psychology" because they are "soul stories," moving us from "the fiction of reality to the reality of fiction."

Dr. Gruber, if Omm Sety had walked into your office for therapy and had proceeded to tell you the story of her life—her case history—as you've now read it, what would you have made of it all?

I assume that, along with having told me her story, she would also have informed me that she worked faithfully for the Egyptian Antiquities Department, that she paid her rent, that she was able to socialize with people, that she did embroidery and made necklaces, that she was a draftsman and wrote books, and that she was able to relate to the people she lived with in her community. So it would have been clear that she lived a functional life in so-called "everyday reality."

Now, she also had a "parallel" reality, so I would have looked at *that* reality from the point of view of her vision or inspiration; and I would have listened, to use James Hillman's language, to the story of her soul that somehow was privy to and had knowledge of another time and that seemed to be focused on one particular and beloved person—or personification—who was Sety the First. I would have then asked myself: Did this personification inhibit her functioning in the world? It did not. Did this "other" reality negate what we call "waking" or "ordinary" reality? It did not. Did the "membership" she had with ancient Egyptian civilization inhibit her being able to work in a productive way? Quite the contrary. . . .

So I think that my role as a therapist—if I had been able to work with her as my patient—would have been to allow her to elaborate the story of her soul rather than to have created a kind of conflict of interest between, say, my adherence to "everyday" reality in distinction to her rather different view of things. . . . Omm Sety was enriched by her experience, and I think it would have been an extreme loss to have seen her simply as someone who was hallucinating or who was out of touch or split off—it would have been a diminution of her being.

What would you say about that catalytic event in her life—the falling down the flight of stairs when she was three years old?

The age of thirty-six months in the life of a child is part of a developmental period during which the process of separating and individuating from the parent is an important psychic phenomenon. So, although Dorothy Eady had an organic accident—a kind of near-death or out-of-the-body experience—one can, from the perspective of the object-relations school of psychology, still talk of this process of separation as a necessary phase in her development.

Now, this "separation" is oftentimes thought of as taking place within the biological family. But Dorothy Eady claimed to have had *two* families. So rather than a kind of simple separation process, one might have to see that it was necessary for Dorothy to separate from her "present" biological family in order for her to link up with her "imaginal" family or, perhaps, with some previously lived experience. The fact of the accident may therefore have been an event in the external world that simply mirrored an internal and psychological event, and which paralleled what Dorothy experienced at precisely that period of her existence in ancient Egypt. If she were going through a kind of psychic separation, which by its nature disorients one from the external world, then we could say that her fall down the stairs might have been a "physicalization" of that disorientation, which perhaps gave her access to another way of life from another time.

Omm Sety once reflected that her accident may have "knocked a screw loose."

The British psychoanalyst D. W. Winnicott talks of a "gap" between the conceptual way we look at the objective world outside of ourselves and the perceptions we have that are subjective. So between this conception/perception, outer/inner movement, there are always gaps. As Winnicott says—and I concur—these gaps should not be thought of as "cracks" that analysts have to smooth over. Rather, I would emphasize, it's out of this "in between" space of the imagination that the creative vision moves and informs us of another reality, and this reality actually takes hold of Omm Sety.

It was once said of William Blake that he was "cracked," to which Edith Sitwell remarked that "that was where the light came through."

Yes. But how the light comes through and how much light one can contain raises the issue of whether one gets illuminated or just becomes overwhelmed by the radiance. Within the Lurianic tradition of *Kabbalah,* there is a process that has to do with the breaking of the vessels. The theory is that these vessels can hold just so much light. Then there occurs the breaking of the vessels . . . yet this breakthrough is precisely what allows light to enter the world and to bring life and wisdom into the world. Dorothy Eady was somebody who embodied so much light that she needed to "crack" in order that another light—known as Omm Sety—could enter into the world . . . someone who had a vision and who had to live out that vision and who made quite creative and wonderful contributions to the world and who recreated a whole universe—the universe at Abydos.

Omm Sety, of course, linked her life to the life of Bentreshyt. It's interesting to notice that Bentreshyt was abandoned and left at the temple when she was three years old; while Dorothy Eady fell down the stairs at exactly that age. Then, when she was fourteen, Bentreshyt met "His Majesty" in the temple garden; and when Dorothy Eady was fourteen, she had her vision-dream of "His Majesty," who appeared to her in the form of a mummy and ravished her. . . . So with regard to these events, the two lives mirror each other exactly.

Using Rupert Sheldrake's term, one might say that a "morphic resonance" exists at the biological level, such that the cells themselves have a memory and a type of knowledge. Once the seed cracks open —once Dorothy Eady becomes three years old—that "resonance" allows for something to break through; and once *that* happens, a momentum is set up that yields up the similar fourteen-year-old experience.

Now, psychoanalytically, all of this could be talked about in terms of an Oedipal development—separation from the mother, desire for the father during the adolescent period. And I have no problem with using that language, and it may sometimes be helpful. But there's a danger that by using it as a kind of "scientific" language, it can become a "final" way of talking about Dorothy's development . . . and then you're left with seeing Omm Sety, and her connection to her life as an ancient Egyptian girl, as a kind of psychotic break. I don't choose to see it that way—I think there are other possibilities that are faithful to lived experience and keep the exploration and expansion of psyche alive.

Using that language, it might then be possible to accuse Omm Sety of suffering from mythomania—the hysterical acting out of a self-created identity.

The adventure she acts out is not only her own. She is not selfish. We have to remember that Omm Sety had an uncanny sense of Abydos, so she wasn't acting out just a *personal* myth . . . and that's the interesting thing to me. The way she seems to have processed the light that entered her after her fall afforded her an intuitive or imaginative glimpse of knowledge that, after all, was only available to initiates during an entirely different period of history. This seems to me to somehow "speak" beyond a personal mania or just an acting out of a personal myth. Of all the myths she could have enacted, one would have to ask: Why Egypt? Even if we could answer that—since we all have a certain fascination for ancient Egypt—how to explain her knowledge that wasn't likely to be accessible to someone who didn't have such a special sense of life in ancient Abydos?

To accuse Omm Sety of "mythomania" or "schizophrenia" is to analyze away her experience. Her experience, as we know, yielded a meaningful life. If our criterion of health or sanity has to do with whether one can live in a creative, compassionate, and disciplined way, then Omm Sety surely did that. She made many contributions to society that were incredibly meaningful. For not only was she an expert draftsman, writer, and scholar, but she ministered to the people in the village where she lived—even if her healing techniques *were* unorthodox and came from some personal interpretations of certain ancient magical texts (though she also used natural medicines and herbs). In addition, she helped women reinstitute faith around the crucial cultural issue for women in Egypt—childbearing. She was able to help in a compassionate way that allowed them to fulfill what they considered to be their proper role.

It is interesting to mention, in this regard, that one finds in both the Egyptian and the Persian traditions the reference to the "physical veil"—which of course refers to the cloth that covers a woman's face so that her relation to the external world is kept pure—and to the "psychic veil"—which has to do with a closing off of insight into the secrets of the world. If one thinks of the Osirion water that Omm Sety used to help cure all kinds of eye problems and diseases, then the notion of "removing the veils"—of attaining clearer and clearer vision—comes easily to mind.

"Which was the veil? . . . Which was the dream?"

For Omm Sety, that would have been the type of question that she would have been less interested in answering and more likely to have laughed at, while continuing to reveal information and secrets that she obviously felt came through her via her lady Isis—a goddess who was also involved with "veiling" and "unveiling."

It's always seemed to me that the story of Omm Sety is, above all, a story about the unveiling power of memory.

Isis, we should also remember, is the goddess of memory—she re-*members* her husband. Osiris, in his own naiveté, ends up being dis-membered by his brother Set—the god of mortality and death—who cuts him into fourteen pieces. Isis re-members her husband . . . re-members him as he was, as one half of the "member" of the divine marriage called Isis-Osiris. She uses the image of them as *one* in order to continue the "membership" and to give birth to Horus. . . . Omm Sety, whose story is also about remembering, is following the example of her lady Isis, because she, too, is involved with that same restorative movement of mind, body, and spirit.

Of course, Dorothy Eady played the role of Isis in a dramatic production in Plymouth, England; and Bentreshyt performed that role, too, in the Osirian Mystery Play in ancient Abydos.

Exactly. The continued devotion to the "heavenly marriage," to the sense of "membership" in the marriage of Isis-Osiris, seems to me to be an archetype available to women as a particular way of understanding their relationship to the "masculine," the "husband," "Osiris."

But Isis and Osiris are also sister and brother.

This relationship is an image of devotion that we confuse with sexuality, and then get frightened by the act of incest. Within a larger cosmology, it can be seen as an archetype of devotion and love.

Omm Sety is, of course, also devoted to Sety the First, who seems to have been her "ghostly lover." In The Way of All Women, *M. Esther Harding describes the ghostly lover as a projection of the woman's animus who "lures his victim away from reality by promises of bliss in another world." Dr. Harding also suggests that, by a supreme effort on the woman's part, the ghostly lover can change his character and become a woman's strength and guide, her "spiritual animus," thereby transforming her life and allowing her to reenter the world.*

It's important to remember that Sety first appears to Dorothy Eady as a mummy. Both of them have to go through a kind of purification and rebirth process so that Sety can appear as a man and so that Dorothy Eady will not be simply victimized or ravished, as she was at fourteen. For Omm Sety and Sety are involved in a process of remembrance that's also an atonement—an atonement for what they had transgressed together during a "previous" lifetime and, on her part, an atonement for her own sense of not being *at one* with herself and for her need to be at one with the "masculine," energetic form that is called "Sety." It is this sense of at-onement that is connected to the notion of the "heavenly marriage" of Isis and Osiris.

So whether there's a spiritual development of the "ghostly lover" idea—enabling the woman to go out into the world—or whether you talk about it more metaphysically—as Omm Sety herself does, in terms of astral or etheric bodies—it's not a static dream or myth. There's a process that both of them go through with regard to their own development—his in another world, perhaps; and hers by doing the work that she needs to do in *this* world (in Giza and Abydos) in preparation for her *own* journey through the underworld. It's therefore important not to take the word "ghost" or "demon" in the way that we usually do in our culture as an apparition or an expression of evil, but rather to see it as an "inspiration" or a "guardian angel." The function of the angel is to *guard* and to *guide* a person through the perilous journey—daytime and nighttime—of life.

Whatever the inspiration or even "otherworldly" origin of Omm Sety's vision, it's important to reassert that she found a way to make that vision meaningful, creative, and of this world. She was able to be faithful to her love at the same time that she loved the world that she was living in. Her life had a meaning to it, it embodied values . . . *that* is what I think important—rather than whether she was sane or insane, whether her vision was real or unreal. For those questions may reveal more of the questioners' insecurity about their *own* sense of reality. And if one were to ignore the presence of the "guiding image" or "daimon" that animated her journey and her work, one would not be able to understand Omm Sety or account for the unwavering courage and faithfulness with which she lived her life.

* * *

"There are a lot of things you can't explain in this world," Dr. Veronica Seton-Williams once remarked, "and you can't explain Omm Sety—she was a very strange creature." And according to Dr. James P. Allen, "Sometimes you weren't sure whether Omm Sety wasn't pulling your leg. Not that she was a phony in what she said or believed—she was absolutely not a con artist—but she knew that some people looked on her as a crackpot, so she kind of fed into that notion and let you go either way with it. I just tried to see her for what she was, but I don't know if I was more successful at it than anybody else. Omm Sety really believed in all the craziness—she *really* did. She believed enough to make it spooky, and it made you doubt your own sense of reality sometimes."

In her beautiful book-length poem entitled *Helen in Egypt*, the poet H.D. draws upon the legendary notion that the Greeks and Trojans alike fought for an illusion, since Helen of Troy was actually a phantom substituted for the "real" Helen, who had been "transposed or translated" into Egypt. In her "defense" of Helen, H.D. presents us with the passionate, out-of-time love affair between Helen and the shade of Achilles, who, in a waking dream, reenact the "heavenly marriage" of Isis and Osiris (with whom they are repeatedly identified). It is a story of "an old enchantment," of "the lure of the invisible," of Egyptian incense "wafting through infinite corridors," of two ghostly lovers, "home-sick for what has been." And, in its essence, it is the same story as that of the girl and the Pharaoh who once, long ago, met each other in a garden by a temple:

> How did we greet each other?
> here in this Amen-temple,
> I have all-time to remember;
>
> he comes, he goes. . . .
>
> I have not answered his question,
> which was the veil?
>
> which was the dream?
> was the dream, Helen upon the ramparts?
> was the veil, Helen in Egypt?
>
> I wander alone and entranced,
> yet I wonder and ask
> numberless questions;
>
> the heart does not wonder?
> the heart does not ask?
> the heart accepts,
>
> encompasses the whole
> of the undecipherable script. . . .

The story of Omm Sety's life was best told by Omm Sety herself. It is therefore fitting that the last words of this story be left to her. As she wrote to her friend Maureen Tracey in a letter dated September 20, 1978:

My dear old Honey-bun,

So glad to get your letter, but want to SEE YOU! It was very kind of you to send the Vit E, which just finished off the ulcers nicely. They were improving slowly, but the Vit E seemed to speed matters up, and also did my general health good. But I assure you that they had *no* effect on my sex-drive! I'm well past that, and I doubt if even the sudden appearance of King Sety would get my reading glasses steamed up!

I'm afraid you'll miss Dr. Hani [Hanny El Zeini] at Kathmandu; he's supposed to have left on September 15, but so far I've not had any news of him. I hope he hasn't gone off rescuing flood-victims, it's the sort of thing he would do!

You're right about the origin of the word "chemist" [from *khemt,* meaning "the Black Land"—the ancient Egyptian word for "Egypt"], but did you know the common Irish name for a cat, Maukey, may be the Egyptian *mau-key,* meaning "another cat"? I think there were far more comings and goings in the ancient world than we give them credit for. From where came the Egyptian beads in the graves around Stonehenge (graves and beads of pre-Roman date!)? And what about the statue of a chap who was a herald for our boy Ramesses II, found 6 feet underground at Sydenham? A herald in those days was a kind of advance publicity-cum-public relations agent, but I doubt if Rammy himself ever went to Britain or else we would have heard a lot about his conquest of a hoard of barbarians dressed in wolf-skins and blue paint!

I did laugh at your reference to "The Green Eye of the Yellow God." I used to have to perform that poem at parties when I was young, and how I hated it! Also the bloody silly musical accompaniment. But worse still, my Dad insisted on my making an appropriate action to nearly every word. But I still remember it, and am sending a copy to you so that you can spout it (with actions!) to your tour group. By the way, there seem to be some very porno sculptures in the temples in Nepal. Dr. Hani sounded quite shocked. But I hope he took some photos so that I can be shocked too! Can you imagine *me* being shocked?!!!

Well, that's about all. Ahmed just blew in and sends his love, and hopes you'll soon be here again.

And now, as promised, the words to "The Green Eye of the Yellow God":

He was known as Mad Carew by the subs at Kathmandu,
He was hotter than they felt inclined to tell,
But for all his foolish pranks, he was worshipped
in the ranks,
And the Colonel's daughter smiled on him as well.

He had loved her all along with the passion of the
strong,
And the fact that she loved him was plain to all.
She was nearly twenty-one and arrangements had
begun
To celebrate her birthday with a ball.

He wrote to ask what present she would like from
Mad Carew,
They met next day as he dismissed his squad,
And jestingly she told him that nothing else would do
But the green eye of the Little Yellow God.

On the night before the dance Mad Carew seemed
in a trance,
And they chaffed him as they puffed at their cigars,
But for once he failed to smile, and sat alone awhile,
Then went out into the night, beneath the stars.

He returned before the dawn, with his shirt and
tunic torn,*
A gash across his temple dripping red.
He was patched up right away, and slept all through
the day,
And the Colonel's daughter watched beside his bed.

He awoke at last and asked if they would send his
tunic through,
She brought it, and he thanked her with a nod,

* Though *I* always insisted on saying "his trousers."

And bade her search the pockets, saying, "That's
    from Mad Carew,"
And she found the little green eye of the god.

She upbraided poor Carew in the way that women do,
Though both her eyes were strangely hot and wet.
But she wouldn't take the stone, and Carew was left alone
With the jewel that he'd chanced his life to get.

When the ball was at its height on that still
    and tropic night,
She thought of him and hastened to his room.
As she crossed the barrack square, she could hear
    the dreamy air
Of a waltz-tune softly stealing through the gloom.

His door was open wide, silver moonlight streaming
    through,
The place was wet and slippery where she trod.
An ugly knife lay buried in the heart of Mad Carew—
'Twas the vengeance of the Little Yellow God.

There's a one-eyed yellow idol to the north of
    Kathmandu,
There's a little marble cross below the town;
There's a broken-hearted woman tends the grave
    of Mad Carew,
And the Yellow God forever gazes down.

I haven't seen a copy of this for nearly 55 years! God
knows what made me remember it all!

                       Tons of love and kisses,
                       Omm Sety

The Kings of Egypt

A Chronology

The dates used in this chronology of the principal kings of Egypt—as in the text of this book—are approximate (since only Twelfth Dynasty dates, and those after 664 B.C., are generally considered precise) and adhere to those employed by John Baines and Jaromír Málek in their *Atlas of Ancient Egypt*.

LATE PREDYNASTIC (c. 3000)
King Scorpion
Narmer

EARLY DYNASTIC PERIOD (2920–2575)
First Dynasty (2920–2770)
Menes
Aha
Djer
Djet
Den

Second Dynasty (2770–2649)
Hotep-sekhemwy
Ra-neb
Ninetjer
Per-ib-sen
Kha-sekhemwy

Third Dynasty (2649–2575)
Zanacht (2649–2630)
Zoser (2630–2611)
Sekhemkhet (2611–2603)
Khaba (2603–2599)
Huni (2599–2575)

OLD KINGDOM (2575–2134)
Fourth Dynasty (2575–2465)
Snefru (2575–2551)
Khufu (Cheops) (2551–2528)
Djedefre (2528–2520)
Khafra (Chephren) (2520–2494)
Men-kau-Ra (Mycerinus) (2490–2472)
Shepses-ka-ef (2472–2467)

Fifth Dynasty (2465–2323)
User-ka-ef (2465–2458)
Sahu-Ra (2458–2446)
Nefer-ir-ka-Ra (2446–2426)
Shepses-ka-Ra (2426–2419)
Nefer-ef-Ra (2419–2416)
Neuser-Ra (2416–2392)
Men-kau-Hor (2396–2388)
Djed-ka-Ra-Izezi (2388–2356)
Unas (2356–2323)

Sixth Dynasty (2323–2150)
Teti (2323–2291)
Pepi I (2289–2255)
Mer-en-Ra (2255–2246)
Pepi II (2246–2152)

FIRST INTERMEDIATE PERIOD (2134–2040)
Seventh to Tenth Dynasties

MIDDLE KINGDOM (2040–1640)
Eleventh Dynasty (2040–1991)
Mentu-hotep II (2061–2010)
Mentu-hotep III (2010–1998)
Mentu-hotep IV (1998–1991)

Twelfth Dynasty (1991–1783)
Amon-em-het I (1991–1962)
Senwosret (Sesostris) I (1971–1926)
Amon-em-het II (1929–1892)

Senwosret (Sesostris) II (1897–1878)
Senwosret (Sesostris) III (1878–1844)
Amon-em-het III (1844–1797)
Amon-em-het IV (1799–1787)
Queen Neferu-Sobek (1787–1783)

SECOND INTERMEDIATE PERIOD (1783–1532)
Thirteenth to Seventeenth Dynasties

NEW KINGDOM (1550–1070)
Eighteenth Dynasty (1550–1307)
Ames (1550–1525)
Amon-Hotep (Amenophis) I (1525–1504)
Thotmes I (1504–1492)
Thotmes II (1492–1479)
Thotmes III (1479–1425)
Queen Hatshepsut (1473–1458)
Amon-Hotep (Amenophis) II (1427–1401)
Thotmes IV (1401–1391)
Amon-Hotep (Amenophis) III (1391–1353)
Amon-Hotep IV (Akhen-Aton) (1353–1335)
Semenkh-ka-Ra (1335–1333)
Tut-ankh-Amon (1333–1323)
Ay (1323–1319)
Hor-em-heb (1319–1307)

Nineteenth Dynasty (1307–1196)
Ramesses I (1307–1306)
Sety I (1306–1290)
Ramesses II (1290–1224)
Mer-en-Ptah (1224–1214)
Sety II (1214–1204)
Amon-messe (1202–1199)
Si-Ptah (1204–1198)
Queen Twosret (1197–1196)

Twentieth Dynasty (1196–1070)
Set-nakht (1196–1194)
Ramesses III (1194–1163)
Ramesses IV (1163–1156)
Ramesses V (1156–1151)
Ramesses VI (1151–1143)
Ramesses VII (1143–1136)
Ramesses VIII (1136–1131)

Ramesses IX (1131–1112)
Ramesses X (1112–1100)
Ramesses XI (1100–1070)

THIRD INTERMEDIATE PERIOD (1070–712)
Twenty-first Dynasty (1070–712) *Tanis*
Smendes (1070–1044)
Amon-em-nisu (1044–1040)
Psusennes I (1040–992)
Amon-em-ope (993–984)
Usarkon I (984–978)
Siamun (978–959)
Psusennes II (959–945)

Twenty-second Dynasty (945–712) *Libyan*
Sheshank I (945–924)
Usarkon II (924–909)
Takalot I (909– ?)
Sheshank II (? –883)
Usarkon III (883–855)
Takalot II (860–835)
Sheshank III (835–783)
Pami (783–773)
Sheshank V (773–735)
Usarkon V (735–712)

Twenty-third Dynasty (878–712) *Nubia and Thebes*
Pedubaste I (828–803)
Usarkon IV (777–749)
Peftjauwybast (740–725)

Twenty-fourth Dynasty (724–712) *Sais*

LATE KINGDOM (712–332)
Twenty-fifth Dynasty (712–657) *Nubia and all Egypt*
Shabaka (712–698)
Shebitku (698–690)
Taharqa (690–664)
Tantamani (664–657)

Twenty-sixth Dynasty (664–525) *Sais*
Psamtik I (664–610)
Psamtik II (610–595)
Apries (589–570)
Amasis (570–526)
Psamtik III (526–525)

Twenty-seventh Dynasty (525–404) *Persian*
Cambyses (525–522)
Darius I (521–486)
Xerxes I (486–466)
Artaxerxes I (465–424)
Darius II (424–404)

Twenty-eighth Dynasty (404–399) *Sais*
Amytaios (404–399)

Twenty-ninth Dynasty (399–380)
Nepherites I (399–393)
Psammuthis (393)
Hakoris (393–380)
Nepherites II (380)

Thirtieth Dynasty (380–343)
Nectanebo I (380–362)
Teos (365–360)
Nectanebo II (360–343)
(Last of the Egyptian-born pharaohs)

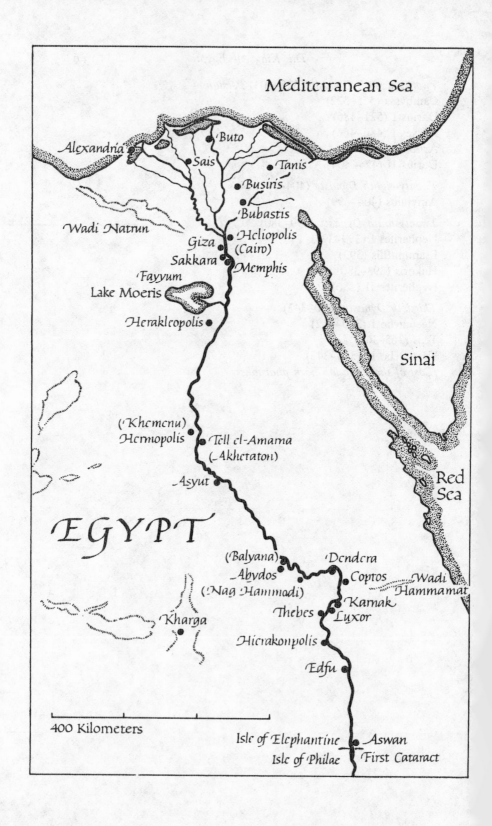

Mediterranean Sea

Alexandria

Buto

Sais

Tanis

Busiris

Bubastis

Heliopolis
(Cairo)

Giza

Wadi Natrun

Sakkara

Memphis

Fayyum

Lake Moeris

Herakleopolis

Sinai

('Khemenu)
Hermopolis

Tell el-Amarna
(Akhetaton)

Asyut

Red
Sea

EGYPT

(Balyana)

Dendera

Abydos

Coptos

Wadi
Hammamat

('Nag Hammadi)

Karnak

Thebes

Luxor

Kharga

Hierakonpolis

Edfu

400 Kilometers

Isle of Elephantine

Aswan

Isle of Philae

First Cataract

Acknowledgments

To the scholars, associates, friends, and acquaintances of Dorothy Eady/Bulbul Abdel Meguid/Omm Sety who shared their personal memories and recollections of her with me, I wish to thank: Dr. James P. Allen, Professor Klaus Baer, Dr. Lanny Bell, Professor Bernard V. Bothmer, Dr. Bob Brier, Julia Cave, Dr. Rosalie A. David, Margaret S. Drower, Mrs. Hanny El Zeini, Zahi Hawass, T. G. H. James, Professor Kenneth Kitchen, Dr. William Murnane, Professor Donald Redford, Stephan A. Schwartz, Dr. Veronica Seton-Williams, Professor William Kelly Simpson, M. Tracey, Dr. Kent R. Weeks, Susan Weeks, Christopher S. Wren.

To the many people who, in other and various ways, helped me to complete this book, I am grateful to: Mohammed Ali Azab, Dr. Robert S. Bianchi, Miriam Birch, Janis Bultman, Ernie Eban, Jesse Effron, Mohammed Abdel Elkelei, Sami El Masri, Nefissa Elsaid, Sherif El Sebai, Randa El Zeini, Mr. Foukay, Margaret Franklin-Plympton, Gad Ali Gad, Hussein Gaffar, Alex Gotfryd, Harold Grabau, Diane Guzman, Metwall Abdel Hakam Hassanein, Nicholas Kendall, Daniel Kolos, Peter Lacovara, Mary MacDonald, Dr. Nicholas B. Millet, Pat Remler, Olivia Robertson, Dr. Carl Sagan, Roberta Shaw, Professor David Silverman, Ehud C. Sperling, Kacy Tebbel, Ann Tunstall, Dr. Paul E. Walker, Dr. Arthur Wallace, Leslie Weisberg, Dr. Paul S. Weisberg, Jane and Jann Wenner, Hannah Wolski.

I am especially indebted to Julia Cave (of the BBC), Dr. Bob Brier, and Norrene Myra Leary (of the Association for Research and Enlightenment) for making available to me invaluable tape-recorded interview material with Omm Sety; to the film scholar and journalist Robert Ainsworth for his help in uncovering the facts about Dorothy Eady's and her family's years in Plymouth, England (and to those citizens of Plymouth who shared with me some of their reminiscences); to Dr. Shawki Hussein (of the Egyptian Tourist Authority) and Mr. Nabil Osman (head of the Press Office of the Permanent Mission of the Arab Republic of Egypt to the United Nations) for their professional courtesies; to Dr. Michael Gruber, Dr. James Hillman, and the late Erlo van Waveren for their discussions with me, which are included in the final chapter of this book; to Judy Sandman for her invaluable help; and, again, to Dr. Bob Brier for his innumerable suggestions and patient instruction.

My deepest thanks go to Michele Napear, for leading me through deserts and tombs; to Ann Druyan for her encouragement, faith, loyalty, and invaluable criticisms; to Russ Galen for his efforts to find a home for this book; to Jean C. Cott for her generous support; and to James Fitzgerald and Jacqueline Onassis—my editorial "guardian spirits"—who guided me "out of the body" back to the manuscript. I am particularly grateful to the former for reminding me, in the words of the anthropologist Hans Peter Duerr, that "it is not the experience of another reality, but rather the experience of another part of *the* reality, that is the precondition for . . . self-knowledge"; and to the latter for sharing with me her knowledge of, devotion to, and enthusiasm for ancient Egypt, and for reminding me, in the words of an ancient Egyptian scribe, that "to speak of the Dead is to make them live again."

In doing research on Dorothy Eady's early years in London, I was unable to discover any surviving relatives (her cousin, a Mr. Charles Williams, had recently died in Sussex, leaving no children) or any still-living teachers, schoolmates, or friends. For the "facts" of Dorothy Eady's first sixteen years, therefore, I have consulted official documents (birth certificate, street directory records), visited her childhood haunts, and drawn on Omm Sety's own recollections as she wrote about them in her monograph *Omm Sety's Abydos* and as she told them, in part, to a number of acquaintances, colleagues, and journalists—and, in more detailed fashion, to Julia Cave and, of course, to Hanny El Zeini.

Indeed, THE SEARCH FOR OMM SETY would not have been possible without the collaboration of Omm Sety's great and trusted friend, Dr. Hanny El Zeini. For his part, Dr. El Zeini wishes to thank and acknowledge the help of the chairmen and directors, past and present, of the Egyptian Antiquities Authority (in particular, of Dr. Ahmed Kadry and Dr. M. Abdel Razik, respectively President and Director-General of the Authority); Dr. A. El Khouly, Dr. A. Sadek, Dr. Ambassador A. Fakhry, Dr. A. Moussa; Bita Doss, Professor Werner Kaiser, Dr. Manfred Bietak, Gawdat Gabra, Gamil Helmy,

Sheriff El Touny; the Gabry family and the Fayeds in Nazlet El Simman; Hanny El Zeini's childhood friend—now living in the United States—Dr. Wilson Nashed ("with whom I took my first hesitant steps into the desert"); and "all the kind people of Abydos who took such loving care of Omm Sety at the end of her life in keeping with the age-old Egyptian countryside traditions."

It was an honor for me to have been able to work with Dr. El Zeini on this book, which we both wish to dedicate to the memory of Omm Sety and which we hope may serve as an example of the possibilities of genuine dialogue, cooperation, and mutual tolerance and respect between and among peoples of different faiths and traditions, and to those who know, as a philosopher once said, that "what is required is a monotheism of reason and heart, a polytheism of imagination and art."

Index

Page numbers in *italics* indicate map.